Special educational needs policy in the 1990s

Warnock in the market place

Edited by Sheila Riddell
and Sally Brown

London and New York

First published 1994
by Routledge
11 New Fetter Lane, London EC4P 4EE

Simultaneously published in the USA and Canada
by Routledge
29 West 35th Street, New York, NY 10001

Typeset in Palatino by LaserScript, Mitcham, Surrey
Printed and bound in Great Britain by
TJ Press (Padstow) Ltd, Padstow, Cornwall

British Library Cataloguing in Publication Data
A catalogue record for this book is available from the British Library

Library of Congress Cataloging in Publication Data

A catalogue record for this book has been requested

ISBN 0-415-09759-2 (pbk)

Contents

Illustrations

Contributors

Julie Allan is a Research Fellow in the Department of Education, University of Stirling and was previously a Research Officer at the Scottish Council for Research in Education. Her main research interest is in special educational needs and she has been involved in a number of studies in this area. Publications have included *Off the Record: Mainstream Provision for Pupils with Non-recorded Learning Difficulties* (with Sally Brown and Pamela Munn: SCRE, 1991) and *Teaming Up: Area Teams for Learning Support* (with Pamela Munn: SCRE, 1992). She is currently engaged in a comparative study of mainstream and special schools in Scotland, funded by the Scottish Office Education Department, and undertaking a PhD.

Derrick Armstrong is a Lecturer in Special Educational Needs in the Department of Educational Research at Lancaster University. He worked with David Galloway and Sally Tomlinson on their recent ESRC research on the 'Identification of Emotional and Behavioural Difficulties: Participant Perspectives'. Their book, *The Assessment of Special Educational Needs: Whose Problem?* is to be published by Longman in March 1994. Currently Derrick Armstrong is carrying out research on the education of transient children and on the transition of young people with emotional and behavioural difficulties into adult life.

Sally Brown is Professor of Education at the University of Stirling and was formerly Director of the Scottish Council for Research in Education. Her current research interests are primarily in the field of special educational needs and teachers' thinking about teaching and learning. Once upon a time she was a physics teacher.

Jenny Corbett has been a Lecturer in the Department of Education and Community Studies in the Faculty of Social Sciences at the University of East London since 1986. Her main area of research interest is post-school provision and policy for students with disabilities and learning difficulties. She has worked in London as a teacher in schools, further education and higher education throughout her career and has developed a particular interest in the effects of social and economic factors upon special educational policy and practice. Her PhD research, completed in 1987, was a study of integration at a London college of further education. She has established close liaison with several schools and colleges in the East London area and has undertaken studies of integration policy, LEA practice on statementing and learning support in further education colleges.

Jill Duffield is a Research Fellow at the Department of Education, University of Stirling, and is a former modern studies teacher. She has worked on projects in the area of specific learning difficulties and in the evaluation of foreign language teaching in Scottish primary schools. She is currently investigating how schools support the progress of lower achieving pupils, with Sally Brown and Sheila Riddell.

Jennifer Evans is currently Lecturer and MA Course Tutor in the Department of Policy Studies, University of London Institute of Education. She has worked in the field of policy research, particularly in relation to special education, since 1983. She is a specialist adviser to the House of Commons Education Select Committee and a consultant to the OECD. Her publications include: *Policy and Provision for Special Educational Needs* (1988) with B. Goacher, J. Welton and K. Wedell, and a number of monographs on the impact of LMS on special education, co-authored with Ingrid Lunt.

David Galloway worked in residential social work before training as a teacher and educational psychologist. After seven years with Sheffield LEA he was appointed to a Senior Lectureship at Victoria University of Wellington, New Zealand. He is now Professor of Primary Education and Head of the School of Education at the University of Durham. He has carried out research on many aspects of special educational needs. His books include *Schools, Pupils and Special Educational Needs* (Croom Helm, 1985), *The Education of Disturbing Children* (with Carole Goodwin,

Longman, 1987), *Primary School Teaching and Educational Psychology* (with Anne Edwards, Longman, 1991) *and The Assessment of Special Educational Needs: Whose Problem?* (with Derrick Armstrong and Sally Tomlinson, Longman, 1994).

Ingrid Lunt is Senior Lecturer in the Department of Educational Psychology and Special Educational Needs of University of London Institute of Education. She has responsibility at the Institute of Education for the professional training of educational psychologists. Her research interests include the area of policy and provision for pupils with special educational needs and in particular the effects of education legislation on these. With Jennifer Evans she has been monitoring the effect of LMS on special needs over the past four years; they have published a number of articles and monographs in this area. Ingrid Lunt and colleagues at the Institute of Education have held ESRC research awards for both a project on Clusters as a form of organisation to meet special educational needs and a project on LMS and special educational needs. The chapters in this volume report some of this work.

Pamela Munn is Professor of Curriculum Research at Moray House Institute of Education, Heriot Watt University. One of her research interests is classroom processes and she has been involved in a number of studies of teachers' perceptions of their role. She has recently completed a major research project on classroom discipline and is currently working on a study of values education in primary schools. Her interests in special needs education centre on how these needs are defined and the consequent implications for mainstream and special needs teaching. The policy context in which teachers operate is an important influence on their practice and she is currently researching the effects of devolved management of schools with colleagues from the University of Edinburgh.

Brahm Norwich is a Senior Lecturer in the Department of Educational Psychology and Special Educational Needs at the London Institute. He is an educational psychologist with interests in a range of areas, including the special educational service, the identification of children with special educational needs, and the emotional and motivational aspects of learning.

Sheila Riddell is a Lecturer in the Department of Education, University of Stirling. Having graduated from Sussex University in 1976, she worked as an English teacher for seven years before enrolling for a PhD at Bristol University in 1984. The topic of her research was gender and option choice in rural comprehensive schools. She moved to Scotland in 1988 and took up a post as a Research Fellow in the Department of Education University of Edinburgh, working on a project in the area of special educational needs. Since joining Stirling University in 1989, she has continued to research and write in the areas of special educational needs and gender and education.

Jane Steedman has taught in Learning Support departments of comprehensives and is an educational researcher. Her publications include reports on the progress in selective and non-selective secondary schools of the National Child Development Survey cohort. Among other research interests of hers are adult literacy and school television. She was from May 1992 to January 1993 a Research Officer on the project, 'Clusters for Special Educational Needs' at London University Institute of Education.

Klaus Wedell worked as an educational psychologist in Bristol and Hull, and taught at the Universities of Bristol and Birmingham, until he became the first Professor in the Education of Children with Special Needs at the Institute of Education, University of London. He has carried out research on many special needs topics, including the implementation of the 1981 Special Education Act in the UK. He is a consultant to the Centre for Educational Research and Innovation of the OECD.

Charles Weedon is Principal Teacher Learning Support and Special Needs at Perth Grammar School, a city comprehensive serving a mixed catchment area. After leaving the Royal Navy, he trained at Moray House, then worked as an English teacher and maths teacher in Shetland and Fife, and as a Learning Support teacher in Fife and Tayside. His research interests have clustered around the difficulties experienced by pupils early in their secondary schooling: primary/secondary transfer, writing skills and the difficulties pupils have in learning from text. He is currently continuing his research with pupils with difficulties in mathematics.

Sheila Wolfendale has been a primary school teacher, a remedial reading teacher and an educational psychologist in several local education authorities and is currently Principal Lecturer in charge of a postgraduate professional training course for educational psychologists in the Psychology Department at the University of East London. She has authored and edited a number of books, booklets, and many articles and papers on particular interests and specialisms, such as reading and learning difficulties, special needs, early years and parental involvement, and has guest- edited national journals on a number of occasions. Recent publications include: *All About Me*, a parental assessment guide (1990); *Empowering Teachers and Parents – Working for Children* (1992); 'The profession and practice of educational psychology' (edited, 1992); 'Assessing special educational needs' (edited, 1993).

Preface

Sally Tomlinson

In almost all countries which have developed special education sub-systems within their state education systems there has been a paucity of research and literature on policy and policy-making for the special. A burgeoning literature on practice, provision, management and training has not been matched by research on, or evaluation and analysis of, the policy development, implementation and change which underpins all practice. Consequently those dealing with special educational needs are in danger of knowing about 'how to do it', while knowing little about why they do it.

The editors of this book have admirably filled a gap by focusing on national and local policies and policy-making which affect the education of those deemed to have special education needs and have widened the analysis by the inclusion of policy and practice in Scotland. Their contributors have, via original research and analysis, examined changing influences and ideologies behind policies, and identified areas of tension which have been exacerbated by policies of market competition between schools and the problematic position of Education Authorities. The book is a valuable contribution to an understanding of the policies and politics of special educational needs.

Yet policy analysis in this area is still immensely difficult. A precondition for understanding implementation and change in policy and provision in any aspect of state education systems is a careful analysis of educational politics, and the ideological framework within which policies are developed – and a study of the social interest groups who have varying degrees of access to the process of educational negotiation and varying degrees of power to influence events. Despite the introduction of a critical literature during the 1980s, special education is still dominated by ideologies of benevolent humanitarianism and the 'feel-good' factor. Politically, no party can afford to ignore special educational needs nor the powerful lobbies for some categories of 'special need'. Educationally, few mainstream headteachers, driven by insufficient funding and greater accountability to credential more children to higher standards, can do other than ration resources and exclude the troublesome – thus failing to satisfy the expectations of parents and other interest groups, raised by legislative promises about the education of the special. It is unsurprising that most policy in the special educational needs area is still developed from the assumption that there are groups of children and young people whose physical or sensory deficits, low intellectual capabilities, or behavioural intransigence, create such difficulties for the 'normal' school system, that they will fail to achieve unless accorded 'special' educational treatment. (The notion of a continuum of hardship, DES 1978, reinforced rather than negated this assumption.) It is unsurprising that the term special educational needs remains confused on both philosophical and political grounds, with no agreed criteria for its use. It could be argued that from the time the Warnock Committee extended the concept to include all low-achieving and largely working-class pupils who had never been seriously offered an education, and whose needs, far from being special, were absolutely normal, the challenge to the school system was to offer an *education*. However, this would have entailed inclusive and expensive educational policies and a re-thinking of the whole relationship between normal and special education, which no government, interest group nor educationalists seem inclined to do at the present time.

Sheila Riddell and Sally Brown are more aware than most of the contradictions, tensions and anxieties generated by special educational needs in the 1980s and 1990s and their book is an eloquent testimony to their determination to bring debates on policy and practice in the area into the open.

22 March, 1994

Chapter 1

Special educational needs provision in the United Kingdom – the policy context

Sheila Riddell and Sally Brown

INTRODUCTION

This book aims to explore the impact of national and local policy on the educational experiences of children and young people with special educational needs, focusing on England and Wales and on Scotland. It traces the impact of Conservative policy-making of the 1980s and 1990s on the thinking of the 1970s and looks forward to future developments in the twenty-first century.

Two broad factors have influenced the development of policy and provision in this area. First, attempts were made throughout the 1970s to reconceptualise learning difficulties not as intrinsic to the child but as arising in the context of interaction between the child and his or her environment. This thinking was reflected in documents such as the Warnock Report (DES, 1978) and the report on learning difficulties by Scottish HMI (SED, 1978). Both reports had implications for the way in which children with special needs should be educated, with learning support in mainstream classes regarded as the preferable option for a wider group of children. The second major influence derives from educational policy and legislation of the 1980s and early 1990s, which established centralised control over the curriculum and assessment, increased competition between schools through the vehicle of parental choice and weakened the power base of local authorities.

The chapters in this book begin to unravel the effect of these influences and to identify both continuities and discontinuities. To some extent, it is possible to trace common themes through policies with different ideological pedigrees; for instance, both Warnock and more recent policy developments affirm the right of parents to an increased say in the education of their children, although Warnock's emphasis on partnership has been replaced by the notion of the parent as critical consumer. There is also evidence of tension in the development of policy, for instance, the acceptance of the benevolent discretion of professionals which tended to characterise special needs provision in the pre-and post-Warnock era does not sit easily alongside the more recent emphasis on choice and accountability of the 1980s and 1990s. In addition, although a number of central principles may be identified in recent government policy, disjunctions are also apparent. For example, the increase in schools' control of finance and pupil selection may be at variance with the principle of parental choice of school. In so far as parents of children with special educational needs opt in large numbers to have their children educated in mainstream schools, special schools will suffer from falling rolls, become less cost-effective and eventually face the possibility of closure. In this sense, the exercise of choice may have the effect of reducing diversity of provision and hence foreclosing on possible avenues of choice in the future. Our contributors have assessed the extent to which policies, perhaps formulated with prime regard to the mainstream majority, have the potential to benefit children with special educational needs by emphasising their common entitlement, or may disenfranchise them further by forcing them to fit into an inappropriate regime. Within this context, the complex processes of policy-making and implementation and the relationship between central policy and local practice must inevitably be addressed.

A central, and perhaps unusual, feature of this book is that it draws on papers based on policy and practice in both Scotland and England and Wales. Summarising the key differences in the two systems, Munn (1991) commented that

> the emphasis on parents as a mechanism for school quality control flows from a U.K. policy agenda, yet that policy has found rather different expression north and south of the border. For example, the 1981 Education (Scotland) Act introduced a much more radical notion of parental choice than the 1980 Education Act for England and Wales. In contrast, the 1988 Education Act gives far more extensive powers to school governing bodies than the 1988 School Boards Act, and Scotland has had a separate Act, the oddly named Self-Governing

Schools etc. (Scotland) Act, 1989, to introduce the right of
schools to opt out of local authority control. We may note in
passing that Scottish curriculum and assessment reforms have
been introduced via guidelines rather than by statute and that
a comparative study of education policy north and south of the
border deserves greater research attention than it has hitherto
attracted.

(Munn, 1991: 173)

In this chapter and the conclusion we endeavour to point up
some of the contrasts between Scotland and England and Wales.
We argue that these differences provide important insights into
the diverse ways in which central policies may be translated into
practice, reflecting not only the different legal frameworks, but
also the distinctive political and social contexts.

In this introduction we begin by outlining some of the features
of the literature on policy-making in education generally and
special educational needs more particularly. We then provide a
brief account of key elements in the two phases of policy-making
which have profoundly affected provision for children with
special educational needs: first, the Warnock and the Scottish
HMI reports and the accompanying legislation and, secondly,
certain aspects of Conservative government policy since 1979. In
particular, we consider the issue of continuity and disjunction
between the conceptual position adopted by Warnock and more
recent policy. Finally we provide an overview of the papers,
focusing on the twin themes of the limits of entitlement and
tensions within and between policies.

EDUCATIONAL POLICY AND SPECIAL EDUCATIONAL NEED

Literature on policy-making in education

Until the start of the 1980s, there was comparatively little
literature on educational policy, despite the fact that other major
areas of public spending, such as health and social services, had
been analysed extensively. Commenting on this absence, Ball
(1990) argued that even those who had written about educational
policy had often failed to make their theoretical perspective
explicit. He suggested that the lack of social policy literature in

the field of education is partly due to the fact that until the late 1970s it was assumed that post-war educational provision represented a consensus of the various political, cultural and ideological perspectives. Texts such as *Unpopular Education* (CCCS, 1981) challenged the uncritical acceptance of notions of consensus, demonstrating that the post-war settlement should be seen as the outcome of contest and struggle between a range of social factions. Since the victory of the Conservative Party in the General Election of 1979, the positioning of education at the centre of the political agenda has led to a marked growth in policy analysis.

The dearth of policy literature in the field of special educational needs has been particularly marked. Tomlinson (1982) argued that both research and policy analysis tended to explain the pattern of provision as reflecting the growth of humanitarian concern for children with special needs. Such uncritical explanations, she suggested, concealed other important factors such as the desire to exclude certain groups of children from mainstream schools and the vested interests of professional groups in promoting career structures in special education. Oliver (1985) maintained that the Warnock Report tended to reflect the 'march of progress' view of special needs provision rather than its social control function, citing the following excerpt:

> As with ordinary education, education for the handicapped began with individual charitable enterprise. There followed in time the intervention of government, first to support voluntary effort and make good deficiencies through state provision, and finally to create a national framework in which public and voluntary agencies could act in partnership to see that all children, whatever the disability, received a suitable education. The framework reached its present form only in this decade.
>
> (DES, 1978: 8, para 2.1)

In Barton's (1986) view, a far more critical perspective was required, holding in question the assumed disinterest and altruism of those providing services for children with special educational needs.

What sociologists have argued is the view that concern for the handicapped has developed as a result of progress, enlightenment and humanitarian interests, is totally unacceptable. The experience of this particular disadvantaged group has generally been one of exploitation, exclusion, dehumanisation and regulation.

(Barton, 1986: 276)

The work of Tomlinson and Barton has been criticised by others, however. Croll and Moses (1985), for instance, suggested that it ignored the very real needs of children with learning difficulties, and the humanitarian concerns of their teachers. Such accounts

fail to do justice to the very real difficulties experienced by some children . . . the fact that standardised testing procedures inevitably force some children to be bottom does not mean that these children do not have considerable difficulties. Similarly, the fact that categories of special needs are socially created and that the application of them to particular children is imperfect does not mean that the difficulties to which they refer are not real.

(Croll and Moses, 1985: 20)

Clearly, there is a danger inherent in conflict theory that *any* action may be interpreted as upholding the interests of privileged groups, and all developments thus become suspect. The problems which this may raise for practitioners are discussed by Oliver (1985). Whilst in general favouring the use of critical perspectives in the analysis of special needs education, he argued that if economic, political and social forces are seen as all-powerful, then practitioners may feel unable to effect change; as Willis (1977) has put it:

If we have nothing to say about what we do on Monday morning everything is yielded to a purist, structuralist, immobilising, relativist tautology. Nothing can be done until the basic structures of society are changed but structures prevent us from making any changes.

(Willis, 1977: 89)

We would argue that whilst a rigidly determinist model is unhelpful, nonetheless critical perspectives are essential to alert us to the economic and political context in which special educational needs are construed, and the power struggles surrounding policy. None of our contributors adopts the view that recent developments in the area of special needs are automatically in the best interests of the children, but their assessment of these changes varies widely. For example, Wolfendale (this volume) comments:

> There is a consensus that the thrust of recent legislation is benign and enabling, reflecting a caring society, despite enduring professional concerns about the imprecision of terminology and consequent difficulty of agreeing criteria and thresholds for assessing special educational needs.

By way of contrast, Corbett (Chapter 4, this volume) emphasises the inhospitable political climate in which inclusive education in Newham is struggling to survive.

A further common theme in this collection is that although politicians might hope that legislation and policy directives would be implemented in a smooth and uncontested manner, the reality may be far removed from this, as policies are interpreted and possibly subverted at all stages. Fulcher (1989), for example, has argued that the distinction between policy and implementation served political purposes since 'it occludes the real politics involved and presents bureaucrats as merely "administrators": it constitutes a discourse of persuasion, of maintaining the view that only politicians hold real power' (Fulcher, 1989: 6).

Hill and Bramley (1986), writing in the context of social policy more generally, also pointed out that the distinction between policy-making and implementation was based upon an important assumption in democratic government that policy is made by a group of politicians who are answerable to the electorate. However, they maintained that

> There is a great deal of empirical evidence to suggest: (a) that 'policies' leave that part of the political system still highly uncertain or ambiguous, or indeed even sometimes containing contradictions; and (b) that actors in the part of the system concerned with implementation frequently operate in ways which create or transform or subvert what might have been regarded as the 'policies' handed down to them.
>
> (Hill and Bramley, 1986: 139)

All the chapters in this book attempt to provide insight into the process of policy formation and implementation. They suggest that even though policies emanating from central government act as a powerful constraint, nonetheless there is still space for the creative responses of individuals and institutions.

The Warnock Report, the Progress Report of Scottish HMI and the 1981 Education Acts for Scotland, England and Wales

We turn now to a brief consideration of the significance of key policy developments in the late 1970s: the policy recommendations of Warnock and Scottish HMI and their translation into statute.

A major theme of the Warnock Report was the need to reconceptualise the position of children with learning difficulties in the school system, recognising them not as a discrete group entirely separate from the rest of the school population, but as part of a broad continuum ranging from those with severe and enduring difficulties to those whose problems were mild and perhaps temporary. Warnock noted that the source of a child's learning difficulties might be his or her social and cultural environment rather than an intrinsic condition. In the light of what was seen as an educationally unhelpful and socially stigmatising system of categorisation, Warnock made the following recommendation:

> We believe that the basis for decisions about the type of educational provision which is required should be not a single label 'handicapped' but rather a detailed description of special educational need. We therefore recommend that statutory categorisation of handicapped pupils should be abolished.
>
> (DES, 1978: 43, para 3.25)

In the committee's view, a system should be put in place to record the educational needs of children

> who, on the basis of a detailed profile of their needs prepared by a multi-professional team, are judged by their local education authority to require special educational provision not generally available in ordinary schools.
>
> (DES, 1978: 45, para 3.31)

Warnock envisaged that an increasing number of children with learning difficulties would be educated in mainstream rather than special schools, but at the same time was convinced that there would continue to be a role for special schools. Citing evidence from the Inner London Education Authority, the report noted that 'in many respects, the special school represents a highly developed technique of positive discrimination' (DES, 1978: 121, para 8.1).

A further major theme of the report was the central role to be played by parents in the identification, assessment and education of their children and their need for continuing co-operative support in the form of information, advice and political help. This support, it was argued,

> must be seen as taking place within a partnership between parents and the members of different services. To the extent that it enables parents more effectively to help their children at home and at school the support should be an integral part of the provision made for children with special educational needs, which parents have a right to expect.
>
> (DES, 1978: 161, para 9.40)

In Scotland, the legislation was also influenced by the Progress Report of Scottish HMI entitled *The Education of Pupils with Learning Difficulties in Primary and Secondary Schools in Scotland* (SED, 1978). This report focused on children with learning difficulties in mainstream schools and the role of the remedial teacher and underlined the value of a curriculum-deficit rather than a child-deficit model. According to HMI, all pupils should follow essentially the same curriculum, differentiated in an appropriate manner. Segregating pupils in separate remedial classes or withdrawing them for individual tuition was likely to exacerbate their problems rather than cure them, since they were likely to lose contact with their peers, lack the stimulation of the mainstream curriculum and become increasingly demotivated. Responsibility for meeting the needs of children with learning difficulties was placed firmly on the shoulders of the class or subject teacher. Even if extra assistance was required from the learning support teacher, this does not reduce the class or subject teacher's responsibility for the pupils, or absolve him from continuing his own endeavours (SED, 1978: 25, para 4.11). HMI also proposed a new role for the remedial teacher. Criticising the trend towards separate remedial departments, it was argued that 'remedial education is a whole-school responsibility and an inherent element of the work of subject departments' (SED, 1978: 27, para 4.17).

It was proposed that remedial teachers should henceforth engage primarily in co-operative teaching and consultancy alongside the mainstream teacher and should give up their separate departmental base, since this was likely to convey the impression that children with learning difficulties required separate provision. This report by HMI was extremely influential in Scotland and some of its implications are discussed in chapters 7 and 10 (this volume) by Munn and Weedon. It is interesting that although the 'whole-school approach' has been advocated by writers south of the border (e.g. Dessent, 1987), there was no equivalent English document at the time.

A number of the recommendations of the Warnock Report were incorporated into the 1981 Education Acts for England and Wales and Scotland. The 1981 Education (Scotland) Act amends the 1980 Education (Scotland) Act, but, for the sake of brevity, the legislation is usually referred to as the 1981 Act rather than the 1980 Act as amended. Both north and south of the border the legislation abolished statutory categories of handicap, established the concept of special educational needs and provided for an assessment procedure and the drawing up of an official document stating the nature of the child's special needs and the measures proposed by the education authority to meet these needs. The definitions of special needs employed in the English and the Scottish legislation were slightly different, but both defined the concept in relation to the performance of other children of the same age and the general level of resourcing.

There were, however, two other important differences between the two Acts. The Scottish legislation incorporated measures to allow all parents choice of their child's school, which went further than the 1980 English legislation (see Adler, 1993, for a detailed discussion of arrangements for parental choice of school in England and Wales and in Scotland), and whereas the English legislation made a commitment to the integration of children with special educational needs wherever possible, the Scottish Act contained no such provision.

Assessments of the Progress Report of Scottish HMI, the Warnock Report and the 1981 Acts

Although the Progress Report of Scottish HMI gained widespread acceptance among special needs advisers and HMI, it received very little critical appraisal at the time. Allan, Brown and Munn (1991), however, revealed considerable tension at grassroots level, as learning support teachers struggled to negotiate their new consultancy role with mainstream teachers, some of whom neither understood nor sympathised with the new philosophy. In addition, abandoning the notion of deficit within the child as the source of learning difficulties and ensuring that, however great the difficulty, no child experienced a sense of failure, were difficult goals to achieve.

By way of contrast, the Warnock Report and the subsequent legislation were subjected to a great deal of critical scrutiny. Some commentators felt that Warnock did not go far enough in effecting a significant shift in the balance of power between parents and professionals. According to Kirp (1982), a major weakness lay in its uncritical acceptance of the benign discretion of professionals as the guiding principle of policy. This reflected the membership of the committee which, he noted,

> was drawn almost entirely from the professionals who had some relation to special education. . . . Its chairman, an Oxford philosophy don, was the only non-specialist. Only one of the committee's 26 members was the parent of a handicapped child. The special interest groups were unrepresented for DES affirmed it was not forming a constituent body. Despite the disproportionately high number of nonwhite children who had been identified as educationally subnormal or mal-adjusted, no nonwhite served on the committee; nor was there a lawyer, who might have spoken to the relevance of a legal rights viewpoint; nor was there a handicapped person.
>
> (Kirp, 1982: 155)

Kirp contrasted the principle of professional discretion under-lying the Warnock Report with the model of individual rights underlying US provision. He observed that within the US framework it was the duty of the state to identify children's special educational needs, which must be met from federal funds regardless of cost. As a result of this policy, 8 per cent of children in the US had their special educational needs recognised and funded from federal sources, a situation he considered preferable to that in the United Kingdom where only about 2 per cent of children had statements or records of needs.

Interestingly, whilst Kirp criticised Warnock for allowing professionals to restrict the number of children recognised as having special educational needs, Tomlinson argued that the

Warnock Report led to an unwelcome expansion of special education. In her view the rhetoric of special needs has been used
to justify the reproduction of a profoundly disadvantaged group.

> Those who find difficulty in moving beyond humanitarian
> rhetoric, and insist that 'all children have special needs' still
> have to explain why a whole sub-system of special education
> has developed and expanded, which is backed by legal
> enforcement and caters largely for the children of the manual
> working class. To do this, attention must turn from the
> psychogenic focus on individual 'needs' to the social interest
> groupings, the educational, political and economic 'needs'
> which an expansion of special education is serving.
>
> (Tomlinson, 1985: 164)

Whilst questions were raised about the extent to which Warnock
signalled a radical change of policy or 'more of the same',
research commissioned by the DES and the SOED into the
operation of the legislation (Goacher et al., 1988; Thomson et al.,
1989) highlighted a number of inconsistencies in its implementation. Both studies, for instance, identified variation among
education authorities in the proportion of children for whom
statements (England and Wales) or records of needs (Scotland)
were opened. In addition, recording policies operated differently
in different areas, with an apparent lack of consistency with
regard to the types of difficulty judged to merit a record or
statement. The research highlighted the difficulties of achieving
the partnership with parents advocated by Warnock and,
although there appeared to be a movement towards the integration of children with special educational needs, there was
great divergence of practice. In general, those with an established
tradition of educating children with special educational needs in
mainstream schools continued to do so, whereas regions with a
high investment in special schools found it difficult to shift
resources from one location to another. Overall, it appeared that
the type of provision experienced by children with special needs
was influenced by a mixture of geography, politics and luck.
Assessments of children's needs reflected educational psychologists' awareness of resource availability as much as dispassionate
professional judgements of the children's requirements.

Many of the criticisms of the Warnock Report and the 1981
Acts arose as a result of anxiety over the open-ended and circular

definition of special educational needs and the abandonment of categories. Elliott (1990) maintained that the US legislation, which retained categories of learning difficulties and criteria for additional resourcing, was both fairer and easier to operate. Warnock herself expressed concern that, because the system only guaranteed additional resourcing to those with records or statements of needs, those who lacked this legal protection were losing out. She is quoted in the *Guardian*, (Berliner, 1993), as commenting:

> I was very naive not to assume that the financial situation would be such that the only way to get money for special needs was to get a statement which means less spending on the ones without a statement. I would like to go back to a position in which only 2 per cent of children have statements, with money allocated to the other 18 per cent. Unless we do that, a lot of children will slip through the net.

Much criticism of the Warnock Report, then, focused on its failure to shift the balance of power sufficiently in the direction of children with special needs and their parents. However, a rather different assessment has emerged in the light of more recent government policy, where the over-riding purpose has been the introduction of market forces into education along with the tightening of central control. The Warnock Report, it would appear, is now perceived by many as representing an important advance for children with special needs, which needs to be defended in an increasingly hostile climate. Heward and Lloyd-Smith (1990), in their analysis of the impact of legislation on special education policy, stated that

> After nearly a century as a Cinderella, special education finally gained a tenuous foothold in the front line of educational policymaking with a Committee of Enquiry reporting in 1978 and an Education Act in 1981. The Warnock Committee set out a framework for the redirection of special educational policy away from its deeply institutionalized practices of categorisation and segregation towards greater flexibility and integration, a policy long commended by advocates of better education for the handicapped.
>
> (Heward and Lloyd-Smith, 1990: 21)

They further argued that undermining the system of categorisation and segregation had represented a major task requiring
both political commitment and resources and progress had been
slow. Nonetheless, they maintained that the new policy
directions signalled by the Education Reform Act threatened to
undermine and dissipate Warnock's essentially progressive
vision. Russell (1990) also maintained that, despite the
burgeoning bureaucracy noted by Goacher *et al*, the 1981 Act had
led to a general improvement in practice, with greater involvement of parents throughout the assessment and decision-making
process, higher parental expectations with regard to the quality
of educational provision and a growth in numbers of children
being integrated into mainstream schools. In order to allow
Warnock's reforms to reach their full fruition, they should be left
undisturbed. In the next section, we look more closely at the
nature of the educational policies of the Conservative Party and
their effect on the field of special educational needs.

THE CONSERVATIVE POLICY AGENDA AND ITS EFFECT ON SPECIAL EDUCATIONAL NEEDS PROVISION

Throughout the 1980s and into the 1990s, the government has
introduced an extensive programme of reforms which has shifted
responsibility for the quality of children's education from the
state to individual families, enhanced the power of schools at the
expense of that of education authorities and centralised control of
important areas such as the curriculum and assessment. Many of
the reforms have been formulated with prime regard for the
mainstream majority, yet all have implications for children with
special educational needs. In this section, we comment on
differences in the implementation of certain aspects of the
reforms north and south of the border.

Recent policy-making in England and Wales and Scotland – the case of the national curriculum

In England and Wales, many of the recent wave of reforms were
incorporated into one wide-ranging piece of legislation, the 1988
Education Reform Act, which was intended to introduce an
entirely new system of educational and social values. As the then
Secretary of State for Education, Kenneth Baker, said in his

speech to the North of England Education Conference at Rotherham in January 1988:

> It is about enhancing the life chances of young people. It is about devolution of authority and responsibility. It is about competition, choice and freedom . . . it is part of the search for – and achievement of – educational excellence. It is about quality and standards . . . ultimately it is about the health and wealth of our country. It is not about enhancing central control.

The government emphasised its determination that the new agenda of competitive individualism would replace former concerns with equality and social justice. Education professionals were seen as an impediment to progress and were left in no doubt that their role was to implement the reforms rather than play a significant part in their shaping.

Although in the late 1980s, educational policy-making in Scotland was also characterised by a lack of sympathy for the views of professionals, in the early 1990s, with a new Scottish education minister, attempts were made to seek common ground with the education profession. For instance, the quest for consensus was evident in the keynote address given by Lord James Douglas Hamilton, the Scottish Secretary of State for Education, to the National Association of Special Educational Needs Conference in May 1993. The speech stressed continuity between the Warnock Report and subsequent educational reforms.

> Now we can see the Warnock Report and the ideas contained within it as a starting point for change. By setting out so clearly the issues which had to be resolved, it acted as a foundation on which to build. Above all, however, the Report was supremely in tune with its time. Its recommendations reflect educational developments which had already begun to be fundamentally influential in education generally: the green shoots of educational change which were to punctuate the early 80s!

Many would of course dispute Lord James' claim that present educational policies are in line with Warnock's reforms, but nonetheless the aim of winning the consent of practitioners rather than intimidating them into acquiescence is apparent.

The manner in which the educational reforms have been introduced in Scotland and England and Wales has led to broadly differing responses from the educational community and this is particularly evident with regard to the national curriculum and assessment. In England and Wales, alarmed by the rapid pace of change and lack of consultation, educationists greeted the national curriculum and assessment with some hostility, suggesting that its consequences for children with special educational needs might be particularly damaging (e.g. Copeland, 1991; Heward and Lloyd-Smith, 1990; Swann, 1992; Wedell, 1988). These commentators argued that teachers might be encouraged to label children with special educational needs as failures throughout their educational careers and important areas of study, such as personal and social development, might be neglected. Others (a rather smaller group) reminded us of the potential benefits of the national curriculum and assessment for children with special educational needs. Galloway (1990), Russell (1990) and Hegarty (1989) suggested that the national curriculum had the potential to provide all children with stimulating and wide-ranging educational experiences, which may not have been universally available in the past. The insistence that assessment should be for all children, it was argued, would have the beneficial effect of forcing practitioners to think about the nature of progress for those with the most severe difficulties as well as the more able and would provide parents with the information needed to allow them to be actively involved in their child's education. As Hegarty pointed out:

> School education is too important, both for the individual and for society, to be determined entirely at local level, and the diversity of curricular practice in schools has been far greater than can be justified by reference to local conditions.
>
> (Hegarty, 1989: 205)

By way of contrast, the 5–14 programme, Scotland's national curriculum, was introduced by national guidelines rather than by legislation and changes have been implemented over a longer time-frame than has been the case south of the border. This lower-key approach has had the advantage of allowing the government to modify its tactics when this has seemed expedient without having to stage a major policy retreat. For example, the SOED was able to respond to the parents' boycott of tests in 1990–91 by reviewing procedures and arriving at a compromise position with teachers and education authorities, abandoning its original intention to test all children in primary 4 and 7. Instead, testing would be used to confirm teachers' judgement that a pupil had attained a given level and the Scottish Office reaffirmed that test results would not be used to construct league tables. Unlike the situation in England and Wales, where it was felt that all children with special educational needs should be tested unless specifically exempted, the SOED has always maintained that testing should 'be left to the discretion of the school in consultation with the parent of the pupil' (SOED, 1991: para 16:3). Revised arrangements for national testing, published in May 1992, stated that pupils with special educational needs and those for whom English is a second language, would not be tested until they had completed level A. This, it was stated, 'would remove a group for whom testing was widely seen to offer few benefits and for whom tests were difficult to construct and time-consuming to administer' (SOED, 1992b: para 20:3). Perhaps as a result of this quest for consensus, and the fact that, particularly at the secondary level, the curriculum was already controlled from the centre, there has been less public debate in Scotland on the implications of the reforms.

The reception of the national curriculum and assessment in England and Wales and Scotland, then, reflects differences in the nature of the schemes, in their manner of introduction and in the educational traditions of the two systems. At the time of writing, it is too early to say whether the new curricular and assessment arrangements will have positive or negative consequences for children with special educational needs, nor whether the harder line approach in England and Wales will prove more or less beneficial than the looser approach adopted in Scotland. However, as both supporters and critics have warned, irrespective of political intentions, much will depend on whether ordinary classroom teachers use the national curriculum and assessment to label and segregate children with learning difficulties, or to press for a broad and enriching educational experience for all.

Choice and diversity – the future policy and legislative context

The reform of education continues, with new measures reflecting the familiar themes of greater choice and accountability accompanied by tighter central control. At the time of writing, the government was in the process of shepherding the 1993

Education Act for England and Wales through Parliament. This Act incorporated measures laid out in the White Paper *Choice and Diversity: A New Framework for Schools* (DFE, 1992a) and the consultation paper *Special Educational Needs: Access to the System* (DFE, 1992b). The five themes permeating educational change since 1979 were identified as: quality, diversity, parental choice, greater school autonomy and greater accountability. Rather than introducing new principles, the 1993 Act was intended to consolidate the movement towards the marketisation of education. To this end, it incorporated measures to simplify the process of attaining grant maintained status for schools and established a funding agency to distribute resources to these schools. In addition, new arrangements for children with special educational needs were introduced, with the stated intention of extending parents' rights to information about and choice of schools, reducing the time taken by LEAs to make assessments and draw up statements of special educational needs and extending parents' rights to appeal. The Act provided for the establishment of an independent tribunal to replace the jurisdiction of both the Secretary of State and appeal committees to hear appeals under the Education Act 1981. Further guidance for authorities on the criteria to be used for making assessments and issuing statements was also provided (DFE, 1993).

In Scotland, two sets of regulations with implications for children with special educational needs were laid before Parliament in 1993. *Better Information for Parents in Scotland* (SOED, 1992a) required the publication of data on examination results, attendance and truancy rates, school leaver destinations, school costs and policy on special educational needs. *Devolved School Management – Guidelines for Progress* (1992c) contained requirements for Scottish education authorities to delegate financial management to schools, a measure introduced earlier in England and Wales under the terms of the 1988 Education Act. In addition, the document *A Parents' Guide to Special Educational Needs* (SOED, 1993) consolidated information on recording, appeals procedures and choice of school.

Both north and south of the border, there appears to be an even greater emphasis on the responsibility of individual parents for the quality of their child's education and a further increase in the power of individual schools, accompanied by a diminution of the power of education authorities. The process of diverting the locus of control from the education authority to the school is further advanced in England and Wales than Scotland. For instance, whereas, at the time of writing, about 1000 schools south of the border had gained grant maintained status, only one Scottish school had opted out of education authority control (although more may apply for opted-out status in the near future). As a result, the power of Scottish education authorities is still largely intact, although the reorganisation of local government in 1996, scheduled to coincide with the devolution of management to schools, is likely to destabilise the system and may contribute to the undermining of education authority power.

The significance of these shifting power relations is explored in a number of chapters in this collection and in the conclusion. A recurrent anxiety is that the principle of parent power may work well for interested and articulate parents who have sufficient cultural and economic resources to use the system to their advantage, but this may be at the expense of less advantaged groups. In the context of waning local authority influence, some notion of collective responsibility is required if quality education is to be made available to all children. In the area of special educational needs, obtaining a helpful balance between collective responsibility and individual rights is far from straightforward. Trusting in the benign discretion of the professionals may lead to parents being subtly steered towards certain outcomes which may promote the smooth functioning of the system, but may not be in the interests of the child or the family. On the other hand, placing responsibility for decision-making entirely on the shoulders of individual parents may work well for the socially advantaged, who feel competent to use appeals procedures if required, but for the majority it may prove too great a burden.

With regard to the effect of the delegation of funds to schools, there is a danger that this will lead to some services being duplicated and others ceasing to exist altogether. As evidence from England and Wales demonstrates (Lunt and Evans, Chapter 2 this volume; Vincent et al., 1993), much depends on the LEA's funding formula, which may channel resources towards pupils with special educational needs or the reverse. However, we should not forget that the provision of services in this area has never been an unmitigated success, and the new obligation on schools to provide better information for parents on their special needs policy may lead to higher levels of participation. Russell

(1992), in her response to the White Paper *Choice and Diversity*, pointed out both the strengths and weaknesses of the new arrangements:

> Devolving power to local schools is right for some aspects of school management. Autonomy and accountability live hand in hand. But such devolution cannot be effective if we end up with a series of Renaissance-style mini-city states, fighting each other and the LEA/Funding Agency for resources and pupils with Machiavellian zeal.
>
> (Russell, 1992: 21)

We have yet to see the extent to which the most recent reforms will intensify competition between schools and the effect this may have on children with special needs, who may be regarded as unattractive customers, particularly if they are not accompanied by additional resources. Furthermore, it will be important to monitor the way in which conflicting principles are resolved. For instance, parents of children with special educational needs may request a place in a grant maintained school, but if the school has opted to become selective such a request may be refused. Particularly in England and Wales, conflicts are likely to arise between the parents' right to choice of school and the school's right to choice of pupils.

To summarise thus far, we have highlighted the key themes to emerge from the major policy documents of the late 1970s with regard to pupils with special educational needs, noting the way in which the Warnock Report demanded a rethink of the conceptualisation of special needs. We described the way in which early responses to Warnock tended to criticise the report for not going far enough in empowering children with special educational needs and their parents, and for failing to be sufficiently precise about the criteria for statementing and recording. Following the introduction of the 1988 Education Reform Act, more sympathetic interpretations of Warnock emerged, with the growing emphasis on market forces in education being seen as a challenge to the higher profile which children with special educational needs had briefly enjoyed. Accounts of the impact of recent educational reforms on children with special educational needs have tended to focus on their potentially negative consequences, although it has generally been acknowledged that the actions of teachers and administrators in interpreting the reforms will be crucial. The relatively quiet reception of measures such as the 5–14 programme in Scotland was discussed and it was suggested that this was partly due to the fact that the existing centralised control of the curriculum made it a less radical departure. In addition, the lower-key implementation strategy led to less hostility among teachers. We now turn to a brief overview of the chapters, all of which address issues to do with continuity and disjunction in policy and provision for children with special educational needs.

THE STRUCTURE OF THE BOOK

In the course of the book, we progress from a consideration of issues connected with national and local government policy initiatives through to a more detailed consideration of the way in which government and local authority policy impacts on teachers' classroom practice. The unifying theme of the entire collection is that policy is made not only in the corridors of power, but by teachers, pupils and parents in their daily interactions.

Lunt and Evans consider (Chapter 2) some of the philosophical and practical dilemmas which arise in relation to provision for children with special educational needs. It is argued that many of these problems are not new, however they are thrown into higher relief by the introduction of local management of school (LMS), under which budgets are allocated to schools on the basis of a formula devised by the LEA. The stated aim of LMS is to increase accountability and openness and reduce anomalies of funding. However, since schools are to be funded on the basis of pupil numbers, it is evident that those which attract more children through open enrolment will be rewarded with more resources and will be able to expand further. Schools with dwindling rolls and resources are likely to be in socially disadvantaged areas and have a high proportion of non-statemented children with learning difficulties, who will not qualify for additional funding. In general, Lunt and Evans fear a retreat to a situation where children with significant special needs were viewed as essentially different from the mainstream population and treated accordingly. For example, they point out that the attachment of funding to a particular child is likely to revive outmoded forms of categorisation and parents may be encouraged to agree to the placement of a child in a special school if additional resources are unavailable in the mainstream. The main positive feature of financial delegation for children with special needs is its emphasis on accountability, which has to date been lacking in this area.

A more optimistic picture is presented by Wolfendale (Chapter 3), who sees some aspects of recent legislation as benign, enabling and having the potential to introduce some consistency into the use of the term 'special educational needs'. She describes the way in which a number of LEAs are creating unified pre-school/special educational needs teams, drawing together the expertise of teachers, nursery nurses and other non-teaching professionals. Parents are becoming increasingly involved in various aspects of the education of pre-5s with special educational needs, participating in education, assessment and the setting up of support groups. She notes that all recent child legislation has shifted the balance of power in favour of parents and that assessment, statementing and appeal procedures now operate in such a way as to enable parents' wishes to be recognised.

However, Wolfendale does not present an entirely rosy picture. Ultimate control continues to rest with the large institutions, increasingly central government. Local accountability mechanisms are being eroded and redress procedures place the parent in opposition to government ministers. The security of early years provision is also under threat. Although education authorities have mandatory duties towards the under-5s, provision of pre-school education remains non-statutory. As an increasingly large proportion of the education budget is devolved to schools, it is unclear who will foot the bill for pre-5s provision. Alongside these uncertainties, Wolfendale notes considerable improvements in practice, a new concern with equal opportunities and rights, and interesting developments arising out of the move towards common European policies.

Corbett (Chapter 4) charts the nature of Newham's inclusive education policy, tracing its roots in radical practice in the former ILEA and considering possibilities for its future development. Difficulties of implementing a radical policy in the context of an inhospitable political climate are highlighted. These include loss of confidence among local policy-makers due to the gradual erosion of local authority power, feelings of stress and overload among teachers, a cautious parental response to the closing of special schools, and the effects of economic recession in an already poverty-stricken area. Conditions for the successful implementation of integration policies are considered, including detailed consultation with all those involved, careful timing of implementation and the ongoing involvement of parents. In particular, consideration of how pupils with severe and profound difficulties may be assisted to access the curriculum in mainstream schools is essential. Overall, it is argued that inclusive education in Newham represents an attempt to implement a caring policy for the education of children with special educational needs. Corbett suggests that, to ensure its survival in the present political climate, more attention will have to be paid to winning the support of parents and staff and ensuring accountability.

Jennifer Evans and colleagues (Chapter 5) highlight the problems and possibilities thrown up by the growing emphasis on the need for schools to work together as clusters in order to pool resources and expertise. Such arrangements are likely to be of growing importance in the future, as the declining power of education authorities makes it increasingly difficult for centralised services to be sustained, particularly for pupils who do not have a statement or record of needs. By looking closely at the operation of two clusters, this paper highlights the key factors which need to be in place for them to work effectively. These include the need for the cluster to remain at a manageable size, to have a key person responsible for its co-ordination and to have a clearly defined role and area of concern. Evans *et al.* consider factors which may hinder the operation of clusters, and the fostering of a competitive culture between schools may be one of these. In addition, if schools attempt to participate in too many collaborative projects, it is likely that their energy will become dissipated.

In Chapter 6, by Riddell, Brown and Duffield, the focus is on the conceptualisation of special educational needs. In advocating the abolition of statutory categories of handicap, Warnock appeared to be reflecting a general consensus that these categories were no longer ethically or practically acceptable as a means of describing a child's problems and educational requirements. Nevertheless, debate persists with regard to the abandonment of labelling. Within psychological literature, discussion continues concerning appropriate taxonomies of learning difficulties. Sociologists and activists have questioned whether an anti-categorisation approach should be regarded automatically as being in the best interests of those with disabilities, since this may deny an important aspect of their identity. And parents have sometimes used their newly acquired power to insist on the potential benefits of having their child identified as experiencing a particular type of difficulty. Based on empirical research in the area of specific learning difficulties, the authors highlight the existence of considerable differences between parents and professionals in their conceptualisation of the problem and their attitudes towards categorisation, with parents generally supporting the use of categories as a means of accessing resources and professionals defending the concept of a continuum of difficulties.

In the context of HMI's insistence that learning difficulties arise as a result of deficiencies in the curriculum, Weedon (Chapter 7) investigates teachers' perceptions of the nature of learning difficulties in mathematics. It would appear that teachers have not incorporated the views of HMI into their work, since the majority believed that children's problems in maths derived mainly from within-child factors. They felt that greater flexibility was needed than that permitted within the framework for the secondary school curriculum, even when individualised teaching methods were used. Weedon considers the implications of this manifest discrepancy between official thinking and teachers' beliefs on the nature and origins of learning difficulties in mathematics. At the very least, he suggests, in-service work is necessary to explore the discrepancy and perhaps encourage teachers to adopt more highly differentiated approaches to the teaching of mathematics. He also suggests, however, that teachers' views should not simply be dismissed as misguided. In his opinion, serious attention should be paid to their contention that a wider group of children would benefit from the degree of curricular flexibility which is currently only considered appropriate for those whose special educational needs are officially recognised. Teachers will clearly play a crucial part in the implementation of the 5–14 programme and, Weedon argues, in the interests of avoiding the alienation of teachers and pupils, it is vital that its flexible rather than its prescriptive aspects are emphasised.

Julie Allan (Chapter 8) provides us with insight into the conditions which may be necessary for integration to work successfully, and the different expectations which may be held by policy-makers and practitioners. Based on case studies undertaken as part of the OECD/CER1 project *Active Life for Disabled Youth* (NFER, 1992), Allan analyses the factors which affect the level of integration of particular children. These include the nature of the child's learning difficulties and the degree of successful collaboration achieved by the learning support and mainstream teacher. In addition, teachers' understandings of the type of integration appears to be crucial. Interestingly, teachers tended to assume that integration had been unsuccessful if it remained at the locational or social level. Senior management and learning support staff, however, revealed that for children with severe learning difficulties, functional integration was often not deemed possible and therefore a lower level of integration might be counted a success. Allan argues for greater clarity of understanding and clearer communication between all concerned in order to ensure that the goals of integration for individual children are clearly understood. If this does not happen, disillusionment with integration as a policy may result.

Armstrong and Galloway (Chapter 9) explore the way in which mainstream schools are responding to children with emotional and behavioural difficulties in the context of an increasingly competitive climate. Although Warnock supported the principle that most children should be integrated, the 1981 Act did not result in a decline of the numbers of children with emotional and behavioral difficulties being educated in special schools. Indeed, at the time of writing there were indications of increasing exclusions of such pupils. Armstrong and Galloway's research explores the way in which teachers legitimise the handing over of responsibility for these children to other professionals. They suggest that this happens first by defining such children as disturbed rather than disruptive, thus locating the source of the problem in the child rather than the teacher or the school. Secondly, teachers define skilful work in terms of teaching 'normal' pupils rather than identifying and planning programmes for children with behavioural problems. Dealing with disturbed pupils is regarded as a the remit of 'experts' working outside mainstream schooling, who have traditionally been regarded as a lower order of professionals. The analysis offered by Armstrong and Galloway provides fascinating insights into ways in which teachers' notions of what counts as legitimate professional activity shifts in order to accommodate the demands set by the marketisation of education. As these new formulations take hold, so there will be less chance of teachers effectively challenging present policy directions.

Pamela Munn explores aspects of the work of the learning support teacher in the context of the HMI Report on children with learning difficulties (SED, 1978). Focusing on one Scottish region, she highlights the way in which primary and secondary learning support teachers construe their tasks differently, with secondary learning support teachers attempting to achieve social integration and to maintain the child's confidence, whilst primary learning support teachers concentrate on enhancing the child's level of academic attainment. Particularly in secondary schools, there appears to be considerable diversity in the role of the learning support teacher and, even within the same school, different departments display a range of understandings of the goals of learning support. Munn points to conflicting elements within the HMI Report, as teachers are enjoined to pursue the same curriculum goals for all pupils whilst at the same time avoiding the development of a sense of failure. In addition, learning support teachers are urged to differentiate their teaching to take account of pupils' needs and abilities, whilst at the same time offering the same curriculum. Finally, the report suggests that the new role of consultant is more professionally demanding than that of remedial teacher, yet at the same time questions whether an independent department is required and maintains that the mainstream teacher must have central responsibility for children with special needs. Munn shows how these confusions affect the way in which learning support and mainstream teachers negotiate their work in the classroom.

Anyone writing on educational policy over the past decade and a half has had to recognise that the next policy rethink, which is inevitably just around the corner, is omitted. We are conscious of the fact that, at the same time as this book is being sent to press, events in the education world are continuing to develop. This book does not attempt to provide a detailed and comprehensive account of all developments which have relevance for special educational needs. We are also aware of some voices that are missing, for instance, we do not have accounts written by parents or pupils of their experiences of policy. Nonetheless, we hope that key elements in the development of policy in the past decade and a half are captured, and their major implications addressed.

REFERENCES

Adler, M. (1993) 'Parental choice and the enhancement of children's interests', in Munn, P. (ed.) *Parents and Schools: Customers, Managers or Partners*. London: Routledge.

Allan, J., Brown, S. and Munn, P. (1991) *Off the Record: Mainstream Provision for Pupils with Non-Recorded Learning Difficulties in Primary and Secondary Schools*. Edinburgh: Scottish Council for Research in Education.

Ball, S.J. (1990) *Politics and Policy-making in Education*. London: Routledge.

Barton, L. (1986) 'The politics of special educational needs', *Disability, Handicap and Society* 1, 3, 273–290.

Berliner, W. (1993) 'Needs that are not being met', *Guardian*, 25 May.

Centre for Contemporary Cultural Studies (CCCS) (1981) *Unpopular Education: Schooling and Social Democracy in England since 1944*. London: Hutchinson University Library.

Copeland, I. (1991) 'Special educational needs and the Education Reform Act, 1988', *British Journal of Educational Studies* 39, 2, 190–206

Croll, P. and Moses, D. (1985) *One in Five: The Assessment and Incidence of Special Educational Needs*. London: Routledge & Kegan Paul.

Department of Education and Science (DES) (1978) *Special Educational Needs* (The Warnock Report). London: HMSO.

Department for Education (DFE) (1992a) *Choice and Diversity: A New Framework for Schools*. London: HMSO.

Department for Education (DFE) (1992b) *Special Educational Needs: Access to the System*. London: Department for Education.

Department for Education (1993) *Draft Code of Practice on the Identification and Assessment of Special Educational Needs. Draft Regulations on Assessments and Statements*. London: Department for Education.

Dessent, T. (1987) *Making the Ordinary School Special*. Lewes: Falmer Press.

Education Act (1981) London: HMSO.

Education Reform Act (1988) London: HMSO.

Education Act (1993) London: HMSO.

Education (Scotland) Act (1980) Edinburgh: HMSO.

Education (Scotland) Act (1981) Edinburgh: HMSO.

Elliott, C.D. (1990) 'The definition and identification of specific learning difficulties', in Pumfrey, P.D. and Elliott, C.D. (eds) *Children's Difficulties in Reading, Spelling and Writing*. London: Falmer Press.

Fulcher, G. (1989) *Disabling Policies? A Comparative Approach to Education Policy and Disability*. Lewes: Falmer Press.

Galloway, D. (1990) 'Was the GERBIL a Marxist mole?' in Evans, P. and Varma, V. (eds) *Special Education: Past, Present, Future*. London: Falmer Press.

Goacher, B., Evans, J., Welton, J. and Wedell, K. (1988) *Policy and Provision for Special Educational Needs: Implementing the 1981 Education Act*. London: Cassell.

Hegarty, S. (1989) 'Special educational needs and national testing', *Support for Learning* 4, 4, 205–208.

Heward, C. and Lloyd-Smith, M. (1990) 'Assessing the impact of legislation on special education policy – an historical analysis', *Journal of Education Policy* 5, 1, 21–36.

Hill, M. and Bramley, G. (1986) *Analysing Social Policy*. Oxford: Basil Blackwell.

Kirp, D. L. (1982) 'Professionalisation as a policy choice: British special education in comparative perspective', *World Politics* 34, 2, 137–174.

Munn, P. (1991) 'School boards, accountability and control', *British Journal of Educational Studies* 39, 2, 173–189.

National Foundation for Educational Research (NFER) (1992) *OECD/CERI Project Integration in the School: Reports of the Case Studies Undertaken in the UK*. Windsor: NFER.

Oliver, M. (1985) 'The integration–segregation debate: some sociological considerations', *British Journal of Sociology of Education* 6, 1, 75–93.

Russell, P. (1990) 'The Education Reform Act – the implications for special educational needs', in Flude, M. and Hammer, M. (eds) *The Education Reform Act, 1988: Its Origins and Implications*. Lewes: Falmer Press.

Russell, P. (1992) 'Choice and diversity – the challenge for pupils with special educational needs: a personal perspective', in Special Educational Consortium, *A Response to the Government's Current Proposals for Education*. London: Special Educational Consortium.

Scottish Education Department (SED) (1978) *The Education of Pupils with Learning Difficulties in Primary and Secondary Schools in Scotland: A Progress Report by HM Inspectors of Schools*. Edinburgh: HMSO.

Scottish Office Education Department (SOED) (1991) *The Framework for National Testing in Session 1991–92*. Edinburgh: SOED.

Scottish Office Education Department (SOED) (1992a) *Better Information for Parents in Scotland*. Edinburgh: The Scottish Office.

Scottish Office Education Department (SOED) (1992b) *Review of Arrangements for National Testing: Consultation Paper by the Scottish Office Education Department*. Edinburgh: SOED.

Scottish Office Education Department (SOED) (1992c) *Devolved School Management: Guidelines for Progress*. Edinburgh: The Scottish Office.

Scottish Office Education Department (1993) *A Parents' Guide to Special Educational Needs*. Edinburgh: SOED.

Scottish Office (1993) 'Keynote address by Lord James Douglas-Hamilton to National Association of Special Educational Needs Conference', 8 May, Edinburgh.

Swann, W. (1992) 'Hardening the hierarchies: the national curriculum as a system of classification', in Booth, T., Swann, W., Masterton, M. and Potts, P. (eds) *Curricula for Diversity in Education*. London: Routledge.

Thomson, G.O.B., Riddell, S. and Dyer, S. (1989) *Policy, Professionals and Parents: Legislating for Change in the Field of Special Educational Needs*. Edinburgh: University of Edinburgh Press.

Tomlinson, S. (1982) *A Sociology of Special Education*. London: Routledge & Kegan Paul.

Tomlinson, S. (1985) 'The expansion of special education', *Oxford Review of Education* 11, 2, 157–165.

Vincent, C., Evans, J., Lunt, I. and Young, P. (1993) 'The Market Forces? The Effect of Local Management of Schools in Special Educational Needs Provision', paper delivered to BERA Conference, University of Liverpool, 10–13 September.

Wedell, K. (1988) 'The new act: a special need for vigilance', *British Journal of Special Education* 15, 3, 98–101.

Willis, P. (1977) *Learning to Labour: How Working-class Kids Get Working-class Jobs*. London: Saxon House.

Chapter 2

Dilemmas in special educational needs
Some effects of local management of schools

Ingrid Lunt and Jennifer Evans

INTRODUCTION

This chapter will report on research carried out over the past three years studying some of the effects of local management of schools (LMS) on special educational needs (SEN). The research has involved three questionnaire surveys to all local education authorities (LEAs) in England (1989–90, 1990–91, 1991–2) and three national day conferences. In addition both authors have had the opportunity to visit several LEAs and to join in discussion and debate concerning special educational needs provision under LMS. The questionnaire findings and conference proceedings have been published in three monographs (Evans and Lunt, 1990, 1992; Lunt and Evans, 1991).

The chapter will focus on a number of dilemmas inherent in making decisions about special educational provision. It is suggested that these have been highlighted by the 1988 Act and, in particular, by LMS. This suggestion has been endorsed by recent reports by the Audit Commission (Audit Commission, 1992a, 1992b) which confirm that the problems in defining and resourcing special needs have become more acute since the implementation of the 1988 Act. It could be argued (in relation to special educational needs) that the implementation of LMS, in and of itself, could have helped both LEAs and schools to greater clarity of definition, greater accountability, more equitable identification of need and allocation of resources, more coherent planning across the continuum of special need and greater evaluation of effectiveness. However, LMS is operating within a context both ideological and economic which makes special educational provision particularly vulnerable. The research reported here (and research by others in the field) is exposing some of these vulnerabilities.

The chapter presents six dilemmas inherent in making special educational needs provision. To a great extent these dilemmas are universal, that is, they have existed over time and are experienced by most other developed countries. The question of how to provide for the more vulnerable members of society clearly raises social, political, economic and ideological issues which are reflected in the problems inherent in making provision for the more needy pupils in our schools. Questions of definition and identification of who is (most) needy, how, where and what to provide, whose responsibility are they and what rights do they have are fundamental issues for decision-makers. However, 'it is as well to remember that the old system, as familiar as it was inequitable and ineffective, was also guilty of "failing" those very same children. . . . LMS did not cut short a 'golden age' of special education' (Lee, 1992a).

THE BACKGROUND OF LMS

LMS (local management of schools) was introduced by the Education Reform Act in 1988.

> Local management of schools represents a major challenge and a major opportunity for the education service. The introduction of needs-based formula funding and the delegation of financial and managerial responsibilities to governing bodies are key elements in the government's overall policy to improve the quality of teaching and learning in schools.
>
> (DES, 1988: para. 9)

LMS introduces the principle of maximum delegation of resources and responsibility to schools. Under LMS, budgets are allocated to schools on the basis of a formula (hence formula-funding) devised by the LEA. The stated intention is to increase accountability and openness and to reduce anomalies of funding and has been expressed thus: 'The government has presented . . . a package, designed to promote accountability and responsiveness of schools and LEAs to their consumers' (Coopers & Lybrand 1987). LEAs are required to devise formulae which are (1) 'simple, clear and predictable'; (2) 'based on an assessment of schools' objective needs, rather than on historic patterns of expenditure'; (3) determined mainly by 'the number of pupils in each school, weighted for their difference in age' (DES, 1988: para 104). LEAs may include a special needs factor in the formula in order to indicate the differing needs of schools in the authority.

LMS thus constitutes the major mechanism for the introduction of market policies into education. If it is possible to quantify the cost of the education of pupils of different ages and different needs, and if schools receive resources mainly according to their pupil numbers, the logic goes, then schools will improve in order to attract more parents' choice under open enrolment. This logic is disarmingly (and misleadingly) simplistic. In the research reported in this chapter we attempt to monitor some of the effects of the introduction of LMS on pupils with special educational needs and to highlight some of the consequences of introducing market mechanisms into an area such as SEN.

THE RESEARCH SO FAR

The three national questionnaire surveys (1990, 1991, 1992) in conjunction with three national day conferences have enabled us to gain both a national overview and some indication of trends over time of some of the effects of LMS on special educational needs policy and provision. Returns were received from 57 per cent, 49 per cent and 52 per cent of the English LEAs respectively over the three years. The questionnaire surveys have focused on the following topics:

1 Provision for SEN and any changes in provision
   • schools and units
   • statemented pupils
   • peripatetic support teams
   • individual support staff
   • exclusions
2 Funding for SEN and any changes in arrangements
   • proportion of aggregated schools' budget (ASB) allocated by age-weighted pupil units (AWPU) and that allocated by other factors
   • mechanism used to allocate SEN funding
   • monitoring of delegated funds
3 Funding of different types of provision
   • special school

- units
- mainstream placements
- non-educational provision
4 Discretionary exceptions
5 Local management of special schools (LMSS)
6 SEN reviews
7 Non-educational provision
8 Other comments

DILEMMAS IN MAKING SPECIAL EDUCATIONAL PROVISION

We have selected six areas where problems or dilemmas arise. These relate to *identification, resourcing, continuity of the special needs continuum, locus of responsibility for provision, integration and effectiveness.* It should be emphasised that these dilemmas are inter-related and interdependent and could also be perceived as the constituent parts of the wider dilemma for special education policy-makers. As Dessent suggests:

> Special education is a part of the wider education system. Its existence is also intimately related to questions of public and professional values and attitudes; to questions of financial resources and costs; to questions concerning teaching, teachers and the nature of schools and schooling in our society.
>
> (Dessent, 1987: 2)

Brahm Norwich summarises the interdependent relationship between special educational provision and ordinary schooling as follows:

> Special educational needs is an educational concept which arises in the context of the compulsory schooling of all children. What unifies the different examples of special educational needs and the different broad areas is the provision of different or additional resources for some children on account of some degree of disability or impairment . . . the question of when additional resources are required also depends on what is available in ordinary schooling and teaching. For this reason what counts as special education varies with the nature of ordinary education.
>
> (Norwich 1990: 4)

Identification

The question of who (how many) to identify as in need of, deserving of, worthy of extra support goes to the heart both of special needs decision-making and of LEAs' LMS policy implementation. The issue is both whether to identify (label) individual pupils in order to target and earmark extra resources and, if identifying individuals, who and how many? Is identification of individual pupils necessary in order to provide the resources to meet their needs or can schools be provided with sufficient resources so that pupils' different needs may be met without labelling individuals as 'different'? It might be argued that if schools were sufficiently generously resourced and supported, there would be very little need to identify individual pupils' needs, and conversely, when schools' own resources are (judged to be) insufficient, there is a greater need to identify individual pupils.

Prior to the Warnock Report of 1978 and the 1981 Education Act, about 2 per cent of the school population in England and Wales was identified as in need of or deserving special (extra) provision or resources. These children were formally identified and their needs met in segregated special schools. DES Statistical Bulletins have regularly published information to show that the cost of placing a child in special school may be between four and eight times as much as in an ordinary school, depending on the type and level of need. Figures for 1983–4, for example, showed net recurrent institutional expenditure per full-time equivalent pupil in primary schools of £730 and in special schools of £3265 (Dessent, 1987). Other developed countries tend to identify a similar proportion of pupils (figures range between 1 and 4 per cent) on whom to spend a considerably enhanced educational resource by making special provision (usually in segregated special school) (Pijl and Meijer, 1991).

It is now well known that, following the 1978 Warnock Report and the 1981 Act, there was a recognition (in England and Wales) that as many as 20 per cent of pupils might at some time in their school career experience difficulties which would lead to their having special educational needs. The question again is whether these children should be identified and therefore labelled as having special needs (and so as in some way different from other children) or whether they should not be individually identified (and thus be taught as members of the diverse and mixed ability groups of pupils found in mainstream schools). In a sense the dilemma hinges on the definition of special educational needs and how it is used. It appears to be the case that there will always be a very small number of pupils who need and deserve considerable extra educational resources. Indeed 'countries seem to "agree" that at least one and a half per cent of the students are difficult to integrate on a curricular level in regular education' (Pijl and Meijer, 1991). However, the difficult question is how to resource schools to provide for the larger group of pupils with less significant and extensive special needs, and whether to identify and label these pupils and, if so, what level of need requires such individual identification.

Since the implementation of the 1981 Act there has been always a lack of clarity and agreement over what (level of need) constitutes 'special educational needs' and a 'prima facie case' for full assessment. This has led to a wide variation across the country in the percentage of pupils formally identified and 'statemented'. In particular a generally 'grey' area in the identification of and provision for pupils whose needs fall in the (numerically very large) 'borderline' groups of pupils with moderate learning difficulties and emotional and behavioural difficulties has led to enormous variation in the proportion of pupils so identified and to what may appear to be a somewhat arbitrary distinction between the 'ordinary' and the 'special' child (for purposes of placement and/or resource allocation). This highlights the concept of the relativity of special needs introduced by the Warnock Report and the 1981 Act.

Some findings

As mentioned above, needs-based formula-funding forms the basis of resource allocation under LMS. LEA formulae are required to be 'simple, clear and predictable', 'based on an assessment of schools' objective needs rather than on historic patterns of expenditure' with AWPUs (age-weighted pupil units) as the central determinant. LMS is forcing LEAs to define the basis by which differential resources are allocated to schools and to identify different pupils' resource-worthiness.

The questionnaire survey has confirmed the wide variation across the country in identification (statementing) rates documented by Swann (1988). There is also a wide range (0 to 12

Table 2.1 Statementing rates in sample LEAs (%)

	1990	1991	(DES 1991)	1992
Highest	5.4	3.99	3.98	3.9
Lowest	1.2	1.1	0.89	1
Average	2.0	2.2		2.4

per cent) in the percentage of resources allocated by LEAs through the formula specifically for special needs and therefore in the numbers of children identified as having SEN and in need of extra resources. This has been reported also by Lee (1992b). As has been widely reported, one of the most noticeable and dramatic findings is the increase in numbers of children with statements or put forward for statementing (i.e. identified as having significant SEN) over the past three years (Table 2.1).

As the LEA services available to support schools with their pupils with SEN appear to be reducing (through constraints on the amount which LEAs are permitted to retain centrally) and as the schools themselves are required to take financial responsibility for meeting the special needs of their own pupils, they are identifying a greater proportion of pupils for statutory assessment and statements in an attempt to gain access to earmarked resources. Thus, the more that resources to support pupils with SEN in mainstream without identification of individuals reduce, the greater the pressures from schools to identify pupils for individual resources through statements. Pressures to calculate 'resource-worthiness' have coincided with the publication of Circular 11/90 (DES, 1990) on staffing for special educational needs which has led many LEAs to develop 'bands' of need which act as 'value added' to the AWPU figure. If pupils are to be thought of as units of funding, then LEAs and schools may be forced to devise means of indicating the value to be added to the AWPU by different levels of SEN.

Resourcing

Closely related to the dilemma of identification is that of resourcing. As mentioned above, England and Wales (and many other developed countries) have historically had a system of allocating substantial extra resources for special education through placement in (segregated) special provision. As stated, the average cost to the LEA of a place in a special school may be four to eight times (depending on the type of special school and therefore the resources and staffing provided) as much as the average cost of a place in an ordinary school. By identifying a child for placement in a special school, the LEA has taken the decision to make considerably greater expenditure on this individual pupil. The two budget systems (special and ordinary) have historically been separate and this separation continues to the present, since the budget for special schools is at the moment outside the General Schools Budget, (though this will alter with the implementation of Local Management of Special Schools – LMSS). The issue involves the questions of how and where to allocate significant extra resources, to permit parental choice and to promote integration.

Following the 1981 Act, a separate means of allocating significant additional resources continued to a large extent through the statementing process, which was intended for approximately that same proportion previously in special schools (approximately 2 per cent) and meant to indicate a need for substantial extra resources. Klaus Wedell has pointed out that 'England . . . became the only developed country to attempt special educational reform without an allocation of additional funds to carry it out' (Wedell, 1990). Following the implementation of the 1981 Act, however, local authorities developed their own services (advisers, advisory teachers, peripatetic teachers, support teachers and assistants, additional educational psychologists) by allocating more of their budget to this area in order to support the so-called '18 per cent' who were considered to have special educational needs in mainstream schools (Goacher et al., 1988).

The nature and extent of these (LEA-based) services have always varied considerably across the country both between LEAs and within LEAs. The dilemma has been highlighted by LMS which raises vital questions concerning how to allocate and target additional resources fairly according to need, how to avoid 'resource drift' and how to avoid categorisation and labelling.

Findings

Under LMS there are various ways of resourcing SEN. First, the most obvious and straightforward is through attaching to the individual pupil the 'label' of a statement whose 'value' is defined in section 3 of the statement. Indeed this has been referred to as giving the child the 'protection of a statement' indicating that this is the only (certain) way to protect or guarantee such resources and to prevent 'resource drift' or alternative uses of extra resources. As mentioned above, the demand for statements has increased considerably and continues to do so.

Second, LEAs may weight the amount delegated to schools for SEN. Under LMS Circular 7/91 (DES, 1991) LEAs are expected to include some SEN weighting ('variations in the additional costs of pupils with special educational needs') in the 20 per cent non-AWPU element of the formula. Figures from the DES, data from surveys by Tim Lee at the University of Bath (Lee, 1992c) and preliminary findings from our questionnaire study have revealed wide variations between LEAs in their SEN weightings.

A third means of enhancing the funding for pupils with SEN was introduced by Circular 7/91 (DES, 1991) which brought in the possibility for LEAs to include additional pupil-related weightings to count towards the 80 per cent AWPU limit in respect of pupils with special educational needs with or without statements. Again, there is wide variation across the country in the use of this aspect of the formula.

Finally, the means used by LEAs to identify special needs in order to target resources varies widely between LEAs (see also Lee, 1992a) with the requirement to be 'simple, clear and predictable' leading several LEAs to use proxy indicators such as take-up or eligibility for free school meals as indicators of SEN (Table 2.2). More sophisticated measures of need such as the former ILEA's Educational Priority Index have been judged (by DES) to be too complex, while measures such as professional judgements have been considered (by DES) to be potentially subjective. A more positive finding is the development by a few LEAs of special needs 'audits' based on teacher judgements moderated across the schools. This method involves teachers in schools across an LEA identifying levels of special need in their own schools, usually through an LEA-wide procedure which is then moderated across schools to attempt to ensure consistency of judgements. Although this method is costly both of school and LEA staff time, it offers staff development opportunities and is considered by some LEAs to provide a more accurate indication of the differing needs of schools in respect of pupil intake and attainment. However, the problem of how and where to target resources continues to lead the majority of LEAs and central government into using simplistic and potentially misleading measures.

The notion of a 'voucher' system has now been lurking in the background of some thinking in the area for a decade. It could be speculated that a 'voucher' system indicating 'level of need' and corresponding 'level of extra resource or value' (possibly defining bands of need along similar lines to those suggested in Circular 11/90) could be an administrative follow-on from some of the developments of LMS. This would have considerable disadvantages which include undermining local SEN planning, preventing economies of scale, individualising provision and potentially reducing the value of the voucher to a minimal value and jeopardising initiatives such as integration.

Continuity of continuum

Following the 1981 Education Act, there was a recognition both of a continuum of special educational needs and the need to match

Table 2.2 Indicators of SEN used by LEAs to target resources to mainstream schools (1992)

Free school meals	28
Socio-economic	1
English as Second Language	1
Tests	12
Audit of SEN	1
Single parent	1
Clothing grant	5
Census data	3
Council tenant	1
In care	3

this by a continuum of provision. The implication was that the previous sharp distinction between 'special' and 'not special i.e. ordinary' was often meaningless, particularly for the 'borderline' groups of pupils judged to have moderate learning difficulties or emotional and behavioural difficulties (see above, p.34) and that pupils' needs could be more appropriately represented as lying on a continuum, as interactive and as changing over time.

> The notion of special needs as forming a continuum is both uncontroversial and readily understood. The implications of the concept are, however, quite revolutionary when the business of resource allocation and special educational provision is considered . . . wherever a line is drawn through the continuum of need (for example, for the administrative purpose of allocating resources, the production of statements etc.) it will always be an arbitrary one.
>
> (Dessent 1987: 5, 8)

The problem is how to resource a continuum of need. Clearly it is administratively much easier to identify, categorise and 'pigeonhole' pupils for resource purposes. It is also administratively easier to define need according to categories which, by definition, mean a break in a continuum as one passes over a threshold into a different category of need and resources. Yet identification in this manner involves labelling and breaking the continuum. Resourcing a continuum (which is, by definition, continuous) is much more complicated. In reality the so-called continuum is likely to continue to have a break in it as at present (at the point of statementing) even if only for the important purpose of protecting earmarked resources. Many would argue that there is in any case a justifiable break in the continuum at the point of greatest need of those with, for example, severe sensory impairment, physical or mental handicap. However, there is the obvious question, of where to make that break. Secondly, there is the question of the nature of the break, since it is clearly not appropriate for the break to be seen as implying 'resourced' versus 'not resourced'. If this latter were to be the case, it is likely that we would see an enormous increase in the numbers of pupils being statemented and so identified as falling on the 'resourced' side of the dividing line. In addition, the so-called 'borderline' needs of those with moderate learning difficulties or emotional and behavioural difficulties are those which pose the greatest problem in terms of provision and for whom the break in the continuum is likely to be the most arbitrary. A final problem involves the implications of simultaneously recognising the relativity of SEN while addressing the question of whether to resource schools or individuals or a combination of both.

Findings

As mentioned above, the requirement to allocate funds mainly through AWPUs (i.e. individual pupil units) is leading many LEAs to attempt to attach an individual 'value added figure' to pupils according to need. As already suggested, this has been encouraged by Circular 11/90 (DES, 1990) and several LEAs have introduced 'steps' or bands into their 'continuum' of SEN in order to indicate increasing levels or categories of resource. This may be in relation only to those pupils who have statements or it may include pupils without statements. The difficulty with this, in addition to the re-introduction of some forms of categories, is the problem of attaching resources to individuals. Special educational needs arise out of an interaction of attributes of the child with factors in the environment. Therefore resourcing the child without considering the environment or as though the child were learning in isolation addresses only part of the situation and has the added disadvantage of possible 'perverse incentives' by 'rewarding' schools which 'fail' their pupils.

Our research and that of others suggests that the pressures for statements are having the effect of reinforcing a discontinuity between statemented and non-statemented pupils with special educational needs. On the one hand, a small percentage of pupils with statements is guaranteed extra resources while, on the other hand, schools see or fear that LEA resources which previously supported non-statemented pupils with SEN in mainstream are being cut as the LEA meets the requirement to delegate at least 85 per cent of the Potential Schools' Budget. Evidence from several LEAs indicates that a continuum of provision is hard to maintain under the pressures of formula-funding based on pupil units and with the threat to centrally provided LEA support services.

Responsibility for provision

Some commentators have felt that since the 1981 Act and the

growth in services for SEN provided by LEAs, schools have increasingly been tempted to see special needs as 'someone else's problem'. One way in which this has manifested itself is that schools which demonstrate their inability to provide for special needs have at times gained extra resources from the LEA (either by having the child removed or by receiving extra support). Following the 1988 Act this problem may become more acute as schools compete for pupils and the ability to provide for pupils with SEN is not necessarily perceived by the wider group of parents to be a reason to choose that school. If statements continue to be the one guaranteed means of gaining extra resources, then schools will continue to feel that SEN is 'someone else's (i.e. the LEA's) problem' and expertise. Furthermore, at present there is little financial incentive for schools to accept pupils with SEN for whom it may be difficult and expensive to provide.

The question of who has responsibility for provision may be asked at two levels. At one level it may be asked whether funding for special educational needs should be provided and allocated at central government, local government, school or some other level. At another level it may be asked which pupils with special educational needs should be the responsibility of the school (and if so which school) and which of the LEA. Following the 1981 Act, as mentioned above, many LEAs developed extensive (LEA) support for pupils with special educational needs, such that it became possible for schools to pass on or 'refer' pupils for whom they found it difficult to provide. Some schools developed a narrow or 'exclusive' notion of the kind of pupils whose needs they felt they could meet, while other schools developed a more 'inclusive' concept of meeting the needs of the children in their community. The proportion of pupils within a particular school's community for whom it feels unable to provide clearly depends on a large number of factors, and schools vary considerably in the numbers of pupils which they feel the need to 'refer out'. Both the pre-1981 Act special education referral and the post-1981 Act statementing procedure allowed schools to consider that there was a small percentage of pupils for whom the ordinary school was not responsible and whose needs were such that they required different provision and should be 'referred out'. This proportion appears to be growing steadily (see also Armstrong and Galloway, Chapter 9, this volume).

As used in the 1981 Act, the term 'special educational needs' does not have an absolute meaning, but is defined in relation to the achievement level of the majority of children in a class. The 1981 Act defined 'special educational provision' as 'provision which is additional to or . . . different from . . . provision made generally . . . '. The lack of an absolute definition of special educational needs and special educational provision accounts for the fact that there have always been 'high referring' schools and those that make very few referrals out. One of the problems which contributes to the difficulty in deciding who has responsibility for provision has been the lack of definition of 'generally available provision' in LEA schools (against which an objective assessment of need may be made) and hence a lack of clarity in who has responsibility for pupils who appear unable to 'fit in'. This has been highlighted in the Audit Commission reports (1992a, 1992b).

Findings

Under the 1981 Act LEAs have responsibility for making special educational provision. This has given rise to considerable confusion. While LEAs have a legal responsibility for meeting the needs of pupils with statements and it remains unclear who has responsibility for meeting the needs of pupils without statements, there is a tendency for schools to increase the numbers of pupils put forward for statements. As mentioned above, both DES statistics and our survey show that this has been the case.

The relativity of the 1981 Act implied that a 'prima facie case' for full assessment was dependent on what was 'generally available' in the school. Although in theory the percentage of children requiring full assessment and a statement was thought (by the Warnock Committee) to be about 2 per cent, the relativity of the definition of special educational need led both to wide variations across and between local authorities in the percentage of children so identified and to a lack of clarity as to what constituted a 'prima facie' case for full assessment. The 1981 Act definition of special educational needs inevitably produced a lack of clarity and objectivity in the level of special need required for a 'prima facie case' for the initiation of a full assessment and the relativity inherent in the definition led, some might say predictably, to a wide variation in practice across the country.

This has been highlighted in the Audit Commission report (1992a): 'as the 1981 Act does not define its client group it is very difficult for LEAs to implement it consistently. LEAs lack a definition of special educational needs and the threshold for issuing statements of special educational needs has not been established.'

Prior to the implementation of the 1981 Act, it was considered possible to identify pupils objectively through the use of standardised tests such as IQ tests, which were widely used for the placement of pupils in special schools. The relativity of the 1981 Act definition and the suggestion of a figure of 20 per cent of pupils with special educational needs, together with moves away from the use of standardised and norm-referenced tests and an abandonment of categories of handicap led to a lack of consistency in judgements of what should be considered to be 'special educational needs'.

Now, for the first time, a number of LEAs are attempting to develop 'objective' criteria for the definition of a 'prima facie case' and, by implication, to define 'generally available provision in the LEA's schools'. However, such criteria are extremely difficult to develop, partly because 'objective' may be thought to imply 'numerical' or 'norm-referenced' and partly because of the relativity of SEN. A House of Commons Select Committee sought views on this in its enquiry into the 'statementing' procedure and national guidance was contained in the Code of Practice following the 1993 education legislation (DFE, 1993). Some observers have commented that this will lead to a long overdue definition and redistribution of responsibility between schools and the LEA, and that by defining the kinds of needs that ordinary schools are expected to meet from their own resources it will be possible to develop a more equitable and efficient means of allocating extra resources. However, it should also be remembered that other provisions of the 1988 Act such as open enrolment, publication of national curriculum assessment results and funding on the basis of pupil numbers encourages competition between schools to attract pupils. Pupils with special educational needs are unlikely to be the pupils that schools are competing to attract, since their performance in tests may detract from the schools' overall position in the league tables, their 'behaviour' may discourage other parents from choosing the school, and meeting their needs may be costly on the school budget. As Warnock said 'the education of children with special educational needs is not cost effective. Therefore it does not fit into a market philosophy of schools' (*Hansard*, 1991).

Integration

The 1981 Act recommended that special educational provision should be made in ordinary schools, subject to certain provisos. One dilemma for parents is whether to choose segregated provision in the knowledge that the extra resources are definitely available and located there or to choose integrated provision knowing that their child is likely to get less resources in this setting (see below). There have been moves towards integration or non-segregation of pupils with special educational needs across most developed countries through the 1970s and 1980s following widespread concern with human rights and equal opportunities. Will Swann of the Open University has made detailed analyses of the statistics on integration in England and Wales. He wrote in 1985 that 'overall there is no evidence of a trend towards integration . . . there is little indication that education authorities at either national or local level take the duty to integrate very seriously' (Swann, 1985: 15).

He continued in 1988 'the evidence for a national trend towards integration after 1982 is very slight indeed . . . no clearly articulated steps have been taken by the DES to reduce the proportion of pupils going to special schools' (Swann, 1988: 156). Even in 1991 he was able to write 'ten years after the 1981 Education Act, the proportion of primary aged children in special schools in England may be on the increase' (Swann, 1991: 1).

So, despite the overall trend towards integration, change in the English context appears to have been remarkably slow, suggesting that the trend might be reversed very easily. One dilemma in relation to integration arises from the way in which additional resources for special educational needs are allocated. This has been alluded to above. The vast majority of special educational resources are based in separate special schools where pupils will receive considerably enhanced funding by a factor of four to eight. The easiest and administratively most straightforward way to gain access to these resources is to place a child in a special school. This 'guarantees' the additional expenditure. Furthermore, so long as considerable resources are 'earmarked' and based in separate special schools, it may make more sense economically to place children there, since the special provision 'plant' is being financed and staffed and placement of pupils there may result in economies of scale and more economic use of expensive facilities. However, the existence of considerable resources in a separate system means that there are correspondingly less resources available for supporting children with special needs with or without statements, in mainstream schools. For administrators, therefore, the dilemma at least economically is how to retain both integrated and segregated systems in order to be able to offer parental choice and how to shift resources from one system (e.g. special school) to the other (e.g. mainstream) while maintaining the integrity and adequacy of both. The failure of LEAs to shift resources from special to mainstream schools following more integration of pupils with SEN into mainstream has been highlighted by the Audit Commission/HMI report (Audit Commission, 1992a).

In addition, in order to gain access to these additional resources, the pupil is required to be identified and 'labelled' through a statement, thus highlighting one of the difficulties inherent in the 1981 Act when it abolished the former categories of disability but set up a system for the identification of a small proportion of children requiring additional provision. Put simply, it may sometimes be the case that in order to gain access to the resources needed, a pupil has to be labelled as having special educational needs and placed in a special school since these resources are not available in mainstream school. Pressure for the efficient use of resources militates against the move towards integration since this requires the wider dispersion of additional resources. This dilemma has also been highlighted in the USA by national reports examining its parallel legislation, Public Law 94-142: 'parents articulated being in the difficult position of choosing between a segregated setting with adequate specialised services and an integrated setting with inadequate specialised services' (Florian and West, 1991).

Findings

The analysis of statistics carried out by Swann (1991) suggests that any move towards integration is very slow and, indeed, that there may be some indications of trends in the opposite direction.

Our questionnaire survey showed that most children with statements are placed in special schools and that there has been an increase in the numbers of pupils in special schools in 50 per cent of the sample LEAs. There has also been an increase in the number of pupils with statements in mainstream schools in 86 per cent of the LEAs. However, since more pupils are being identified and resourced through statements, although larger numbers of pupils with statements are being provided for in mainstream, overall the number attending special schools is not falling significantly. A further concern in the picture is the widely reported rise in the number of pupils excluded from school (DFE, 1992); our questionnaire survey showed 86 per cent of the LEAs reporting an increase in the number of exclusions over the last year. The question of how to resource integration may have become more acute following the implementation of LMS, though the full implications will not become clear until we see the effects of extending LMS to special schools and the inclusion of the special schools budget within the General Schools Budget.

Effectiveness

Questions of effectiveness in relation to special educational needs, whether couched in terms of value for money, quality of provision or outcome, have rarely been addressed. One of the reasons is that effectiveness or 'success' is particularly difficult to measure in relation to special educational needs. A difficulty may be that 'success' of special educational provision (e.g. in reducing or removing special educational needs) should in theory at least lead to a reduction in need for that provision and might be used to justify cuts in expenditure. So long as there are separate budgets and systems for ordinary and special provision, it may not be politically advantageous for special needs staff to be too successful, since this might lead to loss of posts in this area. A further reason relates to responsibility. If special educational provision is the responsibility of the LEA, then, apart from occasional input from external agencies, the LEA is the sole provider. Because it has not hitherto been necessary to choose between a range of service providers, most LEAs have not considered it necessary to consider questions of value for money. A final reason for the lack of attention paid to the assessment of effectiveness lies with the concept of 'need'. The 1981 Act introduced a concept of special educational needs which was (more) open-ended and brought with it an implicit assumption that needs identified should be needs met by the LEA. However this open-ended concept has never been and could never be matched within the constraints of a cash-limited budget; we suggest that the accountability forced by LMS is highlighting this reality.

Findings

The Audit Commission report indicated that

> neither special schools nor ordinary schools are called to serious account for their performance with pupils with special educational needs . . . the inspection process has not been implemented with rigour by LEAs, with the result that schools go virtually unchallenged for their work in this area.
>
> (Audit Commission 1992a: 2)

Our questionnaire survey has not provided data on effectiveness and, as mentioned above, this is an area which is new to most LEAs. However, a large number of LEAs have been carrying out special needs reviews in the course of which questions both of effectiveness and value for money have been asked. In addition the LMS Circulars encourage schools and LEAs to 'shop around' for services and to purchase services from alternative providers where appropriate. For example, a recent DFE publication entitled *Buying for Quality: A Practical Guide for Schools to Purchasing Services* suggests that 'in cases where the school is satisfied with the quality but not the level of provision by the LEA then it may seek to buy additional provision, either from the LEA or from another provider' (Coopers & Lybrand, 1992). Some LEAs have already developed 'agency' arrangements and 'service level agreements' for services which have up to now been provided free of charge to all schools by the LEA. It is early to report on the success or viability of these arrangements and how far pupils' needs will be met within mainstream schools, how far governors will be able to fund their responsibilities in respect of pupils with special educational needs and how far services could improve under these new arrangements.

Our questionnaire addressed the question of monitoring. Of the LEAs in our sample five (11 per cent) did not monitor the use

of funding, twenty-eight (64 per cent) reported that the Inspectorate monitored, four (9 per cent) used school development
plans as a basis for monitoring. The issue of accountability was
raised by the Audit Commission report as a key issue in SEN
provision. A clear recommendation from the Audit Commission
report gives LEAs the responsibility for such accountability,
suggesting that LEAs should hold schools accountable for the
progress which they achieve with pupils with special educational
needs. (Audit Commission, 1992a).

SOME CONCLUSIONS

The 1988 Act, including LMS, was introduced at a time of overall
budget constraints and in a context of market forces and
competition. Although LMS, in and of itself, could lead to an
increase in quality through greater accountability, openness and
value for money, its introduction at this time appears to be having a
significantly negative effect on special educational needs provision.
This has been demonstrated both by our LEA questionnaire surveys
and by other studies. The reduction in centrally provided special
needs support services, the documented increase in demand for
statements, a trend towards more placements in special schools and
the rise in number of pupils excluded from school point to some of
the effects of recent legislation on special educational needs. More
work is needed to study the effects on SEN both at the level of
individual schools, classrooms and individual pupils.

Returning to the original dilemmas, it is clear that there is a
strong trend towards the identification (and labelling) of
individual pupils as the means to secure resources, rather than
the allocation of resources to schools in order to enable them to
meet the range of needs presented by the pupils in their
community. Resourcing special needs thus continues to pose a
dilemma as statementing is increasingly perceived to be the main
way (and in some LEAs the only way) to gain access to scarce
resources. The use of the statementing procedure thus becomes
even more confused as it becomes the means to extra resources
(for as many pupils as possible) rather than an assessment of (a
small minority of) pupils' (extraordinary) needs. The continuity
of the continuum appears to have become increasingly
threatened (at least in some areas of the country) with some LEAs
allocating provision only for pupils with statements, thus reintro-

ducing the notion of the distinction between the 'special' (few) and the 'ordinary' (majority). LMS has highlighted the question of who has responsibility for (which level of) special needs. A positive aspect of LMS is that of forcing LEAs to consider the role of special and ordinary schools in meeting pupils' SEN and the balance of integrated and segregated placements. In their reviews, LEAs are considering the different functions served by different forms of provision to meet different needs. The advent of LMSS may bring a more coherent picture into this area.

However, the move towards integration is very slow, with only a hundred special schools closed since 1982 and 100,000 children still segregated (Swann, 1991). Increases in integration appear to be happening only in LEAs with a high growth in statementing, with little decline in the amount of segregated provision. There is some evidence to suggest that it may be more difficult for LEAs to resource integrated placements at the present time, or that integrated placements may be used as a way of cutting costs. Monitoring and effectiveness are only now featuring on the agenda for SEN though some LEAs have made substantial moves in this direction over the past two to five years and to this extent the effects of LMS have been positive.

It is early to evaluate the positives and negatives of LMS for SEN. This is partly due to the enormous numbers of changes (both macro and micro) which continue to bombard the system. It will be important to continue to monitor developments in order to see how far fears are justified that some of the positive developments in special educational needs provision over recent years may be jeopardised or how far hopes are realised that LMS will lead to improved services and therefore a better educational deal for all children.

REFERENCES

Audit Commission (1992a) *Getting in on the Act. Provision for Pupils with Special Educational Needs*. London: HMSO.

Audit Commission (1992b) *Getting the Act together. Provision for Pupils with Special Educational Needs*. London: HMSO.

Coopers & Lybrand (1987) *Local Management of Schools. A Report to the DES*. London: HMSO.

Coopers & Lybrand (1992) *Buying for Quality. A Practical Guide for Schools to Purchasing Services*. London: DFE.

Department of Education and Science (DES) (1978) *Special Educational Needs* (The Warnock Report). London: HMSO.

Department of Education and Science (DES) (1988) *Education Reform Act: Local Management of Schools* (Circular 7/88). London: DES.

Department of Education and Science (DES) (1990) *Staffing for Special Educational Needs* (Circular 11/90). London: DES.

Department of Education and Science (DES) (1991) *Local Management of Schools: Further Guidance* (Circular 7/91). London: DES.

Department for Education (DFE) (1992) *Exclusions: A Consultation Paper.* London: DFE.

Department for Education (1993) *Draft Code of Practice on the Identification and Assessment of Special Educational Needs. Draft Regulations on Assessments and Statements.* London: DFE.

Dessent, T. (1987) *Making the Ordinary School Special.* Lewes: Falmer Press.

Evans, J. and Lunt, I. (1990) *Local Management of Schools and Special Educational Needs.* London: University of London Institute of Education monograph.

Evans, J. and Lunt, I. (1992) *Developments in Special Education Under LMS.* London: University of London Institute of Education monograph.

Florian, L. and West, J. (1991) 'Beyond access: special education in America', *European Journal of Special Needs Education* 6, 2, 124–132.

Goacher, B., Evans, J., Welton, J. and Wedell, K. (1988) *Policy and Provision for Special Educational Needs.* London: Cassell.

Lee, T. (1992a) 'Finding simple answers to complex questions: funding special needs under LMS', in Wallace, G. (ed.) *Local Management of Schools: Research and Experience.* BERA dialogue no. 6. Clevedon: Multilingual Matters Ltd.

Lee, T. (1992b) 'Local management of schools and special education', in Booth, T., Swann, W., Masterton, M., Maud, P., Potts, P. (eds) *Learning for All 2: Policies for Diversity in Education.* London: Routledge.

Lee, T. (1992c) 'Not the same difference', *Managing Schools Today* 1, 10, 14–15.

Lunt, I. and Evans, J. (1991) *Special Educational Needs under Local Management of Schools.* London: University of London Institute of Education monograph.

Norwich, B. (1990) *Reappraising Special Needs Education,* London: Cassell.

Pijl, S. and Meijer, C. (1991) 'Does integration count for much? An analysis of the practices of integration in eight countries', *European Journal of Special Needs Education* 6, 2, 100–111.

Swann, W. (1985) 'Is the integration of children with special educational needs happening?' *Oxford Review of Education* 11, 1, 3–18.

Swann, W. (1988) 'Trends in special school placement to 1986: measuring, assessing and explaining segregation', *Oxford Review of Education* 14, 2, 139–161.

Swann, W. (1991) *Variations Between LEAs in Levels of Segregation in Special Schools 1982–90 Preliminary Report.* London: CSIE.

Wedell, K. (1990) 'Children with special educational needs: past, present and future', *Special Education: Past, Present and Future.* in Evans, P. and Varma, V. (eds) Lewes: Falmer Press.

Chapter 3

Policy and provision for children with special educational needs in the early years

Sheila Wolfendale

This chapter focuses on special needs in the early years, but begins by examining the broader context of early years provision of care and education, on the premise that 'special needs' cannot be appraised without reference to the wider backcloth of which it is a part. This brief appraisal sets the scene for then considering concepts and definitions of 'need' and 'special need' with reference to the English and Welsh legislative context which in turn will lead on to a review of early years/special educational needs policy and provision. The chapter concludes by noting key issues and concerns. 'Early years' in this chapter is synonymous with 'under-5s' and pre-school.

DEVELOPING SERVICES FOR YOUNG CHILDREN: AN UNCERTAIN IDEOLOGY

An historical survey of the growth in medical and educational provision for young children attests to the patchiness of growth over the last hundred years or so. Accounts of the evolution of voluntary and statutory child health services by Dwork (1987) and of education for handicapped children given in the Warnock Report (DES, 1978: Ch. 1) reveal a mix of ideologies leading to their creation. For example, Dwork cites political and economic expediency that in the past led to the establishment of school health services, and Warnock's chronology of the rise in the number and type of 'special', separate schools for children with a range of disabilities confirms that children below 5 years of age were excluded. Dwork's thesis that 'War is good for babies and other young children' (the title of her book) is echoed by Penn and Riley's (1992: 3) assertion that 'two big spurts in growth in the provision of services for young children have been the creative by-products of destructive world wars'.

Thus the ideological melting pot contains ingredients of political pragmatism to which can be added social and psychological factors – the debate has raged for years as to whether or not young children are advantaged or disadvantaged by separating early on from their mothers, to spend time in nurseries (Clarke-Stewart, 1982), and whether once in nursery, a structured, somewhat directed curriculum is more beneficial than one which provides opportunities for learning in a less controlled way (Jowett and Sylva, 1986).

Successive governments this century have never been ideologically committed to a national policy on childcare and early years education, as can be seen from the way in which such provision has evolved locally. Penn and Riley (1992) provide tables listing services for under-5s which show an amazing array of voluntary and statutory service provision. Each of the three major local providing departments (health, education, social services) run various forms of day care and nurseries whilst playgroups and childminding in the voluntary private sector flourish.

The lack of overall planning and co-ordination has long been deplored by early years workers, who along with parents, bemoan the dearth of sufficient provision. Sylva and Moss (1992) are unequivocal in their view, based on research findings, that a properly resourced national commitment to early childhood provision would lead to

> improved educational performance and better social behaviour, especially for children from disadvantaged backgrounds. There is also a strong case for these services on social and economic grounds. Cost-benefit studies reveal major benefits for children, parents and society.
>
> (Sylva and Moss, 1992: 1)

Pugh (1992), echoing this theme points to the wealth of good practice in early years settings, but warns that this is constantly in jeopardy due to under-resourcing and lack of government commitment. Indeed recent educational legislation, she avers, militates against the secure maintenance of what local provision there is.

Thus far, this section has portrayed the longstanding tension between the evolution of early years provision, the not always altruistic forces that have shaped it, and competing ideologies that have underpinned child-focused legislation over the years. Although, as Fox-Harding (1991: 4) points out, 'there seems to be a broad consensus about the *importance* of children and of the safeguarding of their welfare', there has existed, and continues to exist, a number of differing perspectives regarding the relationship between the state and families, the degree to which state intervention on behalf of children is acceptable, the extent to which adherence to children's rights principles can be at odds with parents' and guardians' rights. Fox-Harding (1991) enumerates four such perspectives, which are enshrined in various aspects of child care law and policy, and King and Trowell (1992) advance the view, supported by reference to case study and case law that 'the law' may not always operate in children's best interests, and may not meet their needs.

CONCEPTUALISING SPECIAL NEEDS

Still within the context of broader societal perspectives, I come on now to consider how the concepts and terms have been and are used, for these are overarching ones that apply to early as well as later years, and which have informed the legislation.

Three terms have been extant for around twenty years, and each has generated a specific literature, whilst concurrently, at times, each has been used interchangeably with one of the other. The three related terms are: 'needs', 'special educational needs' and 'special needs'. Each will be briefly scrutinised. For a longer discussion on terminology see Wolfendale (1993a).

The concept of needs

Mia Kellmer Pringle was influential in propagating the universality of children's needs. In her book (1974) she posited a four-fold classification of *needs*: for love and security; for new experiences; for praise and recognition; for responsibility, perceiving these as constancies throughout life, adding 'of course, their relative importance changes during the different developmental stages as do the ways in which they are met' (p. 34).

A critical scrutiny of this conception of 'need' has been undertaken by Woodhead (1990) who cites innumerable government and other official reports on child welfare provision for children of the last twenty years, each of which invokes the fundamental premise that children have these basic needs. Each report then posits a number of requisites, distinctive to particular settings (home, nursery, care facility, etc.) essential to ensure that these needs are met. Woodhead's particular criticism is that, whilst the notion of 'need' may be seen to be a benign starting point to secure an eventual match between 'need' and provision to meet it, nevertheless each 'need' is presented as immutable, proven, 'timeless and universal' (p. 40). 'Need' becomes a politicised issue when the construct is invoked to argue for or against certain types of provision, e.g. expansion of day care.

Thus, the construct is seen to be flawed in a number of ways, yet it is powerful enough to have influenced policy. Woodhead sets out the main danger thus: 'the inadequacy of making simplistic inferences about children's needs from such complex and often context-specific processes is already abundantly clear' (p. 46) and 'the challenge . . . is to recognise the plurality of pathways to maturity' (p. 50).

The 'in need' concept

From the universality of needs we have come to a definition of children *in need* in the 1989 Children Act which acknowledges adult and societal responsibility (a and b below) whilst at the same time making *need* child-specific, as in c below. In the Children Act:

A child is in need if:
(a) s/he is unlikely to achieve or maintain, or to have the opportunity of achieving or maintaining a reasonable standard of health or development without the provision for him/her of services by the local authority;
(b) his/her health or development is likely to be significantly impaired or further impaired without the provision for him/her of such services, or;
(c) s/he is disabled.

Thus the use of 'need' over time shows that it is a malleable term; perhaps its very imprecision makes it amenable for administrators, policy-makers and practitioners to use to provide or to restrict resources.

The concept of 'special educational needs'

This term has generated tremendous discussion and debate. Many welcomed its advent as it obviated the need for an invidious system of official categories of handicaps; others have believed that 'SEN' is a global replacement label that serves to perpetuate the marginalisation of a minority of children from their peers.

Looking at the origins of the term 'special educational needs' (SEN) we see that it appears in the Younghusband Report (1970) paving the way for the Warnock Report of 1978, which explicitly adopted the SEN term and made it 'official'. A number of authors have critically dissected and analysed the term (Cameron and Sturge-Moore, 1990; Hegarty, 1987; Norwich, 1990, 1992); and see Roaf and Bines (1989) for a conceptualisation of SEN within broader contextual 'rights' issues – which is consistent with the Articles in the United Nations Convention on The Rights of the Child reference to the 'mentally or physically disabled child' (Article 23, see Newell, 1991). Despite the controversies, the SEN term over the years has become common currency, enshrined in law in the 1981 Education Act and re-affirmed in the Education Act 1993.

The term 'special needs'

At the time when the 1981 Education Act came into force on 1 April 1983 the 'purist' approach was to differentiate SEN and *special needs*: SEN by definition referred to educational contexts as mentioned above whereas 'special needs' could encompass non-educational provision. The 1989 Children Act 'in need' conception referred to earlier rather resembles the global 'special needs' in its earlier conception. 'Special needs' has become the least precise of these terms, partly because it is not anchored in law, as are SEN and the 'in need' conceptions, yet paradoxically it is applicable to early years, since much early childhood provision is not resourced by local education authorities. In fact, voluntary services such as pre-school playgroups, have made provision in some localities for under-5s with identified special needs, in 'opportunity playgroups'.

What distinguishes 'special needs' and 'special educational needs' from the needs of all children? There are educationalists who see them as enabling terms, which ensure the right kind of provision for particular children; others see them as marginalising terms, perpetuating a divide between 'normal' and different. From an international survey of twenty-one countries, Curtis (1991) found that there was a remarkable degree of agreement as to the definition of the term 'special needs'. A generally agreed definition was 'children needing special help to be able to function at their full potential'. We see from these various sources that there is an approximate consensus to the idea that 'special' means:

1   universality of all children's needs;
2   acknowledging vulnerability of some children 'at risk' who are there in need of temporary and/or permanent extra, or specified provision/resources/staffing.

THE PLACE OF EARLY YEARS AND SPECIAL EDUCATIONAL NEEDS IN REPORTS AND LEGISLATION

The Warnock Report (DES, 1978) gave under-5s and special needs a higher profile than the area had hitherto had, recommending it as a priority area in terms of teacher training and increased provision. Emphasis was given to the proven effectiveness of Head Start programmes (Nielsen, 1989) including Portage to partly justify this call for increased investment in the early years. Portage, cited in Chapter 5 of the Warnock Report (DES, 1978: paras 33, 34) is a home-based learning programme for young children with learning difficulties and developmental delay, which involves parents as educators. Equally, the Court Report published earlier (1976) had focused attention on health and development in the early years and had recommended implementation of local early screening and surveillance systems to detect developmental delay, early-appearing disability. Other government reports include the Select Committee on implementation of the 1981 Education Act (1987) which included early years and the Rumbold Report (1990), which includes brief mention of special needs.

As we know the Warnock Report paved the way for the legislation that amended existing law on special education, namely the 1981 Education Act which conferred new duties on local education and health authorities in respect of identifying and assessing young children with special needs. The accompanying circular to the 1981 Education Act updated in 1989 (Circular 22/89) to take account of the 1988 Education Reform Act has a whole section on under-5s with special needs, and provides guidelines based on cited successful practice, including Portage and multidisciplinary initiatives.

Parts of the 1981 Education Act have now been repealed and replaced by provisions in Part 3 of the 1993 Education Act. Specific early years notification and assessment procedures are made explicit in the Code of Practice, and parental participation is extended.

The Education Reform Act, whilst not statutorily covering pre-school, nevertheless has implications for the early years in terms of those 4-year-olds who are receiving infant school education (Cleave and Brown, 1991; Pascal, 1990); and, too, in terms of the 'knock on' effect of the national curriculum (NCC 1989).

Finally, in this section devoted to inclusion of early years/ special needs in official reports and legislation, mention is made of the 1989 Children Act. Following the definition of 'need', set out above, the Act sets out general and specific duties of the local authority which are:

- identification of children in need and the provision of information
- maintenance of a register of disabled children
- assessment of children's needs
- prevention of neglect and abuse
- provision of accommodation to protect children
- provision for disabled children
- provision to reduce the need for legal proceedings
- provision for children living with their families
- family centres

These duties encompass all ages of childhood and include day care provision for preschool children 'in need'. Local authorities also have a duty to review day care provision every three years, in co-operation with local education authorities. Indeed, interdisciplinary co-operation is one of the hallmarks of this Act – a theme to which I return, later in the chapter.

Comments on the impact and effects of legislation in respect of special needs in the early years

There is a consensus that the thrust of recent legislation is benign and enabling, reflecting a caring society, despite enduring professional concerns about the imprecision of terminology and consequent difficulty of agreeing criteria and thresholds for assessing special educational needs.

On this latter issue, the government has issued assessment criteria, as part of the Code of Practice referred to in Clause 157 of the 1993 Education Act, to introduce nation-wide consistency which has not yet operated, and to rationalise and control the deployment of resources. In principle, a coherent system ought to be equitable, but, in respect of early years, anomalies in local funding and day care/education provision will probably remain. The issue of 4-year-olds in school is a case in point (see Pascal, 1990; Cleave and Brown, 1991).

Concern has been expressed, too, by SEN *and* early years lobbying groups that, up to the present, there has been no synthesis effected by government departments between the Education Acts and the 1989 Children Act which is a Social Services Act. Although the Children Act requires some degree of co-operation in respect of early years services, there are other early years (SEN) areas in which local practitioners ought to be mandated to work together – over assessment criteria, including definitions of 'special (educational) need' over (joint) funding of day care and education, for example.

As so often happens, however, local practitioners are in advance of statute, building upon existing networks and interdisciplinary practice, to bring about advances in these and other areas.

The next section of this chapter constitutes a brief review of practice that has emerged over the last ten years or so in three key selected areas of special education needs and early years. The review is intended to exemplify an inter-relationship between legal provision, local policy and practice. The three main areas have been chosen because they are overarching and pervasive, covering many facets in the early years/SEN scene.

A number of issues, concerns and directions are picked up from this review and addressed in the final section.

A BRIEF REVIEW OF PRACTICE

Staffing, personnel and co-operation

A notable feature of recent years has been the advent of unified pre-school/SEN teams within a number of LEAs. Janine Wooster (1990) has described the evolution of one such team in the London Borough of Newham and later she and this author (Wolfendale and Wooster, 1992) depicted the working relationships between this team and other services. The two case studies in this chapter illustrate these practice links 'on the ground'.

Identifiable expertise within these preschool/SEN teams has become a hallmark – in the case of Newham, the contributions of teachers, nursery nurses and other non-teaching personnel are pooled. Thus, the combined professional strengths operate in the 'best interests of the child'.

Another significant feature since the 1981 Education Act came into force has been the rise in numbers of welfare assistants with an SEN brief. The terminology varies from LEA to LEA – traditionally they worked in nursery and infant schools as general assistants. Often now they work alongside teachers, with and on behalf of children with statements or special educational needs. As their numbers have grown and their input into special needs has increased so have their training and support needs begun to receive attention, albeit to a variable scale and extent (Balshaw, 1991; Clayton, 1993).

School nurses also claim a legitimate SEN brief, as is evidenced in school nurse in-service training carried out regularly by this author, and indeed the Warnock Report cited the place of school nurses in special educational needs provision.

Since a list first appeared in Wolfendale (1987) entitled 'Collective responsibility for meeting children's special needs – whose?' (p. 235) the idea and practice of co-operation has developed significantly. An expanded diagrammatic version of this original list, showing services coming under the remit of the local education authority, appears in Wolfendale (1992: 137). This formulation does not take account of multidisciplinary links being forged, not only on the ground at practitioner level, but at strategic-policy and planning levels. This is partly a required response to some of the provisions of the Children Act and partly inspired by a need to rationalise and utilise existing resources on a cost-effective basis, and partly based on theoretical rationales (Herbert, 1993). For example, there is an increasing number of examples of unified early years services, under which umbrella are subsumed early years/SEN services.

An HMI survey (1991) had indicated that, although there were pockets of emerging effective interdisciplinary support, practice was indeed very variable. The trend, even since that survey (carried out in 1989–90) is towards a greater degree of co-operation.

Working co-operatively with parents

A number of accounts have already appeared describing the extensive number of initiatives in special educational needs, denoting teamwork if not partnership between parents and professionals (see Wolfendale, 1989: Ch. 8; 1992: Ch. 7; 1993a). The areas of such collaboration include assessment (particularly formal assessment under the 1981 Education Act, and see Wolfendale, 1993b), parents as educators (and see Wells, 1989) parent support and parent groups (and see Hornby, 1988). What these initiatives show is the responsiveness of parents and the desire of many to take up their legitimate rights and entitlement to full participation in provision and decision-making.

Wells' review (1989) shows just how pervasive and integral parental participation has now become. Yet, as Russell (1990) points out, none of us working within these areas can afford to be complacent. As she says, 'research has emphasised the long-term consequences of making children and parents feel more competent and skilled through early education. Such research findings, however, presuppose commitment to parent involvement right from the start' (p. 102).

We know from the findings of the Select Committee (1987) looking into the workings of the 1981 Education Act that not only were the preschool years and special needs relatively neglected but that there were many recorded instances of parents continuing to feel isolated, uninformed and excluded. DES *Circular 22/89* went some way publicly to redress this balance and to provide a clarion call for future improved inclusion of parents into special needs assessment procedures at all ages. The circular explicitly drew attention to the significant number of initiatives in the early years involving co-operative endeavours by professionals and parents.

All the child-focused legislation of recent years has moved in the direction of increasing parental rights and representation (Wolfendale, 1993c), ostensibly giving parents choice of education and access to information. The 1993 Education Act Part 3, aims to streamline the 1981 Education Act assessment, statementing and appeal procedures in favour of parents, following a stream of surveys and reports over recent years which have provided evidence that children's and parents' needs and rights have not been fully redressed.

However, as writers have noted (Beveridge, 1992; Wolfendale, 1993c) control remains vested in the large institutions – decreasingly local authorities, increasingly central government. Both these authors sceptically explore the potential as well as limitations to partnership concepts and practice in circumstances where local accountability mechanisms are being eroded, and redress procedures that replace them are accountable directly to government ministers – see for example the tribunals designed to replace local appeals procedures under the 1981 Education Act, as outlined in Part 3 of the 1993 Education Act.

No system can ever address or legislate for all conflicts of interests. We can note, at this point in time, the advances that have been made, in theory, in application and in law. In particular we can applaud the spirit and sentiments underlying the 1989 Children Act, which, of all recent acts, goes furthest in promoting 'equivalent expertise' of parents and practitioners as well as outlining key underpinning concepts of parental as well as professional responsibility (Children Act, Guidance and Regulations, 1991: Vols 2, 6; Herbert, 1993).

Assessment and intervention

Assessment

This area has come in recent years to epitomise interdisciplinary practice. Whilst under the 1981 Education Act, assessment, as an activity, is the responsibility of designated personnel (teacher, educational psychologist, clinical medical officer) in broader terms it is not viewed as a monopoly activity. Let me expand on this, to depict current practice.

Assessment, whether being carried out under Section 5 of the 1981 Education Act (replaced now by Section 157 of the 1993 Education Act, Part 3) or because of parental or professional concern about a child's development and progress, can take place in the child's home, in his or her pre-school setting, or in a multi-disciplinary child assessment/development centre. Personnel who carry out assessment can include the child's regular teacher, playgroup worker, parent (as in the Portage scheme, for instance) and other professionals already described in this chapter. Under the 1981 Education Act and now the 1993 Education Act, Part 3 pre-school children as young as under 2 years of age can be assessed for special educational needs if their parents ask the LEA to do so.

Assessment calls for careful, skilled administration, sensitive interpretation of the findings, and high levels of inter-professional communication. Wherever possible, it should include skilled observation of the child while teaching and learning are going on. Assessment is a means rather than an end: the goal should be the most suitable provision for the individual child, whether it is a nursery or school place, a special home-based or school-based learning programme.

The purposes of assessment include:

- making initial/periodic checks on development;
- checking on skill acquisition;
- identifying strengths and also areas of slower progress, delay and difficulty;
- providing records of children's development;
- enabling decisions about placement to be made.

Methods of assessment include:

- standardised tests;
- developmental checklists and profiles;
- play-based assessment;
- curriculum-based assessment;
- observation techniques;
- written records.

From this portrayal it can be seen that assessment is multi-faceted and a number of perspectives can be obtained to facilitate a comprehensive profile of a young child's functioning.

An example of well-established practice which encompasses these elements, including the involvement of parents in the assessment process, is the PRESAM model operated in the London Borough of Brent (Smith, nd). The following description is taken from LEA documentation, and Figure 3.1 also shows the inter-relationship of SEN/under-5s services.

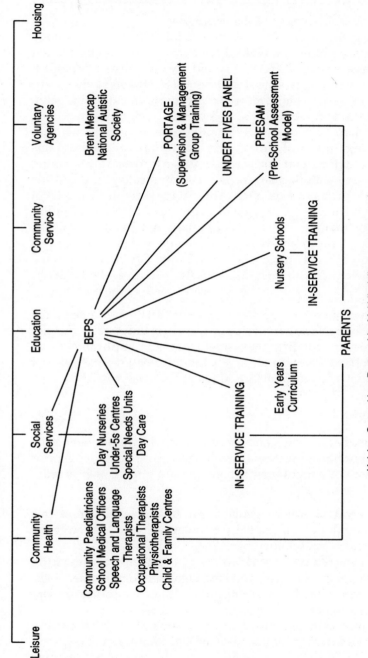

Figure 3.1 Brent Educational Psychology Service (BEPS) and the under-5s

Source: with permission from the London Borough of Brent

Pre-School Assessment Module (PRESAM)

During the past three years, the Educational Psychology Service has offered a multi-disciplinary model of observation and assessment, PRESAM, to aid the diagnosis of complex difficulties in pre-school children. This involves the participation of parents together with professionals from Health, Education and Social Services. This technique has been particularly useful in early identification of children who are showing aspects of autistic behaviour. Implications from this work suggest that further in-borough provision for young children exhibiting severe non-communicating and autistic behaviour may be required. This multi-disciplinary model of assessment may be of particular use under the remit of multi-agency involvement of the Children Act Regulations. The PRESAM Group meets twice per month and referrals for this assessment are made via Jenni Smith, Senior Educational Psychologist, who then discusses the referral at the Under-5s Panel held regularly in the north and south of the borough.

A number of writers present the view that 'good' assessment practice in the SEN/early years area rests on universal principles of successful 'quality' assessment practice applicable to all children (Fox, 1990; Hinton, 1993; Lupton 1990) reminds us that assessment is inextricably linked to appropriate provision.

Intervention

This is defined as action and/or provision which aims to meet the child's special educational needs as identified by the prior assessment. A continuum of contemporary intervention practice includes:

- referral to other agencies, for further assessment (for example by educational psychologists, specialist advisory teachers, speech therapists, physiotherapists);
- mainstream provision with individual learning programmes focusing on language, self-help or other skills, or with some extra teaching and welfare assistance, or with no extra help needed at all;
- mainstream placement in other settings such as a social service nursery, work place or private nursery, playgroup or childminding arrangements, in which a range of learning

and play experiences will be provided based on developing the whole child. Progress will be carefully monitored;

- home-based and/or centre-based programmes with parent links, which aim to promote early learning and specific skills (such as the many Portage early education pro- grammes in operation), support by pre-school teachers, nursery nurses, parent training and support groups, of which home liaison by the staff concerned is an integral part;
- initial assessment may lead to placement in a 'special' class or unit, for further assessment and pending a longer-term placement decision.

All these arrangements exist, to a greater or lesser degree, in local authorities, but there are no current reliable figures on their prevalence.

The two case studies presented by Wolfendale and Wooster (1992) illustrate the inter-relationship between assessment, placement and decision-making. Now, of course, intervention has to be regarded as being explicitly within the remit of Social Services as well as Education (LEA) under the 1981, now 1993, Education Act and the 1989 Children Act (see Herbert, 1993 for practice models).

ISSUES, CONCERNS AND DIRECTIONS OF POLICY AND PRACTICE

At the present time, security of early years provision is under threat as funding arrangements change, due to the effects of provisions within the 1988 Education Reform Act and within the 1993 Education Act. There is a contradiction between a shift of resources to schools themselves, the non-statutory nature of early years education, and the mandatory duties towards early years/SEN as outlined in this chapter. These are huge political and social issues at the 'macro' level, over which practitioners have little control. However, whilst these major issues are or are not being addressed by politicians and policy-makers, there are equally important issues that are currently being addressed by early years organisations and practitioners which reflect a corporate desire to advance good practice.

The final section of this chapter identifies a number of these. Each of them has equal relevance and applicability to *all* early years provision, for a central tenet of this author's thinking is that special needs are not marginal to, or separate from, mainstream issues to do with the rights of all children to quality early learning experiences. Each of the headings below denotes an area of current reflection as well as challenge, developing policy and practice applicable to all young children.

Concerns and challenges

Rights and equal opportunities

Children's rights, as enshrined in the United Nations Convention on the Rights of the Child (Newell, 1991) provide the overarching principle. Slowly but surely practitioners are articulating their own local application of this declaration. For example, the London Borough of Southwark has prepared a leaflet (undated) based on the UN Statement, as well as The Children Act, enumerating nine points of principle underlying local practice.

There has been focus on anti-racist issues in the early years, within the broad umbrella of Equal Opportunities (cf. Cameron and Sturge-Moore, 1990). The CRE (1989: 24) draws our attention to the need to:

- ensure that toys and equipment are neither racist nor unduly sex-stereotyped,
- acknowledge that parental attitudes to child rearing and child management can and do vary,
- guarantee assessment practice that reflects a multi-cultural society. (See also Siraj-Blatchford, 1992.)

These principles equally apply on behalf of young children with special needs from ethnic minorities. Robina Shah (1992) specifically addresses these issues, presenting 'a model of good practice' for effective service delivery (p. 77).

She outlines an equal opportunities policy which clarifies the responsibility of the service providers to assure active and consistent anti-discriminatory practice. This should define what is expected of staff, and be modelled by senior managers and seen to work in practice.

Integration, or inclusive education, which is a term that is increasingly being used (see Corbett, Chapter 4, this volume), is perceived to be an equal opportunities and rights issue. John Hall (1992) has referred to the 'integration salad', the pot-pourri of provision characteristic of the contemporary UK scene, and has criticised the location/social/functional model of integration proposed in the Warnock Report as 'primitive'. He offers a view of 'inclusion':

> The term inclusion has a very specific meaning implying that the child should attend his/her local school or college on a full-time basis in an age-appropriate group and be supported to function as an active member of the learning community such that it matters if he or she is not present.
>
> (Hall, 1992: 12)

Elsewhere the Canadian Inclusive Education experts (Forest and Pierpoint, 1992) have described Inclusive Education: 'it means being with another and caring for one another . . . it means inviting parents, students and community members to be part of a new culture' (p. 10). The rhetoric is matched by the realities of co-operative classroom learning and social interaction, though more such evidence is needed in pre-school and school settings in this country.

Quality assurance

In parallel with other developments in education concerned with ensuring quality service delivery (Woodgate, 1993), this notion is applied to early years.

'Quality' is now enshrined in the Children Act, with specific duties on local authorities to make provision, to inspect, to review. There is increasing acceptance of the notion of performance indicators and of quality frameworks and lists of quality indices (see Elfer and Wedge, 1992, for definition and discussion).

The European Commission Childcare Network (1991) has produced a list of quality criteria, which comprises:

- accessibility and usage
- environment
- learning activities
- relationships
- parents' views
- the community
- valuing diversity
- assessment of children and outcome measures
- cost benefits
- ethos

For each of these in its discussion document the European Commission Childcare Network lists a number of key questions to ask, which constitute performance indicators.

Pascal's (1992) view of quality also encompasses these elements but embraces broader societal dimensions, such that, in her view, any society's commitment to children is reflected in its early years provision.

THE EUROPEAN DIMENSION IN EARLY CHILDHOOD SERVICES

This heading is taken from Moss (1992) who places national issues firmly within the context of European Community policy, directives and recommendations. In comparison with most other EEC countries, the UK is exposed as having poorly-developed, under-resourced preschool and day care services, with a commensurate lack of commitment (Melhuish and Moss, 1991). But, irrespective of the final shape and substance of the Maastricht Treaty, it is imperative that future directions of UK policy and practice be considered within an European context – our societies are multi-cultural, multi-lingual, and trans-country mobility is increasing. In the words of the European Children's Centre leaflet, 'there will be increasing emphasis on developing common policies and practices for children and childcare with Europe'.

FINALE: TOWARDS A CODE OF PRACTICE ON BEHALF OF CHILDREN WITH SPECIAL EDUCATIONAL NEEDS IN THE EARLY YEARS

Passing mention was made earlier in the chapter to the SEN Code of Practice, issued by the government during 1993 for consultation, and in force from September 1994. As hoped, it encompasses early years.

This chapter will end with a blueprint which sets out principles underlying a code of practice focusing on SEN in the early years. This code has been produced by the National Portage Association, is based on the extensive and accumulated experience of Portage workers and families, and is reproduced here, with the permission and agreement of Mollie White, on behalf of the NPA (see White, nd).

This code of practice is a fitting finale to the chapter as it expresses a number of key principles and associated practice which the chapter has sought to address. The code re-affirms commitment to the imperative of identifying and providing for children's developmental, learning and social needs from birth.

The Code of Practice will incorporate criteria for the effective and efficient delivery of pre-school services. The following proposed criteria are focused on under-5s but they can be applied to all special education provision:

1 clear description of services to be provided, expressed in outcomes for the child and family,
2 evidence to be provided of clear measurable outcomes for the child, i.e. against clear developmental objectives,
3 evidence of procedures for publishing data relating to child outcomes for parents, associated professionals, and agencies contributing to the service,
4 evidence of effective collaborative working towards agreed outcomes for the child by agencies responsible for supporting pre-school child and family,
5 evidence of clear and widely published referral procedures readily accessed by parents,
6 evidence of procedures for working in partnership with parents to identify and assess needs of child and to select a service appropriate to child's needs,
7 the inclusion of parent representatives on the managing bodies responsible for pre-school services,
8 evidence of range of pre-school services including home visiting services to be provided appropriate to development needs of children between birth and 5 years and their families,
9 evidence of acceptability of service to parents from all socio-economic categories, single parents and ethnic minorities as well as to teachers, health professional, social workers and other relevant specialists,
10 evidence of independent evaluation of the effectiveness and efficiency of the service,
11 evidence of procedures for providing positive support and appropriate training for staff associated with recommend-ations arising from independent evaluation of service,
12 clear criteria on the efficiency of the form of provision to include costings related to outcomes for the child and family.

CONCLUDING COMMENTS

The National Portage Association code shows us how far we have come in recent years along the road of service provision, for it is a sophisticated declaration based on proven practice, legally-based obligations and an articulated commitment to young children with special educational needs. Thus, we can celebrate an increase in parental rights and participation, in curriculum development and associated supporting materials. At the same time, however, we note with dismay the lack of guarantees that preschool provision will expand or even continue at the same levels, and the shrinking powers of the LEA, and time-honoured local systems for complaint and redress. New legislation (1993 Education Act) which promises to promote parental rights and choice may well exacerbate rather than reduce such tensions in local and national policy. It will take all the efforts and commitment of local and national professional, voluntary and parent groups who currently work on behalf of children with special educational needs to continue to champion their cause, 'in their best interests'.

REFERENCES

Balshaw, M. (1991) *Help in the Classroom*. London: David Fulton Publishers.

Beveridge, S.C. (1992) 'This is your charter – parents as consumers or partners in the educational process?' *Early Years* (journal of TACTYC) 13, 1, 12–16.

Cameron, J. and Sturge-Moore, L. (1990) *Ordinary, Everyday Families*. Mencap, 115 Golden Lane, London EC1Y OTJ.

Children Act, 1989 Guidance and Regulations (1991) Vol. 2, *Family Support, Day Care and Educational Provision for Young Children*; Vol. 6, *Children with Disabilities*. London: HMSO.

Clarke-Stewart, A. (1982) *Day Care*. London: Penguin.

Clayton, T. (1993) 'Welfare assistance in the classroom – problems and solutions', *Educational Psychology in Practice* 8, 4 January.

Cleave, S. and Brown, S. (1991) *Early to School, Four-Year-Olds in Infant Classes*. Windsor: NFER-Nelson.

Court Report (1976) *Fit for the Future*. London: HMSO.

Commission for Racial Equality (CRE) (1989) *From Cradle to School, a Practical Guide to Race Equality and Childcare*. Elliot House, 10–12 Allington Street, London SW1E 5EH.

Curtis, A. (1991) *Children with Special Needs in Mainstream Education*. OMEP Publications, 'Midgecke', 753 Bury Road, Rochdale, Lancs OLII 4BB.

Department of Education and Science (DES) (1978) *Special Educational Needs* (The Warnock Report). London: HMSO.

Department of Education and Science (DES) (1989) Circular 22/89. London: HMSO.

Dwork, D. (1987) *War is Good for Babies and Other Young Children, a History of the Infant and Child Welfare Movement in England, 1898-1918.* London: Tavistock Publications.

Education Act 1981, London: HMSO.

Education Act 1988, London: HMSO.

Education Act 1993, London: HMSO.

Elfer, P. and Wedge, D. (1992) 'Defining, measuring and supporting quality', in Pugh, G. (ed.) *Contemporary Issues in the Early Years,* Chapter 3. London: Paul Chapman and National Children's Bureau.

European Children's Centre, National Children's Bureau, 8 Wakeley Street, London EC1V 7QE.

European Commission Childcare Network (1991) *Quality in Services for Young Children,* a discussion paper. Thomas Coram Research Unit, 27–28 Woburn Square, London WC1H 0AA.

Forest, M. and Pierpoint, J. (1992) 'Inclusion – the bigger picture', *Learning Together* 1, 10–11.

Fox, M. (1990) 'Assessment of special needs – principles and process', *Support for Learning* 2, 83–88.

Fox-Harding, L. (1991) *Perspectives in Child Policy.* London: Longman.

Hall, J. (1992) '"Token" integration: how else can we explain such odd practices?' *Learning Together* 3, 9–13.

Hegarty, S. (1987) *Meeting Special Educational Needs in the Ordinary School.* London: Cassell.

Herbert, M. (1993) *Working with Children and the Children Act.* Leicester: British Psychological Society.

Hinton, S. (1993) 'Assessing for special needs and supporting learning in the early years', in Wolfendale, S. (ed.) *Assessing Special Educational Needs,* Chapter 4. London: Cassell.

HMI Report (1991) *Interdisciplinary Support for Young Children with Special Needs,* ref. 17/91/NS. London: DFE.

Hornby, G. (1988) 'Launching parent-to-parent schemes', *British Journal of Special Education* 15, 2 (June), 77–79.

Jowett, S. and Sylva, K. (1986) 'Does kind of preschool matter?' *Educational Research* 28, 1.

Kellmer Pringle, M. (1974) *The Needs of Children.* London: Hutchinson.

King, M. and Trowell, J. (1992) *Children's Welfare and the Law, the Limits of Legal Intervention.* London: Sage Publications.

Lupton, L. (1990) 'Working with infants and children with special educational needs', in Rouse, D. (ed.) *Babies and Toddlers: Carers and Educators, Quality for Under Threes.* London: National Children's Bureau.

Melhuish, E. and Moss, P. (eds) (1991) *Day Care for Young Children, International Perspectives.* London: Routledge.

Moss, P. (1992) 'Perspectives from Europe', Chapter 2 in Pugh, G. (ed.) *Contemporary Issues in the Early Years.* London: Paul Chapman and National Children's Bureau.

National Curriculum Council (NCC) (1989) *Special Educational Needs in the National Curriculum*, Curriculum Guidance 2. York: NCC.

Newell, P. (1991) *The UN Convention and Children's Rights in the U.K.* London: National Children's Bureau.

Nielsen, W. (1989) 'The longitudinal effects of Project Head Start on students' overall academic success: a review of the literature', *International Journal of Early Childhood* 21, 1, 35–42.

Norwich, B. (1990) *Re-appraising Special Needs Education*. London: Cassell.

Norwich, B. (1992) *Time to Change the 1981 Act*, London File, Institute of Education, London University, Tufnell Press.

Pascal, C. (1990) *Under-Fives in the Infant Classroom*. Stoke-on-Trent: Trentham Books.

Pascal, C. (1992) 'Advocacy, quality and the education of the young child', *Early Years* (journal of TACTYC), 13, 1.

Penn, H. and Riley, K. (1992) *Managing Services for the Under-Fives*. Harlow: Longman.

Pugh, G. (ed.) (1992) *Contemporary Issues in the Early Years*. London: Paul Chapman and National Children's Bureau.

Roaf, C. and Bines, H. (eds) (1989) *Needs, Rights and Opportunities*. Lewes: Falmer Press.

Rumbold Report (1990) *Starting with Quality*. London: HMSO.

Russell, P. (1990) 'Policy and practice for young children with special educational needs: changes and challenges', *Support for Learning* 5, 2 (May).

Select Committee (1987) *Special Educational Needs: Implementation of the Education Act 1982*, 3rd Report from the Education, Science and Arts Committee, Vols 1 and 2. London: HMSO.

Shah, R.C. (1992) *The Silent Minority, Children with Disabilities in Asian Families*. London: National Children's Bureau.

Siraj-Blatchford, I. (1992) 'Why understanding cultural differences is not enough', Chapter 6 in Pugh, G. (ed.) *Contemporary Issues in the Early Years*. London: Paul Chapman and National Children's Bureau.

Smith, J. (nd) Brent Educational Psychology Service Education Department, Chesterfield House, 9 Park Lane, Wembley, Middlesex HA9 7RW.

Southwark LEA (nd) *Declaration of Children's Rights*.

Sylva, K. and Moss, P. (1992) *Learning before School*. National Commission on Education, Suite 24, 10-18 Manor Gardens, London N7 6JY.

Wells, I. (1989) 'Parents and education for severe learning difficulties', Research Supplement, *British Journal for Special Education* 16, 4, 151–161.

White, M. (nd) 4 Clifton Road, Winchester, Hampshire SO22 5BN.

Wolfendale, S. (1987) 'Developing services to meet the special needs of children under five: towards collective responsibility', *Children and Society* 3, 224–238.

Wolfendale, S. (ed.) (1989) *Parental Involvement: Developing Networks between School, Home and Community*. London: Cassell.

Wolfendale, S. (1992) *Primary Schools and Special Needs: Policy, Planning and Provision*, 2nd edn. London: Cassell.

Wolfendale, S. (1993a) 'Thirty years of change – children with special educational needs', *Children and Society* 7, 1, 82–95.

Wolfendale, S. (ed.) (1993b) *Assessing Special Education Needs*. London: Cassell.

Wolfendale, S. (1993c) 'Parents rights in education' *SPECIAL!* (Bulletin of the National Association for Special Educational Needs), February.

Wolfendale, S.and Wooster, J. (1992) 'Meeting special needs in the early years', Chapter 7 in Pugh, G. (ed.) *Contemporary Issues in the Early Years*. London: Paul Chapman and National Children's Bureau.

Woodhead, M. (1990) 'Psychology and the cultural construction of "children's needs"', Chapter 3 in Woodhead, M., Light, P., Carr, R. (eds) *Growing Up in a Changing Society*, Milton Keynes: Open University Press.

Woodgate, D. (1993) 'Applying quality standards to child care and education', Chapter 12 in Miller, A. and Lane, D. (eds) *Silent Conspiracies*, Stoke-on-Trent: Trentham Books.

Wooster, J. (1990) 'The role of the pre-school home visiting team', *Support for Learning* 5, 2, 88–91.

Younghusband Report (1970) *Living with Handicap*. London: National Children's Bureau.

Chapter 4

Challenges in a competitive culture
A policy for inclusive education in Newham

Jenny Corbett

INTRODUCTION

This chapter examines policy and practice in Newham, an innovative borough at a period of rapid change, drawing upon a range of sources which include council policy documents and interviews with teachers and an LEA officer, as well as reflecting upon the findings of earlier fully documented large-scale research projects. Newham has led the field in its policy development on the integration of pupils with special educational needs and in this chapter I provide an account of the historical background, current situation and possible future developments, as progressive ideals struggle to survive in an inhospitable political and economic climate. In the case of Newham, the radical policy of inclusive education was in a relatively early stage of implementation when central government's plans to introduce market forces into education began to bite. The current state of uncertainty in the borough may to some extent be attributed to the fragility of its inclusive education policy.

It is significant that the London Borough of Newham has chosen to adopt the term 'inclusive education' instead of merely referring to 'integrated' provision. This new terminology has become established in Canadian districts such as Toronto, which is the headquarters for the Centre for Integrated Education and Community. In the Summer 1992 edition of its journal, *Inclusion News*, inclusive education is defined in the following terms:

> Inclusion means inclusion! It means affiliation, combination.
> . . . Inclusion does not mean we are all the same. Inclusion does not mean we all agree. Rather, inclusion celebrates our diversity and differences with respect and gratitude. . . .

Inclusion is an antidote to racism and sexism because it welcomes these differences, and celebrates them as capacities rather than deficiencies. . . . Inclusion means all together – supporting one another.

(CIEC, 1992: 1–4)

Such a definition indicates how inclusive education can be seen as one step on from integration: more assertive, life-enhancing and visionary. It also seeks to forge links with other social justice issues, thus avoiding the construction of a hierarchy of oppressions, in which those who champion a particular disadvantaged group claim priority over others.

The particular form of special needs policy in Newham is discussed in subsequent sections. Its origins lie in the vision of the 1978 Warnock Committee which, Mary Warnock (1992: 3) reflected, 'was widely represented as constituting an argument for wholesale integration or mainstreaming of children with special needs'. It is useful to note her sharp observations on the fate of that particular vision, as it serves as a warning to educational innovators working in a culture of market values. She says:

> So enchanted were we by our vision that we never thought to question what motive local education authorities would have to take on this burden. We assumed LEAs would want to educate properly all the other children in their schools according to their needs, that they would have the funds to do so, and they would gradually train teachers to take on the task. This was our naivety. . . . It was all very well as an ideal; indeed, it may have been beneficial in that it may have made children with disabilities seem less of a race apart. But as a basis for legislation, especially at a time when LEAs were increasingly short of money, it was disastrous.

I want to set this chapter in an historical context, as Warnock does in her reflections of changing perceptions between the 1970s and 1990s. We can only understand how we have reached where we are now by examining what led up to this point in history in terms of government policy, changing resource implications and competing demands. As Warnock implies in her evaluation, timing is crucial to successful policy initiatives.

In focusing on one specific London borough and its educational policy, I shall raise issues relevant to LEAs in general.

All LEAs are experiencing a changing role and an uncertain future. London offers a particular example of dramatic changes in educational policy since the demise of ILEA and its ripple effects through the boroughs. Inclusive education in Newham has developed over a period of years and cannot be divorced from Newham's commitment to community education and equal opportunities. Special schools throughout Britain are experiencing changing influences which include the effects of the national curriculum, local management of special schools and policies for integration. In particular, Newham reflects what is developing in other areas committed to special school closures. The situation in the 1990s is uncertain and complex. It is hard to see beyond Warnock's vision towards any secure basis for future legislation. Warnock herself has commented critically on the vagueness which seems inherent in the current special educational needs picture and perhaps this blurred vision of the future is all we can expect in the prevailing culture of disintegration and shifting boundaries. Nonetheless, attempting to understand Warnock's legacy and the tensions created by more recent government policy is essential if we are to develop future policies which will benefit children with 'special needs'.

Among the data sources which I use to investigate this area are the substantial evidence provided by policy documents issued by the Newham Council over the years and the earlier study by Hegarty's research team (London Borough of Newham, 1989). In addition, I draw on my own research, which focused on policy and practice in one Newham special school during the spring and summer terms of 1992. This school served the needs of pupils with profound and complex difficulties and, as such, represented a challenge to the inclusive education policy. I decided to interview the headteacher, who was deeply committed to a policy of inclusive education and was networking nationally in this area. I also asked to interview teachers and welfare staff, who selected themselves. This meant that those I interviewed were committed to inclusion, with some reservations. It inevitably meant that those teachers who were strongly hostile to the initiative were not prepared to be participants. This makes the research limited to the extent that it can only reflect some attitudes and plans for change, whilst neglecting the level of disquiet which could impede its development. Nonetheless, it provides insight into the perspectives of some participants at a time of significant change. I wished to give something tangible back to the school, as well as obtaining a visual image, so my research centred around the making of a video which included extracts from interviews and examples of classroom practice. The classroom activities which were selected included PE in the hall with the use of 'soft play' specialist equipment and with one-to-one staffing. One of the key issues discussed on the video is that of the transferability of these types of resources and staffing into the mainstream. The 20-minute video, when completed, was called, 'Integrating special education in Newham: facing new challenges' and was used by the school and the university, for staff development and teaching purposes. It also serves as a 'snap-shot' of the stage the integration plan had reached in 1992. To supplement this focus on one school, the special needs adviser for Newham, who has worked there over a number of years and seen many developments, was interviewed in the autumn term of 1992.

LEA POLICY AND CHANGE

Within any consideration of the problems encountered in the implementation of inclusive education policies, it is essential to take account of the government's assault on local government. In their comprehensive evaluation of the shifts in policy and power which have occurred as a result of the changing fortunes of LEAs, Heller and Edwards (1992) indicate that a significant cultural revisioning is required if local government is to fulfil a useful role in the future. Personnel who have been conditioned by the LEA framework and mode of operation may find it difficult to adjust and may lose their roles and status in the process of changing power relations, for:

> LEAs of the future are likely to be regulators, planners, supporters, partners and bankers. They may – or may not – be 'leaders' and they will certainly cease to direct and have full and detailed control over the local education service.
>
> (Heller and Edwards, 1992: 110)

The London Borough of Newham, like all other LEAs, is being influenced by this structural change. It may be seen, however, to be more vulnerable than most since, like the London Boroughs of Brent and Haringey, it has been subjected to political attacks from the Tories for its implementation of equal opportunities policies. Education in Newham has always been politically contentious. The relationship between political vision and educational practice is embodied in its anti-racist and anti-sexist policies and in its commitment to inclusive education. Heller and Edwards (1992) note two distinct dimensions to the challenges faced in such a context. These are that 'visions need to be communicated if they are not to remain solipsistic delusions' (p. 122) and that allegiance to visionary policies tends to make LEAs 'the forcing-ground of high political controversy, in which all sides . . . could act out their aspirations, fantasies and resentments' (p. 140). These are difficult and demanding aspects of the problem confronting a borough which seeks to implement an inclusive education policy. In a prevailing climate of accountability and competition, inclusive education has to be presented as an issue of entitlement to the clients of services, of quality assurance in institutional practice and of cost-effectiveness in rationalising staffing and resources to best effect. School services are being closely related to college policies in the emphasis upon quality, assessment and client entitlement. It is significant to note that at this time there is a strong impetus from the Further Education Funding Council (FEFC) to encourage colleges to offer inclusive provision of learning support, rather than discrete course provision (FEFC, 1992). We do not live in a culture which is kind to visionaries, unless their visions are of how to get more out of less. Heller and Edwards (1992) reflect that 'the art of intervention and resource management becomes decisive in times of scarcity' (p. 160) and that 'the bad coinage of survival drives out the good currency of fair resource exchange' (p. 161). They reinforce Warnock's (1991) contention that, in times of scarcity, the underdog has had its day. In such a climate, the least able pupils who require massive intervention are unlikely to be prioritised for restricted resources. Tensions increase as teachers resist being expected to do more with less, albeit under a visionary banner. It is hard for a profession which has undergone such sustained erosion of its autonomy and status to struggle with a vision which rests uneasily in a market culture. There is also the legacy of inevitable in-fighting and empire-building which the politicising of educational issues entails. This can lead to the raising of difficult questions such as 'Have children's needs sometimes been outranked by adults' schisms and self-seeking careerism?' (Heller and Edwards, 1992: 160)

On the one hand, it is important to recognise that you cannot have a vision without inviting detractors, so some criticism of innovative policies is inevitable. On the other hand, education politics can seriously cloud the clarity of what the vision was meant to be in the first place. Like other radical policies, inclusive education may have suffered because of political in-fighting, poor communication, lack of attention to accountability and the erosion of professional confidence at the local level. The development of inclusive education in Newham and reactions to its implementation are discussed more fully in the following sections.

THE DEVELOPMENT OF INCLUSIVE EDUCATION IN NEWHAM

A commitment to integrated educational provision, aligned to a policy of providing equality of opportunity, was embedded in the principles within the Fish Report (ILEA, 1985: 4), which stated that:

> The aims of education for children and young people with disabilities and significant difficulties are the same as those for all children and young people. They should have opportunities to achieve these aims, to associate with their contemporaries, whether similarly disabled or not, and have access to the whole range of opportunities in education, training, leisure and community activities available to all.

It is important to link this review of equal opportunities policies in London schools with the developments in Newham, for the initiatives which brought anti-racist, anti-sexist and the integration of special education policies together under a civil rights banner grew out of this period. Jordan (1992) records how a new Education Committee was formed after the May 1986 elections which set a priority to do something about the high level of under-achievement in Newham.

In its position at the bottom of the examination league tables for years, Newham reflects in stark reality the gross and distorted absurdity of such systems of measurement. It has an almost entirely working-class population, many of whom experience poverty and racial prejudice. The Education Committee set out to improve achievement levels and to increase entry into further and higher education. Jordan (1992) states that:

> Equally important for the Education Committee was to further develop equal opportunities policies. Anti-racism, anti-sexism and the integration of special education had all been central to the two independent inquiries and to the plans for secondary reorganisation.
>
> (Jordan, 1992: 379)

Thus, the decisions which were made were informed by this policy. They were: to set up two independent enquiries, one which examined under-achievement in Newham schools, chaired by Seamus Hegarty, and the other which sought the reasons why Newham people did not go on to higher education, chaired by Professor Peter Toyne. They also drew up a borough plan for special education to show how to achieve the end of segregated schooling, and reorganised secondary education to create a sixth form college to supplement the work of the further education college which was already established. In order to understand how a policy of inclusive education developed in Newham up to the present, it is necessary to set it in the historical context of a borough which systematically planned to tackle the problem of under-achievement in a variety of complementary ways.

In considering the development of policy in the era of the Fish Report (ILEA 1985), it is useful to draw parallels between Newham and former ILEA boroughs, which it resembles in experiencing a high degree of poverty, homelessness and racial prejudice. Barber (1992), who examined schooling in ILEA, is pessimistic about the possibilities of developing successful educational practice in such circumstances, commenting:

> Indeed, while the current obsession with market solutions to all problems remains, the likelihood is that many schools in these areas will fall into a spiral of decline as resources are diverted to the apparently more successful schools in more stable social surroundings.
>
> (Barber, 1992: 34)

Such an attitude, whilst almost unavoidable in the prevailing malaise, was strongly resisted in those recent research reports by

Toyne (London Borough of Newham, 1988) and Hegarty (London Borough of Newham, 1989) on Newham's educational resources and level of achievement. Both reports acknowledge the severe deprivation within the Newham community and the significance of background factors on academic performance. There have undoubtedly been further contributions to economic deprivation in the area during the 1990s. The Hegarty Report recognised that in the late 1980s the area was economically depressed but anticipated that the London Docklands Development Corporation would provide an opportunity for a change in fortunes for Newham's residents. This has proved not to be the case as the recession has made Docklands a ghost town which provides little prosperity as yet to the people of Newham.

It is clearly difficult to implement progressive educational policies in a context of severe deprivation but the over-riding emphasis for Newham is on quality teaching and learning. Gus John (1992) expressed his aspirations for strong equality policies coupled with high educational standards. As a black parent, he resisted 'schools in which mediocrity, a lack of challenge, and low expectations seem to be standard' and, as an education officer, he supported anti-racist policy initiatives designed to highlight 'the structured under-achievement of black and white working-class young people' (p. 144). Newham's commitment to such initiatives is part of an inclusive education vision, yet it has not been implemented without tensions and difficulty. Hegarty's report indicated that the initial response of heads and teachers to these policy initiatives was little different from the subsequent national reaction to the implementation of the national curriculum and assessment tasks by central government initiatives. Commenting on the introduction of inclusive education policies, the report noted:

> The pacing of the initiatives was seen by all heads as appalling – 'too many, too quickly'. Their launch was 'diabolical, we are inundated with paper, nothing is ever finished, the whole thing is badly thought out.'
>
> (London Borough of Newham, 1989: 19)

Some resented the lack of consultation or understanding of the enormity of the task. Teachers felt that the politicians did not appreciate the pressures they were under in trying to operate initiatives which came at them in swift succession. One commented wryly that:

We are forced to jump on too many 'bandwagons'. Someone in authority, either at national or local level, has a 'bright idea' and it's 'all systems change'. There is too little evaluation of existing policies. Change should come about as a result of evolution and evaluation.

Half of the teachers interviewed considered that the policy initiative on the inclusion of pupils with special educational needs was ill-timed compared with 40 per cent who felt this to be true of the anti-racist policy initiative. One teacher noted the inadequacy of provision for implementing the inclusive education policy to its full extent, commenting that:

If we are to proceed with the integration of children with special educational needs, then proper financing, resourcing, training will have to precede such a programme. If this is not done mainstream schools will be undermined.

(from London Borough of Newham, 1989: 65)

As national government is learning in the mid-1990s, withdrawal of goodwill from the teaching force is a real and serious threat. Bangs (1992) records the protests within ILEA over changes in special educational provision, which some teachers found difficult to accept. In adopting a local government policy of inclusive education, Newham is facing significant challenges at a time when teachers are increasingly overwhelmed with changes.

It is important to understand the complex relationship between the publication of reports and the development of policies. Just as the Warnock Report (DES, 1978) did not herald a change in philosophy but mirrored what was already developing in some areas of Britain, so the Hegarty Report (London Borough of Newham, 1989) on educational achievement in Newham was a reflection of an impetus for change which was already under way in the Borough. The value of its focus upon the concept of achievement was that a policy of inclusive education could be aligned to an overall goal of raising expectations and opportunities for progression.

In a recent newspaper interview (Bentley, 1992), Newham councillor, Linda Jordan, is quoted as suggesting that the White Paper on education, *Choice and Diversity* (DFE, 1992), is supportive of integration by giving local authorities control over special education, even if schools opt out, and in preventing state schools from refusing to take a pupil with a statement of special need. This optimism is tempered by the current plight of LEAs, funding cut to the bone, staff morale at an all-time low and in a state of angry confusion. As the comments from teachers in the Hegarty Report implied, practitioners will only give their every effort to new initiatives if they have a sense of stability, confidence and clear direction. This is almost impossible for LEAs to offer in their current state of disarray.

THE CLOSURE OF NEWHAM'S SPECIAL SCHOOLS – TEACHERS' AND PARENTS' RESPONSES

By 1997, the London Borough of Newham planned to be the first area of Britain which offered fully inclusive educational provision. As Allan (Chapter 8, this volume) suggests, integration may be interpreted in a variety of ways, but in Newham the term 'integration' is defined very precisely as meaning 'the closure of all special schools and the inclusion of all children on the registers of mainstream schools irrespective of the type of integration, or the level of resources' (Newham Branch of National Association of Headteachers, April 1992: 3). This policy is far more sweeping than that generally adopted by pro-integration authorities, which tend to concede the case for the continued existence of some special schools.

Plans to close special schools have not been greeted with uproar and perhaps one reason for this is that the special school population in Newham has considerably declined over recent years (Jordan, 1992). There were eight special schools in the borough in 1986, attended by 700 children, with 100 receiving residential special education outside the borough. This changed in the early 1990s to less than 400 children attending six special schools and less than 25 attending special residential schools. In 1988, the school for pupils with emotional and behavioral difficulties was closed and a learning support team established in its place. In 1989, a school for pupils with moderate learning difficulties was closed and one for deaf pupils was closed in July 1992.

Two of the schools which remain cater for pupils with complex and often multiple difficulties, which offer a challenge in arranging inclusive provision. Jupp (1992), however, maintains that starting with children who have severe and multiple difficulties can mean that mainstream schools make particular efforts to ensure that integration works. Maggie Angele, headteacher of one of these schools, catering for pupils with the most complex range of difficulties, presented a positive view of the challenge within the planning process when I interviewed her in June 1992. She clarified the structure of progression, saying:

> We start with the primary age group with possible links with three associate schools in a geographical area where some children are situated. We will look for clusters of children and schools in that area with the access, space and ethos to be part of a project of this type. Having done that, headteachers would discuss it with their parents and their governors and I would have to do the same.

This planned strategy clearly demonstrates the central role which headteachers have to play if change is to be implemented successfully. Clerkin (1992), a Newham primary school head, says:

> In the majority of average-sized Newham primary schools the head can usually work directly with individual staff in planning and co-ordinating new programmes, particularly in the early stages. In larger schools, it will naturally be necessary for the heads to delegate more often and work through department heads or curriculum post holders. . . . When a change is being considered, members of the school team should bear in mind the need to find a shared meaning about what is to be altered and have agreement about how to achieve the vital task of integrating an overall knowledge of the change with a more specific knowledge of the personalities as well as the local politics which are unique to any individual school.
>
> (Clerkin, 1992: 3–4)

For change in practice to be successful, there needs to be a degree of confidence and stability within the school. Such feelings are hardly encouraged by the present uncertainty.

All teachers are feeling stressed by the pressures of change in education. Perhaps this anxiety is particularly acute within special schools which are unsure of their future existence. As the inclusive education policy has been debated over the years in Newham, staff have found it difficult to retain their morale when confronted with the prospect of changes beyond their control.

Among those interviewed in my research, some teachers felt nervous about their new status in a mainstream setting and whether they would be expected to cope with tasks which were unmanageable. At a time when all LEAs are making cuts in education, some special school personnel, especially the welfare assistants, showed anxiety about their jobs. The Inspector for Special Needs in Newham, Chris Dyer, when interviewed in October 1992, expressed this difficulty most succinctly when he said:

> Teachers in special schools find an internal tension between concepts of inclusion for their pupils, often their ambition, against the idea that their schools are being targeted as a purely cost-cutting exercise. What tends to happen with special school personnel is that you get a high fluctuating effect between almost enthusiastic elation on the one hand and a deep depression on the other.

Such an uneasy mix of emotions does not bode well for the required level of sustained stability and steady commitment which has to see a policy through the protracted implementation process.

There is undoubtedly the will and expertise to implement an inclusive education policy but budgetary constraints conspire against the level of staffing which would ideally be required. One possibility to which Newham is drawn is that of using a small squad of floating task-force teachers to act as 'fixers' in mainstream schools, helping to facilitate effective support. What became evident over the last few years was the need for the LEA to demonstrate publicly that it can provide the level of support for children who may have multiple needs, in order to convince anxious parents that there will be no cause for concern.

Under the terms of the citizen's charter (DES, 1992), education authorities are obliged to take note of the wishes of parents in making provision for children with special educational needs. Not all parents are supportive of integrated school provision. Whilst some insist that their children attend mainstream schools, with the appropriate support, there will always be others who are much more tentative, or whose children have met with bad experiences in mainstream which has led them to the sanctuary of special schooling. One mother, for example, sent a letter to the journal of the Spastics Society to say that her disabled son had become withdrawn and unhappy when rejected at his junior school and had only returned to his confident self when transferred to a special school (Atkins, 1992). There have been parent protest groups in Newham, presenting their doubts and fears to the town hall and receiving reassurance and guidance in open meetings with education officers and members of the education committee. Maggie Angele recognised that:

> Some parents are extremely concerned. They see the school as an excellent place. When they say, 'Save the school', they are not saying, 'Save the bricks and mortar', but, 'Save the expertise'. So I hope parents will have the confidence to go forward if the expertise is going with the children. . . . I've got to take the governors and parents with me and to present this in a very positive way so that they feel confident with it. You may need to revamp your reality quite a lot but the word we have to go forward with is schools have done it, but not quite in this way.

Her confidence and commitment are important elements of fostering a challenging approach but individual enthusiasm alone is clearly not enough to create new and workable structures. Nor can the plethora of changes from central government do anything to help establish a stable pattern of provision. I interviewed the special school teachers in June 1992. Their reflections, as I write this in June 1993, would now be influenced by both local developments and national events. Like the video which I made with the special school, this examination of feelings at that point in history is no more than a 'snap-shot' of how it felt then.

The planned closure of Newham's special schools has to be seen as part of its overall commitment to enhanced educational achievement. Those who support it see inclusive education as a philosophical stance related to a policy of equality of opportunity. Not all teachers in the special schools feel comfortable about the integration of the pupils they teach. Neither do all the welfare staff. Some are positively obstructive. Others leave for posts in other boroughs. Some parents are enthusiastic. Others are anxious. Some are so uneasy that they seek placement in other borough special schools. It is important to realise that there cannot be a uniformity of perspectives on so contentious an issue. What is important is that Newham learns from how other LEAs have initiated similar provision and then finds the model which suits its context.

NECESSARY CONDITIONS FOR THE SUCCESSFUL INTEGRATION OF CHILDREN WITH SEVERE LEARNING DIFFICULTIES

In two recent publications (CSIE, 1992; Jupp, 1992), the integration of children with severe learning difficulties has been carefully evaluated. There must certainly be lessons which can be generalised from their findings, but the uniqueness of each school, setting and network of relationships has to be taken into account when evaluating the process of change.

What is particularly interesting in these evaluations is their emphasis upon the importance of giving sufficient attention to practical details. These include careful preliminary planning, making adequate staffing arrangements and ensuring full consultation with parents. Jupp (1992) reflected that the most effective preparation for mainstream staff was to ensure the supported child made several short visits to the school before starting full-time. He felt that this helped staff to see the child as non-threatening instead of 'making themselves the victims of their own imaginations' (p. 161). The CSIE report (1992) stressed the value of providing adequate staff cover for teachers who would be involved in the integration project. If the transfer of pupils from special into mainstream schools is to operate smoothly, there will need to be staff visits and meetings which will require additional staff to cover classes. Teachers must also be receptive to parental perceptions, even if they jar with their own. In the CSIE study, parents from the special school wanted to continue with fund-raising which was an established part of resourcing, even though this could be seen as a legacy of the charitable status of special provision. To discourage this might have had the effect of undermining parents' sense of involvement in their children's education and so it was allowed to continue unchallenged.

Plans for inclusive provision have to be addressed within the broader context of national curriculum requirements and assessment procedures. These developments have fostered a new emphasis upon curriculum entitlement for all pupils. As recent curriculum documents illustrate (e.g. Fagg *et al.*, 1990), planning for a broader and more balanced curriculum for pupils with severe and complex disabilities demands considerable flexibility and skill. If a policy to develop inclusive education is to carry real force, it will need to embrace curriculum entitlement as a central issue. To summarise, the integration of children with severe learning difficulties demands careful planning, particularly in terms of retaining the support of parents and staff and ensuring that all aspects of the curriculum are attended to.

CONCLUSION – FUTURE POSSIBILITIES AND CHALLENGES

In this chapter, I have looked at a move towards inclusive education in one London borough. I have shown how it grew out of a commitment to equal opportunities and the development of anti-sexist, anti-racist and integrated schooling policies. The difficulties which Newham confronts in relation to improving overall educational achievement have been systematically addressed in a series of strategies over recent years, of which the inclusive education plan is one. This policy is being developed at a time when educational disruption and uncertainty are unprecedented. Its future resourcing and progression is dependent upon a range of unforeseeable factors, both at a national and local level.

Some critiques of current developments in LEAs predict the demise of equal opportunities policies. Bangs (1992) suggests that: 'a minimalist role for the LEA will mean a minimalist equal opportunity intervention by the LEA in its own schools' (Bangs, 1992: 166). There seems little likelihood that Newham will follow such a path, but its commitment to inclusion will demand remarkable fortitude.

One of the key lessons to be learnt from the Newham experience is that any policy has to be appropriate for the context in which it is to be implemented. Inclusive education in Toronto does not neatly transfer to the Newham context. Different historical developments, populations, sources of funding, cultures and political climates create different opportunities for growth. There are many factors in the British context which are thwarting the nurturing of progressive innovations, particularly if these conflict with current market ideologies. Educational psychologists have become frightened of managers, 'hard-headed, money-oriented types who have no time for consensus' (Croall, 1992: 8), as town-hall economies over-rule children's needs. Chief education officers are pressured into defending their low league table exam results in the national press, with promises of immediate action plans for improved provision (Kemble and Oborne, 1992). There is a pervasive feeling of fear which breeds caution and retrenchment: not the ideal mood for visionary advances.

Newham is an authority which has long promoted a 'caring' ethos. Chris Dyer, when interviewed in October 1992, spoke of the 'groundswell of firm East End and Socialist interest in the individual and in the individual in the community'. The London Borough can be seen to have established a caring ethic within educational administration. Beck (1992) defines such an approach in the following terms:

> a caring ethic assumes that personal, private concerns and the public good are linked and that solutions to problems must seek to promote both. Indeed, it would argue that administrators who fail to do this and seek to solve social problems at the expense of persons are like the stereotypical physician who describes an operation as a success even if the patient dies.
>
> (Beck, 1992: 480)

Inclusive education, in its very essence, embodies this caring ethic. Shaw (1992) describes the message conveyed by conference leaders at an 'Inclusive Education and Community Living' conference as:

> that inclusion and its components – social justice, love, hospitality, trust, cooperation – must be actively built and nurtured in our schools and communities, in our public services and in other major organisations of society.
>
> (Shaw, 1992: 7)

The Integration Alliance (1992) adds that inclusion is a more profound concept than integration as it includes disability as a human experience which should be a central issue in human service planning.

How does inclusive education, in the Newham context and in the British education system as a whole, meet the challenge to be caring in a harsh culture? Warnock (1991), reflecting on integration in the 1990s, suggests that a hard approach is required in order to marry equality with cost-effectiveness. Inclusive education in Newham will not survive without such an approach, for caring without costing strategies is not enough. If inclusive education in Newham is to proceed, as I hope it will, it has to be rooted in the specific needs and values of its community and reflect the history and future potential of the locality.

REFERENCES

Atkins, L. (1992) 'Successful integration depends on the teachers', *Disability Now*, July: 14.

Bangs, J. (1992) 'Special education: the ILEA and after', in Barber, M. (ed.) *Education in the Capital*, pp. 156–168 London: Cassell.

Barber, M. (1992) *Education in the Capital*. London: Cassell.

Beck, L. (1992) 'Meeting the challenge of the future: the place of a caring ethic in educational administration', *American Journal of Education* 100, 4, 454–496.

Bentley, M. (1992) 'Scarce places among peers', Schools Report, *Observer*, 18 October: 5.

Centre for Integrated Education and Community (CIEC) (1992) 'Inclusion – the bigger picture', *Inclusion News*, Summer: 1–4.

Centre for Studies on Integration in Education (CSIE) (1992) *Bishopswood: Good Practice Transferred*. London: Centre for Studies on Integration in Education.

Clerkin, C. (1992) *Inclusive Education Programme 1992: The Role of Newham Headteachers in the Management of Change*. Newham: Newham Council.

Croall, J. (1992) 'Caught within a climate of fear', *Guardian Education*, 17 November: 8.

Department for Education (1992) *Choice and Diversity*. London: HMSO.

Department of Education and Science (DES) (1978) *Special Educational Needs: Report of the Committee of Enquiry into the Education of Handicapped Children and Young People* (The Warnock Report). London: HMSO.

Department of Education and Science (DES) (1992) *Parents' Charter: Children with Special Needs*. London: DES.

Fagg, S., Aherne, P., Skelton, S. and Thornber, A. (1990) *Entitlement for All in Practice: A Broad, Balanced and Relevant Curriculum for Pupils with Severe and Complex Learning Difficulties in the 1990s*. London: David Fulton.

Further Education Funding Council (FEFC) (1992) *Funding Learning*. Coventry: FEFC.

Heller, H. and Edwards, P. (1992) *Policy and Power in Education: The Rise and Fall of the LEA*. London: Routledge.

Inner London Education Authority (ILEA) (1985) *Educational*

Opportunities For All? The Report of the Committee Reviewing Provision to Meet Special Educational Needs (The Fish Report). London: ILEA.

Integration Alliance (1992) *The Inclusive Education System: A National Policy for Fully Integrated Education.* London: The Integration Alliance.

John, G. (1992) 'Education and the community in a metropolis', in Barber, M. (ed.) *Education in the Capital.* London: Cassell.

Jordan, L. (1992) 'Integration policy in Newham, 1986–90', in Booth, T., Swann, W., Masterton, M. and Potts, P. (eds) *Policies for Diversity in Education,* pp. 377–385. London: Routledge.

Jupp, K. (1992) *Everyone Belongs: Mainstream Education for Children with Severe Learning Difficulties.* London: Souvenir Press.

Kemble, B. and Oborne, P. (1992) 'We'll change says shamed schools chief', *Evening Standard,* 18 November: 2.

London Borough of Newham (1988) *Higher Education for Newham. Report of the Committee of Enquiry chaired by Professor Peter Toyne.*

London Borough of Newham (1989) *Boosting Educational Achievement: A Report of an Enquiry into Educational Achievement in the London Borough of Newham* (The Hegarty Report).

Newham Branch of National Association of Headteachers (1992) *Inclusive Education or Integration of Pupils with Special Educational Needs into Mainstream Schools.* London Borough of Newham.

Shaw, L. (1992) 'From conference to learning community', *Learning Together Magazine* 3, 7.

Warnock, M. (1991) 'Equality fifteen years on', *Oxford Review of Education* 17, 2, 145–154.

Warnock, M. (1992) 'Special case in need of reform', Schools Report. *Observer* 18 October: 3.

Chapter 5

Clusters
A collaborative approach to meeting special educational needs

Jennifer Evans, Ingrid Lunt, Brahm Norwich, Jane Steedman and Klaus Wedell

This chapter begins with a brief overview of the use of school clusters in a number of recent initiatives, such as TVEI. It then considers ways in which clusters may be helpful in making provision for children with special educational needs in the context of the diminishing economic power of local education authorities and the very broad definition of special educational needs introduced by Warnock and the 1981 Act. Finally, drawing on a two-year study funded by the ESRC, it investigates the processes of cluster formation and operation in a small number of schools which have engaged in experimental collaboration to meet the special educational needs of their pupils.

THE NATURE AND FUNCTIONS OF SCHOOL CLUSTERS

The term 'cluster', as employed here, denotes a relatively stable and long-term commitment among a group of schools to share some resources and decision-making about an area of school activity. There is a degree of formality, in that there are regular meetings of cluster schools to plan and monitor the activity concerned. There is some commitment of resource (e.g. teacher time) and some loss of autonomy implied, since schools will have to negotiate some decisions about this area of activity. Clusters can be single phase (i.e. all primary or all secondary) or multi-phase, including special schools. They can include outside agencies such as a health authority or local employers' organisation. Their origins can be 'top-down' (i.e. LEA initiated) or 'bottom-up' (initiated by the schools themselves). Clusters differ from networks, in that the former are more formal and well-defined systems. They also differ from 'federations' in that the latter imply the grouping of schools under one headteacher, and therefore a greater degree of loss of autonomy (see Benford, 1988).

The formation of clusters is not a new phenomenon. It is relatively common in areas where there are numbers of small rural schools, for those schools to combine in order to enhance and enrich the experiences they can offer to their pupils and their staff (Benford, 1988; Bray, 1990; UNESCO-UNICEF, 1987; Wallace, 1988). A recent report (Galton et al., 1991) of a DES-funded evaluation study has highlighted the importance the government has attached to clusters development to support small schools in rural areas in the UK. Over £7 million was spent in fourteen LEAs between 1985 and 1991 on schemes to enrich the curriculum in the schools involved. The report concluded that clusters:

> had the potential to provide stable structures within which advisory teachers could operate more efficiently than they could with separate, individual schools. Resources, and their costs, could be shared between the cluster schools, thus allowing small rural schools access to specialised, large or expensive resources. Finally . . . they provided the bases for teachers' curriculum support groups and larger peer groups for children.
>
> (Galton et al., 1991: 146)

Similar considerations (i.e. the sharing of expertise and resources and the widening of pupils' and teachers' experiences) underpinned another government initiative which required schools to form groups ('consortia') to make bids for funding: that of the Technical and Vocational Education Initiative (TVEI). Evaluations of TVEI (Harland, 1987; Lloyd, 1985) endorse the view that initiating and supporting inter-school collaboration is a useful way of extending the use of scarce resources and enriching the curriculum.

Although these two initiatives do not cater specifically for pupils with SEN, it could be argued that schools (and not necessarily just small rural schools) could benefit from sharing resources to allow access to the specialised or expensive resources that such pupils require. This, among other considerations, was the basis of the recommendation of the Fish Committee (ILEA, 1985) that clusters be set up in the former ILEA to make provision for pupils with special educational needs. The main purposes of the clusters recommended by the Fish Committee were:

1   the sharing of responsibility for most special educational needs which arise in the schools in the cluster and developing means of identifying and meeting them;
2   providing a continuity of concern over the children's education, in particular by facilitating close under-five and primary school links and close secondary and tertiary education links in each cluster, together with sensitive procedures for transfer from primary to secondary schools;
3   to assist decision-making about the forms of provision to meet SENs which are most appropriate for a group of schools and associated under-five and post-school arrangements;
4   to provide a focus for service delivery so that members of all services advising and supporting schools and associated tertiary provision, including health and social services, can deploy staff to work with a small group of schools. Schools in their turn would be enabled to work with a known group of supporting professionals.

(ILEA, 1985: 177)

There were thus ideological and philosophical as well as practical components to the Fish recommendation: it was part of an attempt to ensure that children with SEN were, as far as possible, educated within their local area, and not sent away to school. Alongside the commitment to localised, integrated provision, there was also the acknowledgement that there had been serious problems of co-ordination between services and schools in providing for pupils with SEN and that collaboration, in both planning and making provision, was necessary to improve the service offered to children and their families.

More recent developments in clustering arrangements have been reported by Dyson and Gains (1993). They have described a cluster of schools with a special school acting as a resource base for support services to the cluster. The resource base also acts as a base for training and staff development in SEN. A group of clusters (which they term a 'consortium') is serviced by the psychological services. Dyson and Gains maintain that this model has numerous implications for those concerned with the delivery of special education: LEAs might wish to set up 'enabling structures' to promote clusters; special schools will need to clarify and 'market' what they can offer to a cluster; mainstream schools will have to 'audit' their provision to explore what their discrete contribution to a cluster and skills interchange might be; special needs teachers can choose between becoming highly specialised in delivering aspects of the curriculum within the cluster or they can increase their managerial and organisational skills to support the delivery of the curriculum by classroom teachers (Gains, 1992).

Dyson and Gains suggest that the emergence in, LEAs and schools, of an interest in clustering for special needs is due to several factors within the current post-ERA situation. First, they assert that the current competitive model for delivering special needs provision is seen to be unworkable. Secondly, local authorities can no longer be relied upon to sustain the level of support they have provided in the past. Thirdly, as budgets are devolved, schools will have to make decisions about how they are going to meet special educational needs. They suggest that there is an emerging perception that only by collaborating with other schools in a consortium or cluster can the full range of special needs be addressed (Gains, 1992).

PROBLEMS IN MAKING SPECIAL EDUCATIONAL PROVISION

In order to understand the context in which the need for clusters has been identified, it is important to have a sense of the nature of Warnock's definition of special needs and the disputes which have arisen between schools and local authorities with regard to the loss of responsibility for making provision. Before the 1981 Education Act was implemented in 1983, the structure and decision-making for special educational provision had been relatively straightforward, on the face of it at least. Children who seemed to be in need of special education (who were a 'prima facie case') were assessed and placed into one of ten categories of handicap (nine in Scotland). They were educated at special schools appropriate to their handicap. A similar system is still used in several European countries, for example, Germany and Belgium. All other children (i.e. those in ordinary schools) were assumed not to need specialised provision (although many schools educated the least able in small groups known as 'remedial' or 'bottom stream').

The system of crude categorisation came under attack in the 1970s from parents and professionals, not only because it did not accurately reflect the complexity of children's problems, but also because it segregated children with special educational needs. The numbers of children in segregated provision grew from 0.75 per cent of the total school population in 1950 to 1.39 per cent in 1977; the 1977 figure rises to 2 per cent if children in special classes or awaiting placement are included (Booth, 1981). There was also some concern that the increases were in those groups of pupils categorised as 'maladjusted' and 'educationally sub-normal', which indicated that social rather than physical or sensory problems were leading to increasing segregation. Tomlinson (1982) reported that children from Afro-Caribbean backgrounds were over-represented among pupils in special schools.

These two major problems – *deciding which children have special educational needs and deciding how these needs should be met* – lie at the heart of subsequent legislation and policy-making.

Following the recommendations of the Warnock Report (DES, 1978), the 1981 Act abolished categories of handicap as a method of assigning pupils to provision and substituted a relative definition of 'special educational need' which was normative (i.e. it related a child's difficulties to what would be expected of other children of a similar age) and interactive (i.e. it acknowledged that the context in which provision was being made was an important factor in creating or alleviating a child's difficulties). The 1981 Act also put the emphasis on children's needs being met within ordinary schools wherever possible.

The effect of this more open-ended definition of special educational need was to extend the term to a much larger proportion of the school population (Warnock suggested that 18 per cent of pupils at any one time would have special educational needs). However, in any particular school, depending on the nature of the difficulties of the pupils and the school context, a much larger proportion might have special educational needs. The Act also introduced the requirement for an LEA to identify and assess pupils who may require the LEA to decide on the provision to be made for them. Such pupils must be given a 'statement' which details their needs and the provision to be made. This group was assumed to be around 2 per cent of the school population – roughly equivalent to the proportion who had been 'categorised' under the previous system. Thus, the special needs population is divided into two groups – those with a statement and those without.

From the outset, there have been difficulties in deciding for which children it should be the responsibility of the LEA to provide and for which the responsibility of the school. (Goacher *et al.*, 1988; House of Commons, 1987). Recent research (Evans and Lunt, 1990; Lunt and Evans, 1991) has indicated that the proportion of pupils being given statements is rising by 0.2 per cent each year – from 2 per cent in 1989 to 2.2 per cent in 1991 to 2.4 per cent in 1992. Some LEAs are providing statements to over 3 per cent of their school population. It could be said that this is an inevitable consequence of the relative definition of SEN, since the point at which a school cannot make provision and will need to call on resources provided by the LEA directly will depend, partly, upon the level of resources available within schools. This balance of LEA controlled provision and school-controlled provision varies from LEA to LEA, and the introduction of Local Management of Schools (LMS) in 1992 is changing the balance from year to year. However, it is clear that an ever-increasing proportion of the education budget is being controlled by the school.

Even before LMS, however, there was a mismatch between schools' expectations of what support should be provided for pupils with SEN and what LEAs were making available. The 1981 Act and the duties placed on LEAs and schools had raised expectations and had led to an increase in awareness of SEN among parents and teachers (Goacher *et al.*, 1988). The proportion of pupils being given statements had been increasing since 1983. At the same time, the pattern of provision had been changing, with more pupils with statements being educated in mainstream schools. This had led some commentators to assume that special educational provision was becoming less segregated (Adams, 1990). However, research by Swann (1985, 1988, 1991) has concluded that, although in some LEAs special educational provision has become less segregated, in others it has become more so, and that overall the proportion of pupils in segregated provision has not markedly declined.

The Warnock Report (DES, 1978) talks of a 'continuum of need' which should be matched by a 'continuum of provision'. In practice, the 1981 Act has led to a dichotomised system of provision, with some LEAs taking an increasing responsibility for decision-making about pupils with SEN. A recent report by the Audit Commission (1992), indicates that the dilemmas in special educational provision already described have become, if anything, more acute since the 1988 Act was implemented. The main finding of the Commission was that the 'lack of clarity about what constitutes a special educational need' was at the heart of many of the problems. It also found a lack of accountability from both special and ordinary schools for their performance with pupils with special educational needs.

The 1988 Act gives schools and governors more control over resources, while at the same time exposing them to 'market forces' through a funding system based on pupil numbers and through open enrolment which encourages competition between schools to attract pupils. As a number of commentators have observed (Russell, 1990; Wedell, 1988; Willey, 1989) pupils with special educational needs are relatively expensive to educate and may diminish the attractiveness of a school in the eyes of prospective parents. Given the pressures that schools are under to raise standards, it is not surprising that they, in their turn, are pressuring the LEAs to provide extra resources to help them make provision for a wider group of children that they (the schools) deem to have special educational needs. Thus there has been an increased demand for statements. As the boundaries of what is acceptable performance from children become increasingly well-defined and publicised it will be more and more difficult to make 'the ordinary school special' (Dessent, 1987); therefore schools are expecting the LEA to take responsibility for providing extra resources to meet the special educational needs of an increasing proportion of the pupil population, including those needs which, at one time, would have been met from the schools' own resources. At a time when more and more responsibility is being taken by schools for many aspects of educational provision, and the role of the LEA is being eroded (DES, 1988, 1991; DFE/Welsh Office, 1992), it is somewhat of an anomaly that this should be happening.

A key question, then, is – *where in the education system should responsibility for making special educational provision lie?*

THE EMERGENCE OF CLUSTERS AS A FORM OF ORGANISATION FOR SEN PROVISION

Given the inherent competitiveness engendered by the 1988 Act, subsequent Circulars and impending legislation (DFE Welsh Office, 1992), the expectation that there might be co-operation between schools would seem to be somewhat unrealistic. However, it is clear that schools do have problems with resourcing special educational provision from within their delegated budgets. It is also clear that LEAs cannot continue to expand the resources held centrally for making provision – more and more these will have to be delegated to schools. It may be, then, that LEAs and schools will perceive that they have more to gain than to lose in providing for special educational needs within some form of cluster system, either by the LEA delegating funding for special educational provision to a designated group of schools, or by the schools themselves pooling resources to buy in a particular form of support which they need.

However, clusters, as a method of organising special educational provision, are still relatively rare. At the outset of our research, in January 1991, we had some difficulty in finding examples of clusters for study, although by June 1992, we found many more clusters either operating or planned.

Schools, as organisations, have tended to be relatively closed (Bell, 1988; Everard and Morris, 1985). Therefore they have not had a history of or experience with collaboration with other schools in sharing responsibility for making provision. Schools' relationships, in terms of making provision for pupils with special educational needs, have been mainly with the LEA or with services provided by the LEA, such as the educational psychology service. These relationships have themselves been fraught with difficulty (Evans *et al.*, 1989; Goacher *et al.*, 1988). Hudson (1987), in a review of the literature on inter-organisational collaboration has observed that:

> From an agency's viewpoint, collaborative activity raises two main difficulties. First, it loses some of its freedom to act independently, when it would prefer to maintain control over its domain and affairs. Second, it must invest scarce resources and energy in developing and maintaining relationships with other organisations, when the potential returns on this

investment are often unclear and intangible. Hence it could be posited that an agency prefers not to become involved in interorganisational relationships unless it is compelled to do so and that simple appeals to client well-being may constitute an insufficient motivation.

(Hudson, 1987: 175)

Thus, not until some external motivation was supplied – such as a requirement to collaborate in order to receive resources (a 'top-down' cluster) or a realisation by schools that collaboration would provide them with resources that otherwise they would not have (a 'bottom-up' cluster) – would the extra burdens which collaboration would impose be offset by gains for the schools involved.

Collaboration between a group of schools is a particular and unusual form of inter-organisational co-operation. Most collab-oration in the field of social welfare involves an agency supplying a service to clients of another agency which has primary responsibility for them, for example psychological services supplied to pupils in schools. The difficulties in organising such collaboration arise mainly from differing priorities, structures, funding arrangements, value systems, etc. (Benson, 1985; Hudson, 1987). However, the collaboration *must* take place, because it is part of the *raison d'etre* of the servicing organisation.

Schools are not in this position: they do not exist to service each other – they are independent organisations. Now that the role of the LEA as a broker between schools has virtually disappeared, the dominant feature of the relationship between schools catering for the same age range is that of competition rather than collaboration. However, the relationship between secondary and primary schools is somewhat different, since the primary schools are the source of new clients for the secondary schools. There may be, therefore, more incentive for secondary schools to build up good relationships with neighbouring primary schools.

Thus we have seen two types of cluster emerging: one concerned with aspects of *transition* between primary and secondary school, sometimes known as a 'pyramid' or a 'partnership', and another concerned with *sharing of resources* where scarce or expensive resources are made available through co-operation between schools. In the first case, the main focus of the collaboration consists of setting up structures to allow the smooth transition of pupils between primary and secondary schools, and the building up of good relationships between a secondary school and its feeder primaries. This type of cluster is obviously more effective where there are clear catchment areas for the secondary school. Considerations of special needs may be part of the collaboration over the transition of pupils. In the second case, the key factor is the sharing of resources, for such activities as curriculum development, or to provide scarce teaching expertise, such as instrumental tuition or special needs support. This type of collaboration can be across, as well as within, phases of schooling.

RESEARCH DESIGN AND METHODOLOGY

At the start of the project, advertisements were placed in a number of professional journals inviting practitioners involved in clusters to contact the team. At that time (January 1991) there were, as already noted, few examples of clusters concerned with special educational provision. By making contact with practitioners, who responded to our advertisements, the research team was able to study in detail examples of clusters in four LEAs and to carry out focus group discussions on the subject of clusters in a further twelve. For the purposes of the research, we defined a cluster as a group of schools which were involved, not merely in meetings or exchanges of information, but in some sharing of resources and expertise which might involve some loss of autonomy.

As far as the structure of the clusters was concerned they could be: top-down or bottom-up in origination; cross-phase or single phase; special needs only or wider focus; school-managed or LEA-managed. They might include special schools and involve other services, such as health or social services. A bilateral arrangement between schools would not come within our definition. The crucial dimension was the extent of sharing of resources within the cluster.

The four LEAs chosen for detailed study provided us with a range of cluster organisation. Two of the clusters were LEA-initiated and managed; although these were called clusters by the LEA and by the participating schools, the extent of inter-school collaboration was, in fact, minimal. The third cluster was bottom-up in origin. It was managed by the heads of the schools involved and had been a local initiative, which the LEA had not been involved in until it was well established. The remaining cluster was pump-primed by the LEA, which gave money to support it, but the cluster activities were owned and managed by the schools involved.

Special needs, of some kind, were a focus in all the clusters, but in those which were cross-phase (two), transition was seen as the major focus of activity, with special needs being a sub-set of concerns within this. One of the clusters involved health and social services in decision-making about the allocation of resources. All involved LEA support services in their activities.

As far as the sharing of resources was concerned, only one of the clusters involved schools in putting quantifiable amounts of their own resources into a cluster-based resource. Another involved shared planning and activities, time for which was funded by an LEA grant.

We carried out semi-structured interviews with staff in the schools concerned, LEA officers, educational psychologists, SEN support staff and pupils. The interview structure was formulated around an antecedent–process–outcome model which had provided the basis for our conceptualisation of the research. We were, then, trying to answer two basic questions: (1) what are the processes by which clusters are set up and maintained? and (2) are clusters an effective way of making provision for pupils with special educational needs?

The research design and methodology was derived from the work of Miles and Huberman (1985) who have evolved a structured approach to handling qualitative data to enable causal inferences to be made when carrying out school evaluation studies. The Miles and Huberman approach involves collecting data over time and attempting to link antecedent and process events with outcomes. Miles and Huberman used a system of coding the data and storing it on cards for sorting and analysing. We have used a computer programme designed by the ULIE Computer Service to sort the previously coded qualitative data.

The second phase of the research involved bringing together groups of eight staff (school and LEA-based) and governors from each of four LEAs in three regions of the country. These group meetings provided an opportunity for us to explore the idea of clusters with groups of practitioners, some of whom were already involved in cluster arrangements and some for whom this was a new concept. These data have enabled us to gain some knowledge of other forms of cluster arrangements and to explore the reasons why some LEAs and schools have adopted such a system whilst others have not. The findings reported here are based on data from the four case studies.

THE FOUR CASE STUDIES

The characteristics of the four clusters we studied in detail are given in Table 5.1. This gives some idea of the range of systems which can be designed as 'clusters'.

Cluster 1, Midshire LEA

The cluster consisted of nine schools – one comprehensive and eight feeder primary schools in a rural area. Partnership between the schools was well-established and valued. Links were mainly concerned with transition but also with sharing of resources and curriculum development. The particular link studied was concerned with behaviour management and the aim was to achieve a common approach across the schools. The project was financed by GEST (Grants for Education Support and Training) for work on the Elton Report (DES, 1989). The government had

Table 5.1 Characteristics of clusters

	Origin	Size	Phase	Purpose	Management
Cluster 1	Top-down	9 schools	Cross-phase	Behaviour + transition	Schools
Cluster 2	Bottom-up	6 schools	Secondary	Behaviour	Schools
Cluster 3	Top-down	25 schools	Primary	SEN resource allocation	Area office
Cluster 4	Top-down	9 schools	Cross-phase	SEN resource allocation + transition	LEA central admin

given a high priority to development work in schools for the purpose of implementing the recommendations of the Elton Report on *Discipline in Schools*. The LEA monitored the project, but left the day-to-day running to the schools. There were other clusters to which the schools belonged which cut across this one. Other services involved included the Education Social Worker and the Special Needs Advisory Teacher.

The Midshire clusters were part of a well-established system which was based on a secondary school and its feeder primaries. In order to avoid the inference that the primary schools were the junior members of the groupings, they were called partnerships. In that LEA the term cluster referred to other groupings of schools, which were single phase (i.e. primary or secondary) mainly for in-service work and national curriculum development activities.

The LEA was keen to develop the partnerships and when it received a GEST grant for work on behaviour and discipline in schools, it decided to ask groups of schools within the partnerships to bid for funds to work on projects concerned with behaviour. Thus the group of schools we studied had been working together over a period of a year on developing a partnership approach to behaviour and discipline. This had involved teachers from the primary and the secondary schools visiting each others' schools and observing classroom behaviour and its management. The co-ordinating group, which consisted of the heads of the primary schools (which were small rural schools) and a senior teacher from the secondary school, developed and ran an in-service day for all teachers in the partnership's schools which was designed to begin the process of developing a partnership policy on behaviour. A strong partnership identity had emerged as a consequence of this work, to the extent that the heads of some of the primary schools involved were wanting to drop their links with another cluster, which consisted of a different set of schools (some of which were in the partnership and some not), and to concentrate their collaborative efforts on this partnership.

Cluster 2, Northshire LEA

This cluster consisted of six secondary schools in an urban area in the North-east and was concerned with behaviour. Each school contributed an agreed amount of teacher time to form a

Behaviour Support Team which was ultimately led by a full-time leader and had three other full-time members of staff paid for by the LEA. Teachers supported pupils in another school in the cluster, not in their own. Support took the form of small group work on a withdrawal basis, counselling, and work alongside the teacher in the classroom. Secondment to the team was temporary. The cluster did not appear to operate in other areas of school activity (e.g. INSET).

The cluster in Northshire was initiated and managed by the heads of five of the six comprehensive schools in one town, along with the senior educational psychologist. The sixth school joined the cluster at a later date. It was originally conceived as providing an off-site unit to be used by the schools, but quickly developed into a support team which worked with pupils with behaviour problems in the schools. The resources shared and managed by the group of heads consisted, until recently, of a full-time team leader and a number of part-time team members who were seconded from the staff of the schools concerned. Each head would decide how much teacher time would be put in and allocation of support would be on the basis of the needs of the school. The seconded teachers would receive training from the team leader and would be seconded for one or more years. A rotation of staff meant that the cluster served a staff development function as well as a support role, in that, over the years, a number of teachers from the schools received the training and experience of working in the team. Pupils whose behaviour was causing concern were referred to the team leader who would allocate support time.

The full-time team leader was funded by the LEA, but managed by the heads. The size of the full-time team has now been increased to four and the management of these staff is now shared between a County Head of Service and the heads. However, in this cluster, the sharing of resources and joint management of staff brings it closest to the model which we had developed to describe a cluster. That is to say, the collaboration involved some sharing of resources and expertise.

Cluster 3, Eastshire LEA

This was a cluster of about twenty-five primary schools in an affluent semi-rural area. The cluster was delimited and set up by the LEA. It existed for the purpose of allocating resources for special educational needs through a team of support teachers who served the schools in the cluster. It was managed by LEA officers. The schools themselves did not meet as a cluster. Cluster meetings were multidisciplinary case conferences on individual children put forward for consideration by schools. Resources were not shared within the cluster – they were allocated by the central team. The central team consisted of health, social services, education social workers, psychologists, education officers and support service co-ordinators.

Eastshire LEA had set up clusters of around twenty-five primary schools in order to form administrative units in each of the six LEA local areas. These units were serviced by a team of administrators based in the area offices. Support services for SEN were deployed on a cluster basis, as were, as far as possible, health services and education social workers. As far as SEN provision was concerned, the cluster was the location of a twice-termly meeting of a multidisciplinary team which received requests from the schools for extra resources for children with SEN. It was, in effect, a panel meeting. Individual schools would send representatives to the meeting, who would come before the panel at a designated time to put the case for their school. There was, therefore, no sense of a cluster identity among the schools as far as planning for SEN was concerned.

Cluster 4, Southborough LEA

Nine schools made up this cluster – one comprehensive and eight feeder first and middle schools in an affluent urban area. Within the cluster the comprehensive school and two of the first and middle schools were additionally resourced – that is to say, they were equipped to provide for children with physical impairment and for children with moderate learning difficulties. These additionally resourced schools did not act as a resource for the other cluster schools, they simply received children from those schools who had difficulties. The additionally resourced schools were managed centrally by the LEA. The other schools in the cluster did not control the extra resources. The cluster's main value was thought to be in the area of transition from primary to secondary school – not specifically for special needs.

The Southborough clusters had been set up by the LEA as a

means of systematising the deployment of resources. Support teachers were organised on a cluster basis, as was the Educational Psychology Service. The original conceptualisation of the cluster was that resources would be delegated to the cluster, which would take responsibility for their deployment, but this had not happened. The primary schools' main links were with the secondary school and there was very little joint activity concerned with special educational needs between the primary schools.

DYNAMICS OF CLUSTERS – EMERGING THEMES

From our study of the four clusters, and detailed analysis of the two which most closely approach our model (Midshire and Northshire), the following themes have emerged concerning the factors which have a bearing on the processes of setting up and operating school clusters.

Size

It appears that there is an optimum size for effective clusters of between six to eight schools. Larger groups would make effective decision-making and accountability very difficult. This was also one of the findings of the SCENE (Rural Schools Curriculum Enhancement Evaluation) project (Galton et al., 1991). If clusters were smaller than six to eight schools it is unlikely that the benefits of economies of scale and access to a range of expertise within the cluster would be sufficient to make it worthwhile.

Complexity

Clusters should be kept simple. A six-school single phase cluster focusing on one aspect of SEN provision was very effective. Schools involved in more than one cluster (i.e. a cross-phase as well as a single phase cluster) found keeping all the links going very time-consuming and would have preferred to concentrate on just one cluster. Primary schools find clusters involving a secondary school useful, but these can only be effective if there is a clear catchment area (for example in a rural area where there is only one secondary school). Although there are limits to the degree of complexity of clusters which might be effective, nevertheless there is then potential for schools which cluster effectively for one aspect of their work, to develop links over other areas as well.

Initiation

There needs to be a catalyst, in the form of extra funding, and a key change agent to start the cluster off. Without this, the cost in terms of time and resources needed to set up a cluster would discourage schools from participating. The SCENE research suggested that at least two years was needed for a cluster to move from the 'initiation' to the 'consolidation' phase of its formation.

Co-ordination

There needs to be a key person to act as co-ordinator of the cluster. This person must command the respect and trust of the schools involved. The co-ordinator does not necessarily have to be the head of one of the schools, although there are examples from the SCENE project where the co-ordinator role was taken on a rotating basis by a headteacher. However, a special needs co-ordinator or advisory teacher could perform the role.

Ownership

Those involved in the cluster need to feel ownership of it. This will only occur if the schools involved feel they have control of the common resources of the cluster. This sense of ownership and control means that peer-group pressure will prevent any one school becoming dominant in the cluster.

Task focus

Clusters which involve schools in a particular task or project are more likely to be effective than those which are merely concerned with the allocation of resources. Such tasks or projects can be time limited, but can be part of an evolving development of cluster activities.

Pay-off

There must be a pay-off for participating schools in order to compensate for the time and effort involved in participating in the cluster. This may be in terms of access to staff or resources which would otherwise not be available. It could also be in terms of staff development (see below).

Staff development

Participation in a cluster system is a powerful tool for staff development when that participation allows staff to exchange ideas and expertise across the schools (i.e. to undertake joint tasks). This was a major feature in two of the clusters we studied.

Effectiveness

Measures of effectiveness are notoriously difficult to define. In the clusters we studied, a major gain was the improvement in communication between the schools involved in the clusters or between schools and support services. In one of the clusters there had been a marked reduction in the numbers of children referred for statements over the time that the cluster had been operating.

CONCLUSIONS

Is there, then, a role for clusters as a form of organisation for special educational provision? The White Paper, *Choice and Diversity* (DFE Welsh Office, 1992), has suggested that smaller schools should consider opting out of LEA control in clusters. This would indicate an acknowledgement that small schools will not be able to cater for the full range of needs across the national curriculum unless they collaborate in some way.

The White Paper also envisages a diminishing role for LEAs in the funding and management of schools. It leaves LEAs with a residual role in providing for pupils with statements, but indicates that provision for such pupils will be in ordinary schools 'to the maximum extent possible'. It also suggests that schools will be required to admit pupils where the school is named on the statement. This implies that provision for such pupils will be delegated to the school concerned. The White Paper also indicates that the government will force LEAs to reduce the number of special schools in order to eliminate spare capacity.

If ordinary schools are to be expected to cater for a wide range of special educational needs from resources delegated by the LEA, they may find that some pooling of resources would enable them to extend their facilities. The example of Northshire LEA showed that, if schools put in a small amount of resource, they were enabled to form a team which could support a number of pupils who otherwise would have been suspended or sent into segregated provision. However, this was a simple cluster catering for one aspect of SEN only. It may prove more difficult, given the competition between schools and the complex patterns of transition from primary to secondary schools, for clusters to be formed which would cover a wide range of SEN across a number of primary and secondary schools.

Work on continuity and progression in the national curriculum has given primary and secondary schools a focus for collaborative work, and recent research (Weston and Barrett, 1992) has indicated that schools are increasingly collaborating in this way. If special educational needs were to form part of that collaboration, schools could extend the range of needs that they could cater for.

Now that LEAs are unlikely to be able to force shotgun weddings on groups of schools to form 'top-down' clusters, there is still the possibility that common problems and pressures will persuade schools that a sharing of resources will be to their benefit. The role of the LEA in this would be to provide the resources (financial and managerial) to promote and support such collaboration.

Our research has indicated the factors which promote and sustain collaboration between schools. These include a key role for LEAs in providing resources and support. If large numbers of schools become grant-maintained, the power of the LEA to influence schools' activities will diminish to the extent that it may no longer exist. This indicates that collaboration between schools will have to be generated and sustained at the level of the schools themselves. This would require that schools recognise their responsibilities for meeting special educational needs and give it a high priority. The Code of Practice (DFE, 1993), published after the 1993 Act became law, requires schools to publish policies for special educational needs and clarifies their responsibilities. It may be that, when this becomes clear to schools and governors, then the benefits of collaboration will become more evident despite the obstacles caused by breakdown in catchment areas and competition between schools for pupils.

REFERENCES

Adams, F. (ed.) (1990) *Special Education in the 1990s*. London: Longman.

Audit Commission (1992) *Getting in on the Act: Provision for Pupils with Special Educational Needs: The National Picture*. London: HMSO.

Bell, L. (1988) 'The school as an organisation: a reappraisal', in Westoby, A. (ed.) *Culture and Power in Educational Organisations* pp. 3–14. Milton Keynes: Open University Press.

Benford, M. (1988) 'Beyond clustering', *Education* 23 Sept. 294–295.

Benson, J. (1975) 'The inter-organisational network as political economy', *Administrative Science Quarterly*, 20, 229–249

Booth, T. (1981) 'Demystifying integration', in Swann, W. (ed.) *The Practice of Special Education* pp. 288–313. Oxford: Blackwell.

Bray, M. (1990) 'The role of clusters: a framework for helping small schools', *Education and Society 7*, 53–56.

Department of Education and Science (DES) (1978) *Special Educational Needs* (The Warnock Report). London: HMSO.

Department of Education and Science (DES) (1988) *Local Management of Schools* (Circular 7/88). London: DES.

Department of Education and Science (DES) (1989) *Discipline in Schools* (The Elton Report).

Department of Education and Science (DES) (1991) *Local Management of Schools: Further Guidance* (Circular 7/91). London: DES.

Department for Education (DFE) Welsh Office (1992) *Choice and Diversity. A New Framework for Schools* (White Paper). London: HMSO.

Department for Education (1993) *Draft Code of Practice on the Identification and Assessment of Special Educational Needs. Draft Regulations on Assessment and Statements*. London: DFE.

Dessent, T. (1987) *Making the Ordinary School Special*. Lewes: Falmer Press.

Dyson, A. and Gains, C.W. (1993) *Rethinking Special Needs in Mainstream Schools: Towards the Year 2000*. London: David Fulton.

Evans, J. and Lunt, I. (1990) *Local Management of Schools and Special Educational Needs*. London: University of London, Institute of Education.

Evans, J., Everard, B., Friend, J., Glaser, A., Norwich, B. and Welton, J. (1989) *Decision-making for Special Educational Needs: An Inter-service Resource Pack*. London: University of London, Institute of Education.

Everard, B. and Morris, G. (1985) *Effective School Management*. London: Harper and Row.

Gains, C. (1992) 'Clustering in Kirkby', *Special!* Sept. 24–26.

Galton, M., Fogelman, K., Hargreaves, L. and Cavendish, S. (1991) *The Rural Schools Curriculum Enhancement National Evaluation (SCENE) Project. Final Report*. London: Department of Education and Science.

Goacher, B., Evans, J., Welton, J. and Wedell, K. (1988) *Policy and Provision for Special Educational Needs*. London: Cassell.

Harland, J. (1987) 'The TVEI experience: issues of control, response and the professional role of teachers', in Gleeson, D. (ed.) *TVEI and Secondary Education: A Critical Appraisal*. Milton Keynes: Open University Press.

House of Commons (1987) *Special Educational Needs: The Implementation of the Education Act 1981*, Third Report from the Education Science and Arts Committee, Session 1986–87. London: HMSO.

Hudson, B. (1987) 'Collaboration in social welfare: a framework for analysis', *Policy and Politics* 15, 3, 175–182.

Inner London Education Authority (ILEA) (1985) *Educational Opportunities for All?* (The Fish Report). London: ILEA.

Lloyd, R. (1985) *Some Management Implications of TVEI for Secondary Schools*. Sheffield: Sheffield City Polytechnic.

Lunt, I. and Evans, J. (1991) *Special Educational Needs under LMS*. London: University of London, Institute of Education.

Miles, M.B. and Huberman, A. (1985) *Qualitative Data Analysis: A Sourcebook of New Methods*. New York: Sage.

Russell, P. (1990) 'The Education Reform Act: the implications for special educational needs', in Flude, M. and Hammer, M. (eds) *The Education Reform Act: Its Origins and Implications*, pp. 207–223. Lewes: Falmer Press.

Swann, W. (1985) 'Is the integration of children with special educational needs happening?' *Oxford Review of Education*, 11, 1, 3–18.

Swann, W. (1988) 'Trends in special school placement to 1986: measuring assessing and explaining segregation', *Oxford Review of Education* 14, 2, 139–161.

Swann, W. (1991) *Variations between LEAs in Levels of Segregation in Special Schools: Preliminary Report*. London: CSIE.

Tomlinson, S. (1982) *A Sociology of Special Education*. London: Routledge & Kegan Paul.

UNESCO-UNICEF (1987) *School Clusters in the Third World*. Paris: UNESCO-UNICEF.

Wallace, M. (1988) 'Innovation for all: management development in small primary schools', *Educational Management and Administration* 16, 15–24.

Wedell, K. (1988) 'The new Act: a special need for vigilance', *British Journal of Special Education* 15, 3.

Weston, P. and Barrett, E. (1992) *The Quest for Coherence. Managing the Whole Curriculum 5–16*. Slough: NFER.

Willey, M. (1989) 'LMS: a rising sense of alarm', *British Journal of Special Education* 16, 4.

Chapter 6

Conflicts of policies and models
The case of specific learning difficulties

Sheila Riddell, Sally Brown and Jill Duffield

THE POLICY BACKGROUND

At one time, much of the writing on special educational needs tended to be descriptive rather than analytical and reflected a belief that provision for children with such needs developed as a result of the humanitarian concerns, first of philanthropists and later professional educators. The receivers of the provision were either grateful (the deserving) or not (the undeserving), but whichever was the case, they were passive and had little say in what was offered. When education got around to having policies for this area, it was assumed by most people that such policies were translated directly from the statute or other documents into practice.

Not many of us see things that way any more, and there seem to be two particularly important factors at work here. First, scepticism about good intentions and arguments about the need for social and political analysis abound; they emerge from a recognition that 'special education, like other parts of the education system, is about social control and social engineering as much as about individual self-fulfilment' (Barton and Tomlinson, 1984: 66).

Secondly, changes in the way that government thinks about education, the encouragement of a market forces approach and the elevation of the user/consumer to challenge the decision-making powers of education providers, have offered the potential for a major impact on the policy-into-practice process (whether they have had an impact on the policies or practices themselves in another question). Among policy-makers, providers and users there are considerable opportunities for conflict, at both ideological and practical levels.

In this chapter we focus on a particular aspect of policy for special educational needs that has had a profound influence on debate in that area over the last decade and a half: the abandonment of categories of handicap. Inevitably a policy of this kind has substantial implications for practice, especially for the identification of the needs of young people and provision to meet those needs. When we set the policy in the particular context of 'specific learning difficulties', we shall argue that these implications are especially stark. Much of that starkness may be put down to the willingness and ability of parents of children believed to suffer from conditions like dyslexia to challenge mainstream educational thinking. These parents are atypical of parents of children with special educational needs more generally; that general population is more likely to be working class and less likely to be 'pushy' than is this sub-group.

Our aim is to exemplify what happens at the intersection of what might be called the liberal approaches to special educational needs (manifest in DES, 1978, *The Warnock Report* and SED, 1978, the report from HMI on *The Education of Pupils with Learning Difficulties in Primary and Secondary Schools in Scotland*), the emergence of schools into the accountability of the market place and parents who are prepared to air their views and assert their new rights. We look first at the debate on categorisation in the literature and then turn to some empirical findings which illustrate the ways in which different groups (parents and local authority education officers) construe, interpret and contest received policy and its application in practice. Throughout the paper, the focus is on a sub-set of special educational needs, i.e. specific learning difficulties.

THE ABANDONMENT OF CATEGORIES OF HANDICAP

Several pieces of legislation of the last two decades, such as the Equal Pay Act (1974), the Sex Discrimination Act (1975) and the Race Relations Act (1981), have reflected a concern to remove structural barriers to inequality. The Warnock Report (DES, 1978) and the Progress Report of Scottish HMI (SED, 1978) were informed by similar desires to improve the quality of educational experiences of children with learning difficulties. The 1981 Education (Scotland) Act incorporated aspects of the same thinking, but also reflected some important principles of the then new Conservative government's policy in relation to parental choice as the driving force behind the introduction of a market forces approach to education. A common central theme of all the reports and legislation, however, was the abandonment of categories of handicap.

Throughout the history of special education, the idea of categorisation of handicaps has been associated with the increased segregation of children with disabilities and learning difficulties. The abolition of such categories was seen, therefore, as centrally important by those endeavouring to equalise educational provision for all children. In this spirit, the Warnock Report argued that statutory categories of handicap should be abandoned and a continuum of learning difficulties be recognised embracing a wider group of children than the 2 per cent previously identified as in need of special education. It was suggested that categories of handicap stigmatised children unnecessarily, were based on the false assumption that a child's disability was an indicator of his or her intellectual potential and were confusing when children experienced multiple impairments. In future, it was suggested, the blanket term 'special educational needs' should be used in place of the system of categorisation. A number of criticisms have been made of the Warnock Report, often citing ambiguity or inconsistency in its proposals. For instance, whilst advocating the removal of distinctions between children with special educational needs and others, it was envisaged that special schools would remain in existence and 'distinctive arrangements' made for 'children whose disabilities are marked but whose general ability is at least average' (DES, 1978: para 11.48).

The 1978 Progress Report of Scottish HMI focused on children with learning difficulties who were placed in mainstream schools and it echoed Warnock's anti-categorisation message by arguing that learning difficulties frequently arose not because of within-child problems but because of inappropriate teaching methods and an unsuitable curriculum: 'Many learning problems arise because the demands being made by schools are frequently too great for the linguistic competence of some of the pupils' (SED, 1978: 24, para 4.9).

Remedial teachers had traditionally defined their roles as diagnosing and assisting individual children. HMI now insisted that the prime responsibility for alleviating the learning difficulties of individual children should lie with the class or subject teacher and that co-operative teaching and consultancy should henceforth be regarded as the major role of the learning support teacher. This 'whole-school' responsibility for children with learning difficulties indicated that there would no longer be a need for separate remedial departments with their aura of expertise.

Following these two documents, the abolition of statutory categories of handicap was a central provision of the Education (Scotland) Act 1981. Under the terms of the Act, and following a multidisciplinary assessment, a Record of Needs could be opened for a child whose needs were regarded as pronounced, specific or complex, requiring continuing review and of such a degree that they could not be met by the classroom teacher unaided. The Record of Needs should contain a statement of the child's special educational needs and an education authority would be legally obliged to meet those needs, subject to the availability of resources.

Since the publication of the documents and the introduction of the 1981 Act, there has been an increasing acceptance of the principle of anti-categorisation among education authorities (e.g. Strathclyde Regional Council's policy statement published in 1992 entitled *Every Child is Special – A Policy for All*). However, despite the Scottish Office's implicit endorsement of these steps, other aspects of government policy in the general sphere of education may have the effect of encouraging, and perhaps reintroducing, the categorisation (though not necessarily in the traditional categories) of children with special educational needs by parents and schools. For instance, the transfer of funds from education authorities to schools ('local management of schools' in England and Wales and 'devolved school management' in Scotland) is likely to result in fiercer competition for resources as schools attempt to balance budgets. Since children with Records of Needs are more likely to receive preferential funding, parents may argue that their child belongs to a particular group for whom recording is indicated. In addition, south of the border there is already evidence that more children are being formally identified as experiencing emotional and behavioural difficulties as schools seek to protect their image and ensure that levels of measured educational attainment compare favourably with those of other institutions (see Armstrong and Galloway, Chapter 9, this volume). These and other factors help to sustain the debates around the abolition of categories of handicap. It is to these debates we now briefly turn, looking at some of the more general implications of the policy and relating them to the particular case of specific learning difficulties.

THE SOCIAL AND POLITICAL IMPLICATIONS OF THE ABOLITION OF CATEGORIES

There is disagreement about whether the abolition of categories of handicap has been helpful to children with special educational needs. Heward and Lloyd-Smith (1990), for example, have argued that Warnock's recommendations should be seen as essentially progressive.

> The ideological assumptions, organisational practices and institutional frameworks implied in these proposals represented at the very least a radical redirection and in some cases a reversal of those enshrined in special education in the previous century of its development. Their implementation requires the creation of an education service which has a special commitment to children and young people who are difficult to teach and less likely to succeed.
>
> (Heward and Lloyd-Smith, 1990: 22)

Others, however, have been sceptical about the automatic benefits of the demise of categories. Barton and Tomlinson (1984), for instance, have acknowledged the influence of egalitarian beliefs in the Warnock Report but have also reminded us that special education has always been constrained by the desire to select out the least able and to curtail expenditure. The motives of those who devise policy

> are a product of complex social, economic and political considerations which may relate more to the 'needs' of the wider society, the whole education system and professionals working within the system, rather than simply to the 'needs' of individual children.
>
> (Barton and Tomlinson, 1984: 65)

A continuation of this kind of argument could claim that the blurring of distinctions between children with special educational needs and others may be used as a justification for failing to provide adequate resources. In relation to children with specific learning difficulties, Elliott (1990) has asserted that the abolition of categories and the failure to provide a precise definition of what is meant by special educational needs simply releases authorities from their legal obligations. He has drawn attention to the United States Public Law 94-142 (*The Education for All Handicapped Children Act*, 1975) which defined eleven categories of handicap and specified that federal resources would be made available for the education of all children whose learning difficulties fell within one of these categories; there has been much debate around the precise definition of the categories, but no one has advocated the abandonment of them. In Britain the loss of categories, together with a lack of a precise definition of special educational needs, has led to wider diversity of practice than in the United States, particularly in relation to assessment procedures. In conclusion, Elliott stated rather acidly, 'If we do not quite know what we are looking for, or why, it is not surprising that the method we use to achieve this nebulous end-result are both ill-defined and diverse' (p. 24).

In relation to concern about the impact of categorisation on individuals, a continuing debate has featured in the *European Journal of Special Needs Education* on whether labelling theory is helpful or damaging to disabled people. Soder (1989, 1991) has argued that labels need not have negative connotations and that to reject any form of categorisation is to undermine the reality of disabled people's experience. Booth (1991), in reply to Soder, has maintained that labels are automatically stigmatising and therefore should be opposed. Oliver (1992) has subsequently accused both of 'intellectual masturbation' and suggested that labels could be used in positive or negative ways depending on the political context; in his view, disabled people themselves should be the ultimate arbiters of terminology. It appears, therefore, that although the abandonment of categories has received official acceptance, its helpfulness to those with disabilities and learning difficulties is by no means universally accepted.

CATEGORISATION AND PARENTAL RIGHTS

The theme of parental rights can be traced from Warnock through more recent policy documents and has been used to underpin very different ideologies. Whereas Warnock's primary concern was to achieve a better working relationship between parents and professionals, the Conservative government's thrust has been to introduce a market approach which forces schools into competition with each other, weakens education authorities by removing their power to determine admission policies and places a major emphasis on parental choice. Brown (1990) has criticised this aspect of Conservative policy on the grounds that the wealth of parents and their ability to manipulate the system become the ultimate arbiter of a child's educational opportunities.

The principle of parental choice in education will be inconsistent with the principle that no distinctions should be made between children with special educational needs and others, if parents themselves wish for a system of categorisation to be adopted. The British Dyslexia Association, for instance, a well-organised voluntary organisation for parents, has directly challenged the principle of non-categorisation, arguing that children with specific learning difficulties have distinctive constitutional problems that cannot be merged with the general continuum of learning difficulties. The Association has maintained that children with specific learning difficulties are recognised as a distinct group by the 1981 Act. 'During parliamentary debates on the Bill, children with the specific learning difficulty of dyslexia were particularly included among those the new legislation is designed to help' (British Dyslexia Association, nd a).

The School Boards Pack published by the Scottish branch of the British Dyslexia Association also insisted that dyslexia was recognised as a category by the 1981 Act and invoked earlier legislation in support of the claim. 'Dyslexia constitutes a special educational need as defined by the Education Act (Scotland) 1981 having been first recognised by Parliament in the Chronically Sick and Disabled Person's Act 1970' (British Dyslexia Association, nd b).

The scope for parental advocacy groups to challenge the principle of non-categorisation in order to claim additional resources for a particular section of the school population, is, therefore, considerable.

CATEGORISATION AND RESEARCH ON LEARNING DIFFICULTIES

We have illustrated the debates on the social and political

consequences of categorisation, the legitimacy of labelling theory and the tensions between parents' views and official policy. Now we should ask whether research on learning difficulties themselves (as opposed to research on the political context in which they occur) has anything definitive to say about categorisation. Specific learning difficulties provide an area where categorisation is seen by many as especially appropriate; what has research to say about the matter?

As in research on other aspects of special educational needs, studies of specific learning difficulties vary in the emphasis placed on within-child, within-school and wider social and political influences. The debate continues about whether children who experience such problems form a discrete group with difficulties that are qualitatively different from those of other children with learning difficulties. For example, working within a medical framework, Critchley (1981) has insisted that specific learning difficulties are due to neurological problems and hence such children are distinctively different from others whose difficulties may have been caused by environmental factors. Researchers operating within a psychological framework have disagreed among themselves. Bryant and Impey (1986), for instance, have argued that the difficulties experienced by all children in acquiring literacy skills are qualitatively similar, although some will experience more severe problems than others. Snowling (1985), however, has maintained that whilst some children simply experience developmental delays in the acquisition of literacy, others exhibit a pattern of difficulties which deviates from the norm. It is important, in her view, to pay particular attention to, and to categorise, these different patterns of difficulty in order to facilitate diagnosis and remediation. Identification of the literacy problem in isolation is not enough.

It seems, therefore, that researchers are as embroiled in the categorisation/non-categorisation debate as everyone else. They seem unlikely to be able to provide a clear-cut 'answer' to the question and, indeed, it seems unreasonable to expect that they would. But what about a different kind of research that looks at the human effects of different perspectives on the categorisation issue? In the next section we introduce an empirical study which explores the contrasting perspectives of (1) a group of parents who are firmly committed to the view that children with specific learning difficulties are a discrete group and should be categorised as such, and (2) education authority personnel who generally, although not entirely, conceptualise children with specific learning difficulties as forming part of a wider continuum of those with special educational needs.

PARENTS' PERSPECTIVES ON SPECIFIC LEARNING DIFFICULTIES

Specific learning difficulties – a category?

This research was part of a wider study, funded by the Scottish Office Education Department between 1990 and 1992, which investigated policy and provision for children with specific learning difficulties. It used a variety of methods to investigate the perspectives of several groups; full details are available in Riddell, Duffield, Brown and Ogilvy (1992). The main data on parents' perspectives were collected by postal questionnaire.

Because there is no universally shared understanding of the meaning of the term 'specific learning difficulties', or even agreement that it exists as a distinctive condition, the identification of a representative sample of parents of children with such difficulties presents particular problems. As an approximation, we organised a sample of which half were parents identified by educational psychologists as having children with specific learning difficulties, and half were contacted through local branches of the Scottish Dyslexia Association (i.e. members of, or parents who had been in touch with, the Association). The sample covered all parts of Scotland and the overall response rate was 77 per cent ($n = 153$), with roughly equal numbers of parents contacted through education authorities and voluntary organisations. Using a version of the Registrar General's classification of occupations, modified to take account of mother's as well as father's work, we found that about two-thirds of the sample were identified as middle class and one-third as working class. This ratio does not reflect the class distribution of all families of children with learning difficulties; among that whole population a majority are working class.

We have already reported that the Dyslexia Association has argued strongly that children with specific learning difficulties are constitutionally different from those with more global learning difficulties. It has also displayed some resistance to the term itself. A vast majority (90 per cent) of the parents who responded to our survey stated that they would use the term 'dyslexia' to describe their children's learning difficulties. Those contacted through voluntary organisations were more likely to use the term than those contacted through the psychological service, as were middle-class than working-class parents. Comments written on the questionnaire revealed some of the reasons why the term was favoured. For some, it appeared that the use of the term dyslexia legitimated their claim for additional resources. As one parent put it,

> Up until last year no one at my son's school would agree that he was dyslexic. I have since found out that once they agree he is dyslexic they have to provide help with teaching and in this area they don't have either the resources or the know-how. They are forced to make political judgements about the children and not look at what the problem is. You shouldn't have to fight to have your children properly educated and look at private education just to achieve this!

In the eyes of this parent, the use or rejection of the term dyslexia was essentially a political matter and was connected with gaining access to resources. A number of other comments suggested that parents were willing to stake their claim against those of other disabled groups and were resentful when they felt others were receiving preferential treatment. 'A deaf child has been given extra support by a 2:1 ratio since day 1. This, in my view, is not equal opportunity.'

In other cases, however, it was not equal opportunities with others with learning difficulties that was called for, but separate (and better?) treatment. In particular, parents wished to draw a distinction between their child and others experiencing more global learning difficulties. 'There is a comparison/lumping together of dyslexic children and those who are mentally retarded. Dyslexic children are NOT MENTALLY RETARDED!' This parent's view implied an awareness of a social stigma attached to overall low ability which she did not wish to be associated with her child.

Although the vast majority of these parents wished their children to be classified as dyslexic, some interpreted this as a specific condition common to all children so identified whereas others placed emphasis on individual diversity within a broad syndrome. So, on the one hand, we had one parent indicating that in her view children with dyslexia should be educated in separate schools, a sentiment far removed from the spirit of Warnock.

> I would like to see special units or schools for dyslexia children. C was never happier than when he was being educated by teachers who understood his needs and children who were the same as he was.

On the other hand, a different view, expressed by another parent, saw dyslexia as a broad term covering a wide range of difficulties requiring different types of educational provision: 'A lot of people do not realise that all dyslexic children are different and the help when given should suit that particular child and not be treated as a blanket issue.'

Identification and assessment

The stance taken on categorisation can have far-reaching implications. For example, many parents reported considerable difficulties encountered during the process of identification and assessment. Since they believed their child to be suffering from a clearly identifiable condition, they expected psychometric tests to be administered to confirm or deny its existence. The view sometimes suggested by teachers that the child was simply a slow reader was vehemently rejected.

> My main complaint about the education system/school is that from primary 2 onwards I pointed out that my son had difficulty in decoding unfamiliar words, splitting words into syllables and particular difficulty with vowel sounds. If my husband and I had not taken the initiative to get him assessed, the school would still be happy to classify him as a slow reader.

About 10 per cent (a significant majority of whom were middle class) of parents in our sample went to a voluntary association psychologist for an initial assessment, mainly because of delays in assessment by an education authority psychologist.

Provision

The dissatisfaction with identification and assessment extended to the type of educational provision for children with specific learning difficulties. Overall, 37 per cent said that they were satisfied, 42 per cent were dissatisfied and 20 per cent were unsure. Middle-class parents and those contacted through voluntary organisations were more likely to express dissatisfaction than working-class parents and those contacted through psychological services. Again, dissatisfaction appeared to be rooted in a perception that educational provision did not reflect sufficiently clearly the distinctive nature of this group and their need for particular forms of teaching, and that the teaching methods used by the mainstream class teachers, particularly for the teaching of reading, were not sufficiently systematic.

> Whoever thought up the look and say method (otherwise known as glimpse and guess) should have been shot. Had my son been taught at school by phonics, sounding, spelling rules, etc., his problem would have been minimised instead of maximised. By using computers, tutoring, etc., we are now attempting to round up the horse and put it back in the stable.

Some parents specifically rejected the view of the progress report of HM Scottish Inspectorate (SED, 1978) which took the stance that it is not possible to make firm distinctions between children with learning difficulties and others. Its subsequent conclusion that the mainstream class teacher should be able, in collaboration with the learning support teacher, to adapt the curriculum to meet the needs of all children was clearly unwelcome.

> I certainly do not agree with the learning support teacher working in the class situation as I feel these children need to have their confidence built up so that they can cope with the class work and this can be done on a one-to-one basis.

In so far as parents did express approval of educational provision, it was generally where learning support appeared to be geared to the particular needs of dyslexic children. Reading centres, special units for dyslexic children and learning support delivered by specialist peripatetic teachers were all regarded favourably and appreciative comments were made: 'It took a long time to get support but now we have a place in a reading unit. The staff are wonderful. Reading age up two years. Spelling improved. Now mixes with other children. Confidence up 100 per cent.'

There was also evidence that parents were asserting their right to a significant say over the direction of policy. Weatherley and Lipsky (1977) have commented on the way in which 'street-level bureaucrats' deal with impossible demands on limited resources by stereotyping and pathologising some of their clients, thus undermining their claims. Parents in our survey clearly sensed that they were the potential victims of such a process and strongly resisted it.

> H's learning difficulties have been put down by the school and the psychological service to my single parent status and having a stressful job. The Education Authority will not consider that it is inappropriate teaching methods which have led to her difficulties.
>
> Schools tend to be very ignorant about dyslexia. Teachers tend to dismiss the problems of dyslexic children because they are unable to help them. They also tend to view the parents of dyslexic children as 'neurotic' or 'troublemaking', causing great distress to families who have to fight for their children's right to be educated.

Awareness of their power encouraged parents to challenge education authorities who disregarded their wishes. One parent explained her decision to resort to legal action.

> From the discovery of dyslexia it took two years to get any qualified help. This involved making an appeal, then the appeals committee passing on the case to the Secretary of State. We did eventually win, but two very precious years were wasted in the battle.

Another parent, whose child was in the process of transferring from primary to secondary, described the process of ensuring that her child received adequate learning support in the secondary school. Having been told that the secondary school had only very limited learning support, the parent commented

> I shall be writing back to the educational psychologist asking what provision they can supply. It depends what he replies how far we shall take it. If we have to go to court we shall. Under the 1981 Act, the Region must provide educational facilities no matter what your child's difficulties.

Enquiries made of the SOED during the course of the project supported the view that parents were becoming increasingly confident in using the legislation. The number of appeals was still small but several official complaints had been received under Section 70 of the Education Scotland Act 1980.

It appeared from our analysis, therefore, that far from rejecting categories of handicap, these parents were anxious for their children to be located within a particular category in order to access resources and avoid the stigmatisation of other labels which might be applied. They were unwilling to accept the idea that their children's difficulties should be lumped in with those of children with more global problems, and there was evidence of increasing use of existing legislation to achieve the type of education they felt was required by their children. Throughout the study it was apparent that middle-class parents and those contacted through the voluntary organisations were the most dissatisfied with assessment and provision.

There was substantial evidence that many parents saw themselves as having been in conflict with 'the system'. We now turn to the views of the system in the form of the perspectives of education authority personnel. This group might be expected to conceptualise specific learning difficulties as part of a general continuum in line with the official policy documents reviewed earlier.

EDUCATION AUTHORITIES' PERSPECTIVES ON SPECIFIC LEARNING DIFFICULTIES

Specific learning difficulties – a category?

To gain an overview of policy and provision in Scottish education authorities, three key personnel were interviewed in each of eleven regions and six divisions of the largest authority. Our intention was to speak to the principal educational psychologist, special needs adviser and senior education officer with responsibility for special educational needs in each regional/ divisional authority. In practice, some posts were not filled at the time of the interviews and in a few small authorities the same individual fulfilled more than one role. In total, forty-four responses were analysed both on an individual basis and in order to ascertain the dominant view in each authority.

Three broad conceptualisations of specific learning difficulties emerged, which were identified as the discrete, the continuum and the anti-categorisation perspectives. Each perspective led to distinctive views on educational provision.

Professionals who held the 'discrete' group perspective considered that the problems of children with specific learning difficulties were qualitatively different from those of others with more global learning difficulties and could be readily distinguished from them: 'Their difficulties are not similar to those of slow learning children; they are often more intelligent and able to conceptualise in a way that other children can't' (Adviser).

Others, whilst not opposing absolutely the use of labels, felt that learning difficulties occurred along a 'continuum' with no absolute dividing line between children with different types of difficulty. Specific learning difficulties was certainly not construed as a distinctive category.

> [These children] do not exist as a separate group showing identical characteristics, having identical needs or having identical causes of their learning difficulties.
>
> (Psychologist)

> There are common elements between these kids but the variability among them is greater than any commonality.
>
> (Psychologist)

The remaining group, labelled by us as 'anti-categorisation', refused to countenance the use of labels even when conceptualised as part of a continuum of learning difficulties. Although recognising that specific learning difficulties might exist, they preferred to focus on children's individual needs which, in their view, defied categorisation. 'These difficulties are recognised and accepted as special educational needs. . . . We do not 'label' or distinguish between different special needs' (Adviser).

Analysis of the views of individuals and the dominant views in particular authorities revealed that the continuum perspective was the most common (see Tables 6.1 and 6.2). This emphasis was largely determined, however, by the psychologists' perceptions of specific learning difficulties. An important finding was that in only two regions/divisions did the dominant view appear to match the 'discrete' model favoured by the parents.

Table 6.1 Views of individual education Authority officers on the definition of specific learning difficulties

	Discrete	*Continuum*	*Other*	*Total*
Psychologists	3	12	2	17
Education Officers	4	5	2	11
Advisers	6	4	6	16
Total	13	21	10	44

Identification and assessment

The advisers and psychologists were also asked to describe forms of assessment which were used. A majority described a mixture of normative and criterion-referenced tests, diagnostic teaching and observation. However, those who adopted an anti-categorisation perspective were opposed to the use of psychometric tests and in three authorities both the principal educational psychologist and the special needs adviser rejected them. A psychologist explained that: 'Psychometric tests are about putting children in categories and if you're not using a categorical frame of reference they don't help.' Another felt that, 'Viewing the whole child in the whole context is the important thing and how the child extracts learning from the context.'

Table 6.2 Dominant view of specific learning difficulties in regional/divisional authorities where three individuals were interviewed

Discrete	*2*
Continuum	7
Anti-categorisation	2
No dominant view	1
Total	12

Provision

The form of educational provision made available for children with specific learning difficulties again reflected the dominant perspective. In most cases, provision was within normal mainstream resources, consisting of help from learning support staff in addition to that provided by the class/subject teacher. Where the distinct qualities of children with specific learning difficulties were recognised by at least some of the key personnel there was a greater likelihood that some form of separate provision would be made for them. Thus in two regions and some divisions of the largest region, there were specialist reading centres. In one other region, peripatetic learning support staff were attached to the psychological service and provided additional learning support. The role deemed appropriate for learning support staff also reflected the overall perspective of education authority personnel. Most said that learning support staff offered both one-to-one tuition and mainstream classroom support. Those who saw children with specific learning difficulties as a discrete group, however, felt that the amount of individual tuition provided was inadequate. One psychologist identified learning support teachers' conceptions of their own role as a major problem: 'Learning support teachers often see themselves in an advisory role and some are actively hostile to the idea of working with children one-to-one.'

Sometimes, there was disagreement between the view expressed by the principal educational psychologist and the special needs adviser. In one case, for example, the psychologist recommended once-a-day learning support withdrawal in the case of the very small percentage of extreme specific learning difficulties, and saw this as especially important since there were no reading centres in that region. The special needs adviser, on the other hand, felt that too much direct tuition was against the interests of the child since it was 'not a question of the more he gets the more likely he is to be cured'. She favoured support in class backed up by appropriate learning support materials, with the emphasis on helping the child to develop coping strategies through, for example, the use of computers or coloured overlays.

Although in most regions there was a view that there would be some differences in teaching methods for children with specific learning difficulties compared with children with more global difficulties, many of the professionals felt that emphasis should be on good basic teaching methods for all children – 'good teaching practice and attitude' was recommended for *all* children in order to 'quell the panic' amongst teachers about ignorance of how to teach a dyslexic child (quotations from advisers). On the issue of the effectiveness of provision, the view in two-thirds of authorities was that it was fairly satisfactory, although further staff development was necessary to help teachers meet the needs of children across the continuum of learning difficulties. Dissatisfaction was expressed in a third of regions, however, where specialised provision was regarded as inadequate. One psychologist felt that since the region did not have a specialist centre there was a 'definite gap' in provision and that 'the needs of the severest cases are not being met'.

Although the overall perspective of this group of education authority personnel was clearly not identical with that of the parents, there was evidence of some appreciation of the distinctive needs of pupils with specific learning difficulties. It could be argued that the main difference between parents and education authorities is the responsibility that the latter have for *all* pupils with learning difficulties and the (understandable) preoccupation of the former with the plight of their own children. One area where this is well illustrated relates to the national examination arrangements (Scottish Certificate of Education) for children with specific learning difficulties. These have been welcomed by parents; what kind of reaction has there been from the regions? This was explored with both education authority personnel and the Scottish Examination Board.

Scottish Examination Board arrangements

In 1990 new arrangements were introduced by the Scottish Examination Board for candidates with special educational needs to reflect the principles of the right of every child to assessment and the need to reflect classroom approaches in examination arrangements. These arrangements enabled special assistance, such as scribes and readers, to be provided in examinations but only on condition that the child was certified by the education authority as experiencing specific learning difficulties and not more global learning difficulties. The Scottish Examination Board's special needs officer described the problems which arose when educational psychologists and teachers attempted to dissolve these boundaries.

> After one year of the diet of exams it became apparent that we were having great problems with using that terminology . . . there was a feeling that it was for all special educational needs; it was never intended to be that. We were allowing special arrangements to get over a disability but the whole ethos out on the teaching side is enabling the pupil with special needs to get there. Where do you draw the line? Any pupil at the bottom end of Foundation might be helped by extra time in an exam, by a reader or scribe, but that was never the Board's intention; the Board is working on the presence of an identifiable disability that can be removed by using the arrangements, not to make up for a lack of ability.

Since education authorities were responsible for validating teachers' requests for special dispensations, it was important that they concur with the Scottish Examination Board's definition of specific learning difficulties. However, this definition was unclear and the view in many regions was that this approach was, in any case, retrogressive; it was reintroducing forms of categorisation that had been rejected. There was a marked degree of tension over terminology, with some interviewees reporting that requests had been rejected because the term 'dyslexia' had not been used. One psychologist commented that

> I thought we'd got rid of this dyslexia differentiation and any child who had difficulties in demonstrating knowledge would be eligible for a scribe/word processor or whatever. It should be negotiable regardless of the disability that gave rise to it. They still want a diagnosis. If a school has had to modify the class approach to the child, special provision should be available; it shouldn't depend on classification.

As well as this concern that *any* child who might be able to benefit from the support available should be able to have it, there was also uneasiness generated by the perception that middle-class parents were more able to take advantage of the regulations than others: 'Most [nominations] come from middle-class areas and least from areas of priority treatment. One school is 2000 per cent more in terms of its demands' (Education Officer).

Even though most authorities acknowledged a loose grouping

of children with specific learning difficulties within the general continuum, they were unhappy about what they saw as discrimination by the Scottish Examination Board against pupils with more global difficulties. Although in future Standard grade courses will be available based on spoken rather than written English, it is likely that some children with specific learning difficulties will wish to take the normal Standard grade examination in English and the controversy will continue.

Voluntary organisations

We have already commented on the importance of voluntary organisations' support of parents. The education authorities' views of such organisations were, therefore, of interest. Half of the regions had some form of contact with voluntary organisations, and most of the comments were adversely critical. Issue was taken with the British Dyslexia Association's reported claim that dyslexia is a congenital neurological problem affecting 4–10 per cent of the population, and disbelief was expressed at the coincidence of this proportion living in certain middle-class areas without corresponding occurrence in less privileged localities. It was said that the Dyslexia Association was not dealing with the most needy cases, just those who could afford the fee for a private psychological assessment. The forms of assessment used by psychologists contacted through the Association were criticised as 'old-fashioned', 'deficit focused' and ignoring contextual and emotional factors.

> We believe [in terms of theory] that the Dyslexia Association are peddling an outmoded concept of learning difficulties. . . . The psychometric model is wrong. The assessment techniques are wrong – we abandoned that approach years ago.
>
> (Psychologist)

Many interviewees were most scathing about the number of 'false positive' identifications.

> Any child that goes to the Dyslexia Institute for assessment is automatically diagnosed as dyslexic. This is not right in our experience. The definition [of dyslexia] is so broad as to be meaningless.
>
> (Psychologist)

One psychologist claimed that children whose reading age was tested as six months below their scholastic attainment were being diagnosed as dyslexic. These children, it was suggested, were suffering from over-anxious parents rather than a special condition.

Respondents also disagreed strongly with the view which they felt was promoted by voluntary organisations that a 'special kind of teacher' was required.

> They give parents the impression that the only teaching that is worthwhile is by Dyslexia Institute-trained teachers. Parents then try to ask the Record of Needs to specify teaching by Dyslexia Institute-trained teachers.
>
> (Adviser)

Some professionals felt that voluntary organisations did not understand the approach adopted by the education authority, which is based on a notion of curriculum-deficit rather than child-deficit.

> They don't really understand our argument about learning support and the curriculum. They're still looking for 'the cure' therefore they feel we're not giving them what they want. They really want the child to have his own teacher and we can't produce that.
>
> (Adviser)

(We regard this as a misinterpretation of the Dyslexia Association view, which is that dyslexia is a permanent condition and the aim of education should be to help children to cope with or circumvent it.)

The most extreme views were expressed by respondents in two regions. One of these espoused an anti-categorisation view and claimed that the Dyslexia Association encouraged articulate, middle-class people in demanding Records of Needs for their children whose learning difficulties could be met within existing provision; such people, it was argued, prevented the authority from directing its resources towards the most disadvantaged. In the other region, it was reported that all liaison with the Dyslexia Association was discouraged for a similar reason. However, this state of affairs was regretted by some. An adviser commented that:

> Voluntary organisations come about because the system is not

providing adequate input. I might not agree with how they go about things but there is a degree of expertise there which we should listen to. We ought to open the door to them, and should enter into some discussion with them. We can't just dismiss them out of hand saying we don't agree with their views. We have to talk to them.

(Adviser)

DISCUSSION

The striking feature of the findings of research on this aspect of special educational needs has been the plethora of contrasts they displayed. At the most obvious level they demonstrated that the dominant view among the majority of education authorities in Scotland regarded specific learning difficulties in a rather different way from those parents who see their children as suffering from such problems. The authorities saw such children as part of a continuum of all those with learning difficulties (albeit forming a loose grouping within that continuum), as best assessed by a mixture of psychometric tests and observation, and as most appropriately provided for within mainstream classrooms where class or subject teachers and learning support staff share responsibility. The parents, however, regarded their children as forming a discrete group distinct from other children with more global learning difficulties, as best assessed by special-ised psychometric tests and as most appropriately provided for by one-to-one tuition tailored to their needs and outwith mainstream classrooms. The polarisation of the two groups was not of course, complete. A minority of education authorities favoured the 'discrete group' view with emphasis on specialised provision, sometimes in the form of reading centres or special units; others, however, went in the opposite direction and were opposed to even loose grouping on the continuum – for them children with specific learning difficulties were indistinguishable from other children with learning difficulties, and so psycho-metric tests and specialised provision were eschewed.

Despite these differences in conceptualisation and views on suitable provision, two common aims were evident across virtually everyone interviewed. These asserted, as did the Warnock and Scottish HMI reports of 1978, the central importance of improving the quality of educational experiences of these children and removing the stigma associated with their difficulties. It could be argued, therefore, that the conflict is about means not ends. On the one hand, parents' concern for their own children led them to try to secure resources for individualised provision, if necessary at the expense of other children (there was little in our evidence from parents or voluntary organisations to suggest a campaign for extra resources for special educational needs in *general*). They dealt with the matter of stigma by dissociating specific learning difficulties from more global difficulties and so from the unfortunate connotations of 'less able', 'retarded', 'stupid', 'under-privileged' and so on. On the other hand, education authorities have responsibility for *all* children and for the distribution of scarce resources in ways that are in some sense equitable; unsurprisingly, a majority did not support the view that children with specific learning difficulties should receive privileged treatment. Their concern was with the removal of the stigma associated with *all* learning difficulties, and so mainstream provision for everyone, with a minimum of segregation of any kind, was seen as the strategy most likely to avoid damaging labels. This strategy takes pains not to single out groups with specific difficulties, though it does accept that within-mainstream support will have to be given to individuals with a variety of problems.

These contrasts between the ways in which education authorities and parents construe specific learning difficulties have to be interpreted within a framework of national policy. At this level, it is clear that there are tensions between different strands of the government's thinking. The support which the centre has provided for the 1978 reports' ways of thinking about a continuum of learning difficulties rather than categories of handicap has been complemented by education authorities' efforts to translate that thinking into practice. In contrast, the more recent emphasis in government policy on the empowerment of parents has opened the door to quite different views on how to conceptualise learning difficulties and provide for them. Although Warnock was also concerned about the extension of parental rights, it is more recent policies manifest in the *Parents' Charter in Scotland* (Scottish Office, 1991) that have given some parents, supported by voluntary organisations, the confidence to press firmly for the re-introduction of some form of categories.

This state of affairs illustrates two more general features of the Conservative government's education policies. First, the overall thrust for a market forces approach inevitably has beneath it competing philosophies for education. So, for example, during the 1980s we saw side-by-side the highly centralist approach of the Department of Education and Science (national curriculum and testing) and the much more libertarian stance of the Departments of Trade and Industry and of Employment (Technical and Vocational Education Initiative). It is not surprising, therefore, to find competing and largely incompatible approaches in the area of special educational needs. Second, the empowerment of parents is bound to present difficulties that are not open to resolution. The education system has to provide for *all* children and, if it not to disintegrate, its work has to be principled. Parental views will never be in universal agreement, and many may profoundly diverge from the schools' or government's (local or central) principles. As illustration, anti-sexism and anti-racism present particular problems. Not only do parents' ways of construing these aspects of education vary, but some hold rigid gender-stereotypes and are racist. Are these parents' preferences to be taken into account by schools and, if so, how would that be done? Specific learning difficulties prevents a less stark case, but it still exemplifies circumstances in which parental views may challenge principles sincerely held by those in the education system about the nature of special needs and equal opportunities.

Although this disorder is largely the responsibility of the policies of the current Conservative government, it is likely that it is endemic to policy in a complex and contested area like education. It certainly is a prime reason why policy is never straightforwardly translated from official documents into practice.

Parents and professionals are not simply the passive recipients of policy, but are actively involved in its construction in line with their material interests, personal preferences, social networks and political beliefs. In the case of specific learning difficulties, the pressure from parents and voluntary organisations to categorise and implement some form of segregation (out-of-class, one-to-one tuition) is extraordinarily strong and engagement in battle centring on the power to define the nature of learning difficulties is apparent.

But what can we say about the nature of learning difficulties from an 'independent' perspective. Does the evidence favour categorisation or a continuum? It seems to be unhelpful to look for some kind of balancing of evidence for and against, or to expect some eventual resolution, of the argument about the relative merits of the two constructs. In some circumstances, depending on purposes and priorities, it appears that the most helpful way to structure thinking about special needs is according with a continuum; in other cases, categorisation is more helpful. There is an analogy with elementary particle physics in the early part of this century before the Second World War. For many years models of the nature of matter and energy were of either a particulate nature or a wave nature. Great controversy ensued about which was the 'right' one. As time went on, however, it was accepted that matter and energy both exhibited duality. That is, in some circumstances they behaved as if they were particles and in others as if they were waves. Both the competing models were of value in understanding behaviour and predicting events, but neither of these human constructs, of particles or of waves, were adequate to explain matter and energy.

It is not surprising that simple category or continuum models fail to reflect comprehensively the complexities of learning difficulties. Whether we can get over the political and practical discomforts of having two apparently conflicting constructs in centre stage remains to be seen. The most recent document reflecting policy in Scotland has been published by the Scottish Consultative Council on the Curriculum (1993) as an outcome of an initiative on staff development carried out in collaboration with the Scottish Office Education Department. The publication is entitled *Support for Learning: Special Needs within the 5–14 Curriculum* and makes it clear that the idea of a 'continuum of special educational needs which required to be met through a range of provision' (SCCC, 1993, part 1: 5) is still central. What is not clear is what this is a continuum of; it could be a spectrum of difficulty from mild to severe, or barriers to learning from easy to hard. In either case, it tells us little about the diversity in the nature of the different kinds of needs. There is, however, also a gesture towards categorisation. Some pupils are acknowledged to have 'specific problems', a major diagram is included to show 'learning difficulties considered from the standpoint of individual problems' (part 1, p. 6) and this diagram includes specific learning difficulties as one distinct element. Furthermore, under a heading of teaching and tuition, special programmes are recommended for pupils with dyslexia (a return to a label which much of education has replaced with 'specific learning difficulties' in recent years).

The document takes care to inform parents of the power they have and to remind schools that:

> Parents of pupils with special educational needs should be fully involved in the planning process. Their views will be of particular importance in specifying programme aims and in analysing decisions about the selection of curriculum content.
>
> (SCCC, 1993, part 1: 16)

It is difficult to predict how things will change in the future. The readiness of one group of parents to demand more resources for their children may redistribute provision to their advantage. Other parents might follow suit, but the predominantly working-class parents of, say, those children with moderate learning difficulties have a much weaker lobby and may well lose out overall. The potential for conflict continues between parents who want resources without stigma for their offspring, and education authorities whose priority is likely to be one of spreading those resources to achieve high quality educational experiences for *all* those with special needs.

REFERENCES

Barton, L. and Tomlinson, S. (1984) 'The politics of integration in England', in Barton, L. and Tomlinson, S. (eds) *Special Education and Social Interests*. Beckenham: Croom Helm.

Booth, T. (1991) 'Integration, disability and commitment: a response to Marten Soder', *European Journal of Special Needs Education* 6, 1, 1–16.

British Dyslexia Association (nd a) *Dyslexia: The Hidden Handicap*. London: BDA.

British Dyslexia Association (nd b) *School Boards Pack*. London: BDA.

Brown, P. (1990) 'The third wave: education and the ideology of parentocracy', *British Journal of Sociology of Education* 11, 1, 65–87.

Bryant, P.E. and Impey, L. (1986) 'The similarities between normal readers and development and acquired dyslexics', *Cognition* 24, 121–137.

Critchley, M. (1981) 'Dyslexia: an overview', in Pavlidis, G. and Miles, T.R. (eds) *Dyslexia Research and its Applications to Education*. Chichester: Wiley.

Department of Education and Science (DES) (1978) *Special Educational Needs* (The Warnock Report). London: HMSO.

Elliott, C.D. (1990) 'The definition and identification of specific learning difficulties', in Pumfrey, D. and Elliott, C. (eds) *Children's Difficulties in Reading, Spelling and Writing*. Basingstoke: Falmer Press.

Heward, C. and Lloyd-Smith, M. (1990) 'Assessing the impact of legislation on special education policy – an historical analysis', *Journal of Education Policy* 5, 1, 21–36.

Oliver, M. (1989) 'Intellectual masturbation: a rejoinder to Soder and Booth', *European Journal of Special Needs Education* 7, 1, 20–28.

Riddell, S., Duffield, J., Brown, S. and Ogilvy, C. (1992) *Final Report of the Project Policy, Practice and Provision for Children with Specific Learning Difficulties*. Stirling University.

Scottish Consultative Council on the Curriculum (1993) *Support for Learning: Special Educational Needs within the 5–14 Curriculum*. Dundee: SCCC.

Scottish Education Department (SED) (1978) *The Education of Pupils with Learning Difficulties in Primary and Secondary Schools in Scotland: A Progress Report by HM Inspectors of Schools*. Edinburgh: HMSO.

Scottish Office (1991) *The Parents' Charter for Scotland*. Edinburgh: HMSO.

Snowling, M.J. (ed.) (1985) *Children's Written Language Difficulties: Assessment and Management*. Windsor, NFER-Nelson.

Soder, M. (1989) 'Disability as a social construct: the labelling approach revisited', *European Journal of Special Needs Education* 4, 2, 117–129.

Soder, M. (1991) 'Theory, ideology and research: a response to Tony Booth', *European Journal of Special Needs Education* 6, 1, 17–23.

Strathclyde Regional Council, Department of Education (1992) *Every Child is Special – A Policy for All*. Glasgow: Strathclyde Region.

Weatherley, R. and Lipsky, M. (1977) 'Street-level bureaucrats and institutional innovation: implementing special education reform', *Harvard Educational Review* 47, 2, 171–197.

Chapter 7

Learning difficulties and mathematics

Charles Weedon

The project reported in this chapter was linked to Scottish Office sponsored research at Stirling University, 'Policies, Practices and Provision for Children with Specific Learning Difficulties', which concentrated on reading and writing. The study in mathematics, however, was conducted by teaching staff of Tayside Region, one teacher (myself) being seconded on a part-time basis to act as a link with colleagues involved in the research. The project explored teachers' perceptions of the nature of difficulties in mathematics, and the consequent implications for our responses to these difficulties.

The most striking of these implications seemed to concern our curriculum philosophy – teachers expressed the view that difficulties with mathematics might not always result from inadequate teaching methods and might sometimes be attributable to within-pupil characteristics. For such learners, difficulties may best be met through flexibility and choice, rather than adjustments within the existing framework of a generally prescriptive core curriculum. This is in direct conflict with some of the assumptions underpinning Warnock (DES, 1978), the 1978 Inspectorate Report (SED, 1978) and the 5–14 programme. These 'official' documents emphasise common curricular goals for all but the most severely disabled. The paper concludes by considering some ways of resolving the mismatch between teachers' thinking and official policies.

PRESENT POLICIES AND PHILOSOPHIES

The curriculum framework within which mathematics is taught is quite explicit (Scottish Consultative Council for the

Curriculum, 1989). The ideas of the Munn Report (1977), adapted to some degree, continue to lay down the parameters of the curriculum: there is to be systematic and active study within each of the eight modes – language and communication, mathematical studies and applications, scientific studies and applications, social and environmental studies, technological activities and applications, creative and aesthetic activities, physical education, religious and moral education. The national guidelines for mathematics 5–14 (SOED, 1991), in considering pupils with special educational needs, discuss the benefits of 'programmes with mathematically restricted pathways' while emphasising that 'these programmes, would, nevertheless, be built upon the principles of the existing curriculum' (p. 63). At the same time, appropriacy is urged – SCCC curriculum guidelines emphasise balanced study across the eight modes, while urging the importance of achieving a curriculum balance that is appropriate for each individual pupil: 'A curriculum which wholly fails to take account of the components recommended would be inappropriate; one which disregards special circumstances is equally inappropriate' (SCCC, 1989: 19).

In *The Addressing of Special Educational Needs* (SCCC, 1992), COSPEN (Committee on Special Educational Needs) explores this further. The need for a curriculum that is broad, balanced and relevant is stressed, while teachers are urged to be flexible. The Committee is confident that 'the eight mode curriculum structure is appropriate' (p. 26), exempting only those with profound learning difficulties. Differentiation is recommended as 'a powerful way to meet the needs of all pupils, including those with special educational needs' (p. 33), but it is recognised that this 'may pose complex and difficult challenges to schools'. The implications of these statements are potentially contradictory. On the one hand, teachers are told that the curriculum must be flexible, but on the other they are reminded that essentially the same curriculum must be followed by all except those with the most marked learning difficulties.

The entitlement of all children to a common curriculum was affirmed by the enormously influential thinking of the Warnock Report (DES, 1978) and the HMI Progress Report (SED, 1978). These seminal reports focus upon how profoundly damaging it can be to attribute failure to the pupil: better by far to attribute it to the curriculum, to inappropriate presentation and levels of difficulty. By labelling and separating out we reduce teacher expectations, create negative expectations, and form self-fulfilling prophecies. By retaining instead positive expectations and a curriculum structure that emphasises a shared and common experience in an integrated setting, we can remain non-judgemental, keep pupils together and keep options open for them in a way that is precluded in a system that tests, labels and segregates.

These two currents of thought – balanced study within a range of modes, coupled to high expectations and an unwillingness to think in terms of pupil-deficits – have validated an extended core curriculum, where all pupils work towards related goals. This trend towards an extensive core curriculum has been fleshed out and formalised with the advent of the national curriculum in England and Wales, and the 5–14 curriculum guidelines in Scotland. There is provision for a basic curriculum structure for almost all learners, with an element of flexibility, as yet sketchily defined and only for those who are statemented (or recorded in Scotland). It is an all-embracing structure, and it has been welcomed by some as an important way of militating against the marginalising of pupils with special needs (e.g. Galloway, 1990).

But, it is argued in this chapter, teachers appear to recognise a small proportion of Warnock's 20 per cent estimate of children with learning difficulties for whom the relative inflexibility of the national curriculum and the 5–14 programme is unhelpful, and potentially damaging. These are pupils who may not at present be statemented or recorded, and who perhaps have no need of such support. Further, they may be pupils whose teachers and schools are fully committed to the principles of mainstream integration, and who practise it effectively. At present, however, and perhaps increasingly, statements or records may be sought for these pupils as the sole means of gaining for them some measure of curricular flexibility. This was surely never intended.

DIFFICULTIES IN MATHEMATICS

There is some factor-analytic evidence (Spiers, 1987) that mathematical ability is, statistically at least, an independent cognitive entity. Although attention has been given to within-child origins of difficulties in mathematics, especially those arising from neurological sources (DeLoche and Seron, 1987; Farnham-Diggory,

1978; Joffe, 1980a, b, 1990; Kosc, 1974; Krutetskii, 1976; Orton, 1987; Sharma, 1979; Wheatley, 1977) or problems with the symbolic nature of mathematics (Cockcroft, 1982; Dickson et al., 1984; Floyd, 1981; Harvey et al., 1982; Shuard and Rothery, 1984), or learning styles and personality (Chinn, 1992; Orton, 1987; Pask, 1976), greater emphasis has been placed upon instructional, curricular and social factors as probable causes. There is a frequently recurring theme throughout the literature that mathematics failure is school-induced (e.g. Dickson et al., 1984; Giles, 1981; Ginsburg, 1977; Larcombe, 1985; Liebeck, 1984; Plunkett, 1979). Schools, it is suggested, place too much emphasis on standard algorithms and too little upon understanding in a way that obscures and suppresses intuitive mathematical ability rather than builds upon it (e.g. Allardyce and Ginsburg, 1983; Dickson et al., 1984; Giles, 1981; Ginsburg, 1977; Liebeck, 1984; Plunkett, 1979).

Success levels in mathematics are generally quite low – if teachers test a skill taught and practised some time ago, they do not expect a generally high level of competence. Given our recognition of the rigorously linear nature of mathematics, we teach with a high tolerance, even an expectation, of failure. With failure built in in this way, perhaps it is not surprising that mathematics is associated with varying degrees of boredom, dislike, anxiety, alarm and fear (Allardyce and Ginsburg, 1983; Giles, 1981; Orton, 1987).

While these descriptions of schools are harsh, and may appeal intuitively to an individual's remembered experience within the mathematics classroom, they seem to pay little heed to within-child explanations of difficulty. Explanations tend to be polarised, emphasising either factors within the child, or those beyond. They seem too seldom to attend to both – thereby perhaps giving rise to the kind of tensions between practitioners and policy-makers reflected in this project. There remains a need for a perspective that seeks to reflect both sets of factors.

This project focused upon teachers' understandings of the routine performance of pupils with mathematics difficulties. It sought to identify teachers' perceptions of the factors contributing most significantly to mathematical difficulty, and their views of how pupils with such difficulties cope within their classrooms, and how their classrooms cope with them.

THE RESEARCH QUESTIONS, DESIGN AND METHODOLOGY

Whatever the causes or precise nature of a difficulty, the educator's central concern is the ways in which it might manifest itself in the classroom, and how it might interact with the processes of learning. Accordingly, teachers were interviewed to explore their perceptions and understandings of the nature of difficulties in mathematics, and the ways in which schools respond to these difficulties. Accessing teacher perceptions in this way allowed for subsequent comparison between the perceptions of teachers, who implement policies, and the perceptions of policy-makers, as reflected in prevalent curriculum rhetoric. The mismatch thus revealed pointed up the importance of attending to the understandings of teachers: any serious incongruence of understanding must threaten successful development, and can only be damaging.

Teachers were asked first to reflect in general terms about the factors that might cause a pupil to be perceived as poor in mathematics, i.e. on what constitutes a mathematics difficulty, how is it conceptualised, and what criteria and evidence are used. Each teacher was then asked to identify those pupils who were experiencing such difficulties in his/her own S1 and S2 classes (12 and 13-year-olds), and to reflect in detail about each of these children in turn. For most teachers, this involved one class in each year group, and typically three or four pupils were identified from each class. In each school, interviews were conducted with mathematics and learning support staff. In addition, heads of department were asked to complete a questionnaire about provision for pupils with mathematics difficulties.

During a period of secondment from full-time work as Head of Learning Support, I formulated the research questions, devised the research instruments and piloted them within my own school. At this stage, mathematics and learning support teachers from schools throughout the Region became involved in the project; they engaged in discussion about the purposes of the research, and then carried out the research within their own schools. Initial interest was expressed by staff in twenty-one secondary schools across the Region, and data finally received from seventeen. Sixty-one mathematics teachers and twenty-one learning support teachers were interviewed by colleagues involved in the project, with data gathered for about 341 pupils with difficulties in mathematics. The coding scheme used to analyse the data was developed by the seconded researcher and adapted in light of recommendations from teacher colleagues involved in the project.

RESULTS AND DISCUSSION

Interview responses: perceptions of the nature of pupils' difficulties

The coding scheme developed to analyse teachers' interview responses was fine-grained and extensive, comprising fifty-eight separate factors. It was derived by reading and rereading interview responses, noting patterns and categories until all comments and perceptions fell comfortably within the emerging categories. For ease of access, these were then allocated to ten main groupings:

- factors intrinsic to the nature of maths – e.g. its linearity and dependency upon mastery of earlier skills;
- factors stemming from language/symbolic features – e.g. difficulty in extracting the problem from the written text;
- factors stemming from general skills/qualities needed for maths – e.g. inadequate memory;
- motivational factors – e.g. perceived irrelevance and remoteness from the everyday;
- factors deriving from personality traits – e.g. rushed/impulsive working style;
- factors stemming from pupils' past experience – e.g. frequent absence;
- medical factors – e.g. vision or hearing difficulties;
- methodological factors – e.g. class organisation/methodologies inappropriate;
- factors stemming from schools and/or teachers – e.g. poor teacher training and/or teaching.

The results under these ten main groupings are summarised in Table 7.1 below. The interviews first explored teachers' perceptions of difficulties *in general*, asking them why mathematics might be a difficult subject for some pupils. The first column shows these responses. The teachers then identified and considered *specific*

Table 7.1 Teachers' perceptions of sources of difficulty

Factor	Teachers mentioning statements in this category	
	In general	When considering specific pupils
Intrinsic nature of maths	52	8
Language/symbolic features	44	67
Mathematical skills/qualities	97	105
General skills/qualities	20	87
Personality	32	183
Motivation	69	51
Methodology	44	14
Schools and/or teachers	11	6
Pupils' past experiences	3	29
Medical	–	12

Notes:
(1) Teachers typically suggested several sources of difficulty when considering learning difficulties in maths, both in general terms and in relation to particular pupils.
(2) When discussing the difficulties experienced by particular pupils, teachers referred on average to six pupils.
n (staff) = 82 (61 maths staff, 21 LS staff)
n (pupils) = 341

pupils in their own classes, and reflected upon the apparent reasons for the difficulties in each case. The second column shows these responses. This parallel presentation of data allows inspection of the ways in which perceptions shift as teachers move from general considerations to the consideration of specific individuals.

Table 7.2 summarises the data still further, considering the perceptions in three main categories: difficulties arising from the nature of the subject, pupil-based difficulties, and those caused by schools.

As shown in Table 7.2, teachers tend to see mathematics difficulties as predominantly pupil-based, while recognising that school and curricular factors might also play a part. When considering these difficulties in general (column 1), they attribute some responsibility to the intrinsic nature of mathematics and some to what happens in the schools; but they see these factors as

Table 7.2 Comparison of subject, pupil and school as sources of
difficulty – teachers' perceptions

Factor	Teachers mentioning factors in this category	
	In general	*When considering specific pupils*
Subject-based	52	8
Pupil-based	265	534
School-based	55	20

Notes:
subject-based: structural factors intrinsic to the nature of maths.
pupil-based: language skills, general and mathematical skills/qualities needed,
personality, motivation, past experience and medical.
school-based: methodological, and other factors caused by schools/teachers.
n (staff) = 82 (61 maths staff, 21 LS staff)
n (pupils) = 341

comprising only a modest contribution, and their role diminishes
still further once the attention of teachers turns to specific pupils
(column 2). Throughout, there tends to be this clear shift of
emphasis as teachers move from considering difficulties in
general to considering difficulties in relation to specific pupils:
the locus of responsibility moves decisively towards the pupil,
and away from the school and the nature of the subject. To some
extent this is inevitable; when asked to focus on specific children
the teacher is encouraged to provide an account that centres on
individuals. But even taking account of that, the evidence
suggests that teachers see the pupil's own attributes – intellectual,
mathematical and personal – as being at the centre of mathematical difficulties. There is a clear sense that these qualities
have already determined success or failure long before the child
reaches the eighth year of study. After that, the feeling is that
despite the best efforts of teachers, and the range of method-
ologies and organisational approaches employed, the linear
nature of the subject and its inherent abstraction and difficulty set
in motion a down-cycle of failure and decreasing expectation on
the part of pupils, parents and teachers.

The responses demonstrate that, among these secondary
teachers, there was little widespread fundamental optimism.
Allan, Brown and Munn (1991) had found that primary support
staff tended to be more optimistic about pupils' difficulties than

their secondary colleagues, and more likely to see them as short term; others have written positively of the way that, properly presented, mathematics can be meaningful and exciting for pupils with very considerable difficulties (Ahmed and Williams, 1989; Bennett and Williams, 1992). The responses here, however, are pervaded by a sense that these pupils are engaged in studying a subject where their relatively poor performance probably reflects their potential as mathematicians. This may be seen as an attempt by teachers to escape responsibility for their failure to teach effectively, though teachers' responses in this project do not attribute learning failure to the home or other social factors. Or it may be that it is an honest reflection of a real problem, the difficulty of accommodating individual needs within a common curriculum allowing only a limited degree of flexibility. This issue is discussed again in the conclusion.

Provision for pupils with mathematics difficulties

A questionnaire was used to ascertain the nature of provision for S1 and S2 within each participating school. In it, the promoted member of staff responsible for S1/S2 maths provision described and reflected upon the courses, methods, organisation and materials used in that school. The results are summarised in Table 7.3.

Table 7.3 Principal teachers' accounts of class organisation and type of provision in their departments (*n* = 16)

	Number of schools	Class organisation	
		Mixed ability throughout	Mixed ability in S1, with some streaming/ setting in S2
Wholly individualised	5	5	0
Mixed methods with significant individualisation	5	4	1
Primarily class taught	6	4	2

Responses demonstrated that all participating schools worked within the framework of common curricular goals, with approaches being fairly equally distributed between individualisation, class texts, and combinations of the two. While there were satisfactions and dissatisfactions expressed concerning each, no pattern emerged from the overall data indicating decisively that any one approach would meet with general approval. However, the mixed methods gave strong emphasis to individualised learning, so that individualised provision did emerge as the most dominant single strand in the schools surveyed.

When promoted teachers were describing the advantages of their provision, individualised schemes were seen as having many strengths. They allowed for individual differences, different starting points, different pace and differing levels of mathematical aptitude. They were seen as allowing continuity of pupil experience, even where there might be extended absence from school. With frequent in-built diagnostic testing, they allowed identification of strengths and weaknesses, and consequent remediation. Independent, self-organised work was encouraged; tasks were short and varied, and often enjoyed; and the less-skilled might enjoy success without invidious comparison invited by materials too evidently different from those of their peers. These were all qualities that might allow common curricular goals, albeit with differentiated materials, that remained appropriate for all.

However, significant weaknesses and drawbacks of individualised schemes were discussed. They were seen as taking considerable teacher time to organise and administer, at the direct expense of time spent in teaching and in explanation and assistance to pupils. The scope they allowed for pupils to 'coast' concerned teachers, and some felt that such schemes did not make the most effective use of teachers' skills. It was felt, too, that pupils on individualised schemes lacked opportunities for discussion and shared experiences; and the need for learning to depend on reading skills that might be limited was regretted.

Given the climate of opinion among mathematics educators, the substantial number of schools retaining whole-class approaches is interesting – though in considering these results it is important not to equate whole-class teaching with undifferentiated teaching: one of the most widely used whole-class texts provides pupils with opportunities to practice and apply each

taught concept at up to three levels of difficulty. Those
supporting whole-class teaching from texts or prepared materials
felt that it ensured adequate and uniform coverage; that it
allowed pupils to be pressed, with scope for extending the more
competent; and that it offered pupils a secure, predictable and
familiar context for learning. Set against that, it was acknowledged as sometimes inflexible, over-demanding and insensitive
to the very wide range of skills and competencies to be found
within a class, sometimes leading to a sense of hopelessness,
frustration and anxiety.

Discussion of provision

The original research question asked whether provision reflected
teachers' perceptions of difficulties with mathematics. It seems
that teachers see these difficulties as deriving mainly from the
demands made by the peculiar nature of the subject in interaction
with the particular attributes of the pupil in difficulty:
mathematics is seen as linear, abstract, uncompromising and
demanding – success with it demands the ability to grasp abstract
concepts, retain them, understand them enough to apply them,
and a learning style that can accept continuing challenge and
some experience of failure. Individualised schemes, despite their
disadvantages, were seen as most helpful to pupils experiencing
difficulty, with their inherent flexibility of delivery and with the
reduced threat to self-esteem that they pose.

But even so, individualised schemes were perceived as failing
to meet fully the needs of pupils whose difficulties were various
and stubborn. Most who favoured individualised schemes spoke
too of the need to develop further materials and resources.
Teachers felt that, while such schemes went a long way towards
sensitive provision, they remained essentially uniformly paced:
there was little structural accommodation for extended work at
one level, in one area, if or when such a need arose. Individualised schemes seemed premised upon an assumption that a
certain level of exposure to a certain topic should allow it to be
mastered. Teachers, however, spoke of pupils who seemed
sometimes to come to a sudden and complete halt in one or more
topics or concepts. For these pupils, the teachers felt there was a
need to work and rework these topics and concepts, with a range
of approaches and extensive consolidation, returning for

rehearsal and revision before mastery could be expected. No individualised schemes allowed for this.

CONCLUSIONS

The results suggested that while teachers recognised the way in which some learning difficulties in mathematics may stem from the curriculum and factors within the school, they felt that they were more likely to stem from within-pupil factors. Descriptions of provision indicated some use of individualised approaches, and their proponents certainly saw them as the most effective available response to individual differences in mathematics performance. Yet even the best of these schemes were seen as failing to meet fully the needs of the unsuccessful pupil. Official curriculum rhetoric, in emphasising study in all modes and common curricular goals for all (SCCC, 1989, 1992; SED, 1978), tends to imply that an adequately differentiated common experience is the best way to overcome the difficulties experienced by pupils in their learning. As noted, there is a lack of clarity about how much curricular flexibility is appropriate. Teachers appeared to feel that, for some pupils, present arrangements were insufficiently flexible and that attempts to pursue common learning goals could result in repeated and damaging failure.

In addition to the insights it provided into teachers' understandings of pupils' difficulties with mathematics, the project raised two key issues, one research-based and one curricular.

Research implications

The research issue carries implications for the valuing and utilisation of teacher understandings. It is argued that in designing educational policies, the views of teachers are often neglected, and that this neglect has contributed to our failure to develop learning support strategies that are effective for all learners.

Much educational research seeks to explore and understand what happens in the classroom, but very little of it is conducted by teachers. Yet teachers are the only educated and adult participants in the whole education field who have an intimate and continuous experience of both the delivery of the curriculum, and of how learners respond to it. Kemmis (1988) argues that, 'since only the practitioner has access to the commitments and practical theories which inform praxis, only the practitioner can study praxis'.

Moreover, teachers are the arbiters of the very successes and failures that educational research addresses: they are the main agents in defining it and attributing it. Their perceptions structure and create the learning environment within which success occurs, or does not occur. They provide the mirror in which the pupil sees him or herself as a successful or unsuccessful learner. Without their understandings, there can be no understanding – certainly none that can be regarded confidently as valid.

Curricular implications

How, then, are we to respond to the view that has emerged from this research that mathematics teachers tend to believe that, for some pupils in difficulty, the roots of the problem may lie within the child rather than within the school or the presentation of the curriculum? It may be that teachers simply do not understand the policy, or that factors embedded within their work or subject culture make them resistant to it. Considerable resources have been channelled into transforming remedial teaching into learning support – but perhaps important in-service work remains to be done with subject specialists, more fully to alert them to the nature and implications of learning support policy. Indeed, for learning support and subject teachers to collaborate effectively such understanding is vital.

Additionally, however, it is important that when the views of teachers and policy-makers diverge, policy-makers do not see teachers simply as misguided – or, worse, incompetent. The views of teachers represent insights that may imply necessary changes in present curriculum structures. In the following paragraphs, I consider possible policy developments which might stem from teachers' views.

Current curriculum guidelines (SCCC, 1989; SOED, 1991), born of the very evident flaws of a past system that divided and directed according to abilities, ensure that all pupils travel in similar directions with their pathways adjusted and tailored to suit their aptitudes. Difficulties, where they arise, are attributed to the curriculum. About each individual pupil in difficulty, a determined optimism is sustained. We have seen the damage that can be done by segregation and labelling, in the form of down-spiralling self images – and accordingly we work on the basis that there is no learning difficulty that cannot be overcome by appropriate methods and effective differentiation. Thus, by implication we validate the concept of a core curriculum. It is a way of thinking that makes all areas of study theoretically accessible for all children, and therefore valid. It is a model that legitimises a high level of compulsion within the curriculum, while at the same time perhaps militating against flexibility and choice.

For a small number of pupils, however, such a model constrains and diverts our attention when we seek for solutions to learning difficulties. We look only to the curriculum for a deficit, not to the child. We have accepted (for the most part, it must be stressed, to great advantage) that a child-deficit model of learning difficulties is likely to be unhelpful and damaging. However, for all the rhetoric to the contrary, we do utilise a child-deficit model within our schools for a small number of pupils with significant special educational needs. But it is not generally available to the whole school population – only for the very end of the continuum.

For the vast majority of pupils, most difficulties are tackled on a curriculum-deficit basis. Common goals can be made to make sense, at least enough sense for the approach to remain the best one we are likely to come up with. Then, at the far end of the continuum, are the pupils who self-evidently will get but little from a full mainstream curriculum. These pupils generally have a statement or record of needs, and their curriculum tends to be individually constructed and tailored, built up from a genuine attempt to discover where each individual child is, and just where each one might usefully try to go. Most people accept that there are some pupils for whom a full national curriculum is simply not appropriate. Yet, in the secondary sector at least, there are no such considerations for pupils with significant difficulties that are not officially recognised. These pupils are locked into a mainstream curriculum philosophy that has been successful for most – but not for all. It has some flexibility, but not nearly enough. These pupils are trapped in a model they do not fit.

We can respond with a great deal of flexibility to pupils whose needs are recognised officially as special, who are statemented or recorded. If teachers are right, we need to look for ways of extending this flexibility and choice to those other pupils who may need it. A core curriculum must retain a central role if schools are to allow learners experience of all modes of learning – but at what stage in a learner's development it may be modified, and the extent to which it may be modified, have not yet been made clear. National guidelines recognise the tensions – but they do not resolve them with any clarity. In the absence of such resolution, the way in which national structures are interpreted by teachers will prove crucial; and in the meantime, some pupils may continue to be exposed to avoidable frustration and failure.

This research cannot determine the extent to which teachers are right in their views of learning difficulties; as reflected here, they do not accept that schools and teachers should carry all the responsibility for learning failure. These views should not be accepted uncritically but nor should they be ignored. A dialogue is needed between those who make policy and those who implement it – in this case a dialogue centred around ways of rendering less arbitrary and inflexible that cut-off point between mainstream pupils and those who might have statements or records. For the great majority, the curriculum deficit model has worked and worked well; for a small minority, it has never been applied. It is at the interface between these two groups that teachers and policy-makers should meet. The best of both worlds is available to some pupils – together, and cautiously, we should look for ways of making it available to more. Otherwise the core curriculum, far from representing an entitlement, might well become a straitjacket.

REFERENCES

Ahmed, A. and Williams, W. (1989) 'A maths curriculum for all', *Support for Learning* 4, 4, 221–226.

Allan, J., Brown, S. and Munn, P. (1991) *Off the Record: Mainstream Provision for Pupils with Non-recorded Learning Difficulties in Primary and Secondary Schools*. Edinburgh: SCRE Project Report.

Allardyce, B. and Ginsburg, H. (1983) 'Children's psychological difficulties in mathematics', in Ginsburg, H. (ed.) *The Development of Mathematical Thinking*, pp. 319–350. Orlando: Academic Press.

Bennett, A. and Williams, H. (1992) 'What will happen if . . .', in Booth, T. Swann, W., Masterton, M. and Potts, P. (eds) *Curricula for Diversity in Education*, pp. 63–75. London: Routledge/Open University Press.

Brown, S. and Riddell, S. (1992) *Class, Race and Gender in Education*. Edinburgh: SCRE.

Chinn, S.J. (1992) 'Individual diagnosis and cognitive style', in Miles, T.R. and Miles, E. (eds) *Dyslexia and Mathematics*. London: Routledge.

Cockcroft, W.H. (1982) *Mathematics Counts*. London: HMSO.

DeLoche, G. and Seron, X. (eds) (1987) *Mathematical Disabilities: A Cognitive Neuropsychological Perspective*. Hillsdale N J: Erlbaum.

Department of Education and Science (DES) (1978) *Special Educational Needs* (The Warnock Report). London: HMSO.

Dickson, L., Brown, M. and Gibson, O. (1984) *Children Learning Mathematics*. London: Holt, Rhinehart and Winston.

Farnham-Diggory, S. (1978) *Learning Disabilities*. London: Fontana/Open Books.

Floyd, A. (ed.) (1981) *Developing Mathematical Thinking*. Wokingham: Addison Wesley/Open University Press.

Galloway, D. (1990) 'Was the GERBIL a Marxist mole?' in Evans, P. and Varma, V. (eds) *Special Education: Past, Present and Future*, pp. 371–379. London: Falmer Press.

Giles, G. (1981) *School Mathematics under Examination: Part 3, Factors Affecting the Learning of Mathematics*. Stirling: University of Stirling, Department of Education, DIME Projects.

Ginsburg, H.P. (1977) *Children's Arithmetic: The Learning Process*. New York: Van Nostrand.

Harvey, R., Kerslake, D., Shuard, H. and Torbe, M. (1982) *Language Teaching and Learning: 6 – Mathematics*. London: Ward Lock Educational.

Joffe, L. (1980a) 'Dsylexia and attainment in school mathematics: Part 1', *Dyslexia Review* 3, 1, 10–14.

Joffe, L. (1980b) 'Dyslexia and attainment in school mathematics: Part 2', *Dyslexia Review* 3, 2, 12–18.

Joffe, L. (1990) 'The mathematical aspects of dyslexia: a recap of general issues and some implications for teaching', *Links* 15, 2, 7–10.

Kemmis, S. (1988) 'Action research', in Keeves, J.P. (ed.) *Educational Research, Methodology and Measurement: an International Handbook*. Oxford: Pergamon Press.

Kosc, L. (1974) 'Developmental dyscalculia', *Journal of Learning Disabilities* 7, 3, 164–177.

Kosc, L. (1986) 'Dyscalculia – a special issue on the work of Dr Ladislav Kosc', *Focus on Learning Problems in Mathematics* 8, 3–4.

Krutetskii, V.A. (1976) *The Psychology of Mathematical Abilities in Schoolchildren*. Chicago: University of Chicago Press.

Larcombe, T. (1985) *Mathematical Learning Difficulties in the Secondary School*. Milton Keynes: Open University Press.

Lewis, C., Hitch, G. and Walker, P. (in press) 'The prevalence of specific arithmetic difficulties and specific reading difficulties in 9–10-year-old boys and girls', *Journal of Child Psychology and Psychiatry*.

Liebeck, P. (1984) *How Children Learn Mathematics*. Harmondsworth: Penguin.

McNamara, D.R. (1989) 'The outsider's arrogance: the failure of participant observers to understand classroom events', *British Educational Research Journal* 6, 113–126.

Munn Report (1977) *The Structure of the Curriculum in the Third and Fourth Years of the Scottish Secondary School*. Edinburgh: SED/CCC.

Orton, A. (1987) *Learning Mathematics: Issues, Theory and Classroom Practice*. London: Cassell.

Pask, G. (1976) 'Styles and strategies of learning', *British Journal of Educational Psychology* 46, 128–148.

Plunkett, S. (1979) 'Decomposition and all that rot', *Mathematics in Schools* 8, 3, 2–5.

Rourke, B.P. and Finlayson, M.A.J. (1978) 'Neuropsychological signficance of variations in patterns of academic performance: verbal and visuo-spatial abilities', *Journal of Abnormal Child Psychology* 6, 121–123.

Rourke, B.P. and Strand, J.D. (1978) 'Subtypes of reading and arithmetic disabilities: a neuropsychological analysis', in Rutter, M. (ed.) *Developmental Neuropsychiatry*, pp. 473–488. New York: Guilford Press.

Rourke, B.P. and Strand, J.D. (1983) 'Neuropsychological significance of variations in patterns of academic performance: motor, psychomotor and tactile-perceptual abilities', *Journal of Paediatric Psychology* 3, 62–66.

Scottish Consultative Council on the Curriculum (SCCC) (1989) *Curriculum Design for the Secondary Stages*. Edinburgh: SCCC.

Scottish Consultative Council on the Curriculum (SCCC) (1992) *The Addressing of Special Educational Needs*. Edinburgh: SCCC.

Scottish Education Department (SED) (1978) *The Education of Pupils with Learning Difficulties in Primary and Secondary Schools in Scotland*. Edinburgh: HMSO.

Scottish Office Education Department (SOED) (1991) *National Guidelines Mathematics 5–14*. Edinburgh: SOED.

Share, D.L., Moffitt, T.E. and Silva, P.A. (1988) 'Factors associated with arithmetic-and-reading disability and specific arithmetic disability', *Journal of Learning Disabilities* 21, 313–320.

Sharma, M.C. (1979) 'Children at risk for disabilities in mathematics', *Focus on Learning Problems in Mathematics* 1, 2, 63–64.

Sharma, M.C. (1986) 'Dyscalculia and other learning problems in arithmetic: a historical perspective', *Focus on Learning Problems in Mathematics* 8, 3–4.

Sharma, M.C. and Loveless, E.J. (eds) (1986) 'Dyscalculia – a special issue on the work of Dr Ladislav Kosc', *Focus on Learning Problems in Mathematics* 8, 3–4.

Shuard, H. and Rothery, A. (eds) (1984) *Children Reading Mathematics*. London: John Murray.

Skemp, R.R. (1971) *The Psychology of Learning Mathematics*. Harmondsworth: Penguin Books.

Spiers, P.A. (1987) 'Acalculia revisited: current issues', in DeLoche, G. and Seron, X. (eds) *Mathematical Disabilities: A Cognitive Neuropsychological Perspective*. Hillsdale, NJ: Erlbaum.

Wheatley, G.H. (1977) 'The right hemisphere's role in problem solving', *Arithmetic Teacher* 25, 2, 37–38.

Chapter 8

Integration in the United Kingdom

Julie Allan

LOOKING AT INTEGRATION

Integration, as Warnock pointed out, is not achieved by legislation alone, but has to be 'contrived and patiently nurtured' (DES, 1978: 102). Research on the integration of pupils with special educational needs was carried out as part of an OECD/CERI project, *Active Life for Disabled Youth* (NFER, 1992). The aims were to identify the factors which contributed to successful integration and to make comparisons across the member countries. Within the United Kingdom, seven case studies were conducted by the National Foundation for Educational Research, the Northern Ireland Council for Educational Research and the Scottish Council for Research in Education. Comparisons within the United Kingdom highlighted the different ways in which integration could be interpreted. This raises questions regarding the usefulness of Warnock's construct to describe the social and educational experiences of children with special educational needs. The seven UK case studies were selected because they represented a range of provision for pupils with special educational needs, each of whom had a statement or a record of needs and covered a wide age range. The sample also reflected different degrees of integration, as defined by Warnock. Six mainstream schools (one case study was of a primary and a secondary school) and two special schools were chosen. One of the special schools was part of a cluster arrangement of several schools. Three of the mainstream schools in England and Wales had relatively high proportions of pupils with statements (20 per cent, 15 per cent and 6 per cent). This had resulted from a decision to concentrate specialist resources on particular sites, but raised the question of whether the schools had become 'special' as a consequence.

The researchers adopted a common approach to the collection of data. This involved mainly semi-structured interviews with school staff, local authority personnel and, where possible, parents. There was also some observation of lessons and scrutiny of official documentation, such as statements or records of needs. The case studies were analysed by the researchers with responsibility for them and the team met regularly to exchange findings and explore emergent issues.

Three aspects of integration were identified as of particular interest to the funders of the United Kingdom study: access to the national curriculum; resourcing; and the role of the special school. This chapter focuses on the first of these themes and reports on the findings from the Scottish case study, with some comparisons across the United Kingdom. It is important to bear in mind, however, that the possibilities for generalisation from case studies are limited. In the Scottish case study, some distinctive differences in approaches to integration were apparent in an associated primary and secondary school. These differences are the focus of the second part of the chapter. It concludes by exploring the extent to which the integration of the pupils in each of the case studies was successful and considers the usefulness of Warnock's conceptualisation of integration.

WHAT COUNTS AS INTEGRATION IN THE WARNOCK FRAMEWORK?

Warnock distinguished three forms of integration. *Locational* integration occurs where pupils with special educational needs are taught on the same site as their mainstream peers. Opportunities for *social* integration might arise for pupils with special educational needs to interact with mainstream pupils, for instance at intervals or assemblies. *Functional* integration, the most demanding of all, takes place where pupils with special educational needs participate in main- stream classes alongside their peers, either part-time or full-time, and pursue similar goals.

It is mainly with functional integration that differences in interpretation arise. This is not surprising, since, as Warnock said, 'the functional element is perhaps uppermost in most people's minds when they speak of integration' (DES, 1978: 101). It is also the aspect of integration on which the Warnock report is least clear. Functional and curricular integration are often discussed synonymously, but Pijl and Meijer (1991) see the notion of function as being unhelpful. They prefer the term 'curricular integration', meaning a situation in which 'the same curriculum and long-term goals apply for handicapped and non-handicapped pupils'. Hegarty, Pocklington and Lucas (1981) are critical of many definitions of integration, because they relate more to the physical location of the pupil, rather than to his or her educational experiences and Hegarty (1991) suggests abandoning the term altogether. It seems inappropriate to describe pupils as functionally integrated if they are following a special curriculum, with distinctive educational goals, even if they are taught within a mainstream classroom. However, this could be a feature of the unhelpfulness of the term itself, rather than of its interpretation.

The variety of ways in which integration has been interpreted made a comparative study a complex task. There had to be consensus among the researchers regarding what would count as integration in the case studies, otherwise there would be no basis for comparison. However, the case studies were concerned with the extent to which integration was judged to be successful by teachers. It was important, therefore, to ascertain their understanding of the type of integration they were aiming to achieve and how they assessed its success. Warnock's three forms of integration were used as a framework for interviews with staff and observation in the UK case studies.

Teachers in each of the case studies were asked indirectly about locational, social and functional integration. They were asked to describe the time spent by pupils with special educational needs in mainstream classrooms or elsewhere, about the work they did in different settings and how this compared with the work done by mainstream pupils. The pupils' inter-action with their peers was also discussed. They were then asked to indicate in what sense they saw particular children as being integrated and to elaborate on their school's aims for children with special educational needs. It was clear from the interviews that while there was agreement on what was meant by locational and social integration, functional integration was understood in different ways. In some cases, teachers referred to sharing the same classroom; others indicated the pursuit of common curriculum goals. Functional integration was often taken to mean the same as curricular integration.

THE NATIONAL CURRICULUM AND THE 5–14 PROGRAMME

Official policy documents indicate that pupils with special educational needs have a right of access to the national curriculum in England and Wales, the Northern Ireland curriculum, and the non-statutory 5–14 programme of curriculum and assessment in Scotland. Provision has been made in England and Wales for disapplication of all or part of the national curriculum for pupils with special educational needs or for modifications to be made to the curriculum where necessary. This, however, is discouraged by the National Curriculum Council, which calls for maximum participation in the national curriculum for all pupils with special educational needs (NCC, 1989). In Scotland, there are no formal mechanisms for exemption from or modification to the 5–14 programme of curriculum and assessment. The national guidelines state that all pupils would be expected to try to achieve the attainment targets, acknowledging that there will be different rates of progress through the curriculum. However, unlike England and Wales, the guidelines are non-statutory and state:

> If schools, classes or units decide that pupils for whom a record of needs has been opened should become involved in the system of assessment described here, alternative ways of attaining targets should be available to them.
>
> (SOED, 1991: 50)

So far, little advice appears to be available to teachers on how they might accomplish this, although the SCCC has recently issued guidelines on the 5–14 programme for pupils with special educational needs (SCCC, 1993). Previous work on mainstream provision for non-recorded pupils with learning difficulties suggested that help of this kind was needed, since it appeared to be very difficult to find alternative means of attaining the same goals (Allan, Brown and Munn, 1991).

In the case studies of Northern Ireland, and England and Wales, all pupils with special educational needs had access to the national curriculum, although the attainment targets they achieved were often well below those of pupils within the same age group. For pupils who were taught in special schools, or in special classes within mainstream schools, these peer comparisons may not be a salient feature; for those pupils with special educational needs taught in mainstream classes, however, they may be much more apparent. In Scotland, where the implementation of the 5–14 programme was still at an early stage, pupils with special educational needs had varying degrees of access to the mainstream curriculum. In each of the case studies, the integration experienced by pupils with special educational needs was influenced by two major factors: the nature of the pupils' difficulties and the collaborative teaching approaches used.

THE INTEGRATION OF PUPILS WITH PARTICULAR DIFFICULTIES

In the case studies, the difficulties experienced by the pupils were wide ranging and included moderate, severe and profound learning difficulties, specific learning difficulties, physical handicap and sensory impairment. The nature and extent of integration experienced by children seemed to be related to the kinds of difficulties they had. In some cases, practical factors made it easier to provide full integration for children with certain difficulties than for others. Differing levels of support also contributed to the kind of integration experienced. Most importantly, the teachers' perceptions of particular difficulties appeared to influence their views of appropriate goals and the kind of integration the children experienced.

Functional integration was viewed as a realistic goal for many of the children with physical disabilities or sensory impairment. Teachers clearly saw them as capable of following the same curriculum as their peers, providing their difficulties could be circumvented. Physical aids, such as wheelchairs or phonic ears were provided, or special arrangements were made for seating or amplification of sound. These pupils were often withdrawn temporarily from classes, however, for occupational therapy, speech therapy, physiotherapy or swimming. While this was a vital part of provision, it frequently disrupted their mainstream timetable. Clearly there were logistical problems in arranging therapy that involved paramedical staff, but it was seen as unreasonable by teachers that physiotherapy, for example, should count as a substitute for physical education. Not only did the two activities serve quite different purposes, but the with-drawal of the pupils could interrupt their progress and so make it difficult for them to cope with the mainstream curriculum. It could also contribute to damaging 'labels' for particular pupils.

Some of the children with specific learning difficulties were also viewed as capable of being integrated functionally. For this to occur, however, teachers thought it necessary to introduce some measure of withdrawal for discrete language or mathe-matics programmes up to year 9 in their education to enable them to make better progress in the mainstream (becoming a more skilled reader was a particularly important element of this). Functional integration was not seen as a realistic aim for pupils with more pronounced difficulties. Withdrawal for these pupils was aimed at providing individual tuition in basic skills and building confidence. They could be described as integrated in locational and social, but hardly at all in functional terms; children with severe and profound difficulties, who were withdrawn from the mainstream for discrete programmes of work, had virtually no functional integration.

Children with moderate learning difficulties constituted the group for whom functional integration provided the greatest challenge for education; it was in relation to these children that most of the differences of interpretation over functional integration arose. In principle, many of the pupils might have significant achievement potential, but they lacked fundamental skills, especially, in reading and writing, and teachers faced a major task in making adaptations to the curriculum to try to take account of their difficulties. Major changes had to be made to the mainstream curriculum to assist them in gaining access. The most common strategies were to provide tasks that required less reading or writing from the pupils with special educational needs or for the non-teaching assistants to help the pupils with special educational needs by, for instance, completing some of the writing for them. These strategies did not, of course, address the inherent difficulty; to do that, it was suggested, would not be feasible within a mainstream classroom.

Some teachers argued that children with moderate learning difficulties were being integrated functionally where they were being taught alongside their peers, even if the curriculum they were following was distinctively different. This distinctiveness could take different forms. In one case, for example, all children were involved in the same art activity, but different outcomes were expected for a child with moderate learning difficulties. Another class was working on activities related to the theme of weather with differentiation according to task; a child with moderate learning difficulties was tracing a map while the rest of the class was examining satellite pictures. Functional integration was said to be occurring either through shared activities or, in the second example, because the two diverse activities were linked by a common theme. Official documents appear to recognise examples of this kind as appropriate means of differentiation (SCCC, 1993; SOED, 1993) within mainstream classes in general.

While it seems clear that the nature of the children's difficulties played an important part in determining what the teachers saw as appropriate provision and the type of integration which was likely to be experienced, it would be unhelpful to assert that pupils were seen as belonging to homogeneous groups characterised by particular difficulties. In general, teachers acknowledged Warnock's notion of a continuum and based decisions about integration on their view of the needs of individual pupils.

COLLABORATIVE TEACHING APPROACHES

A second factor affecting the nature of integration was the level of collaboration between mainstream and learning support staff. In general, curricular integration was highly dependent on the quality of the working relationship between the mainstream and learning support teacher. In the Northern Ireland case study, where provision was made for hearing impaired pupils, integration appeared to be assisted by the explicitly structured collaboration among staff. The specialist teacher of the hearing impaired had provided guidelines to mainstream staff on such matters as the positioning of teachers and pupils in relation to light sources and strategies for pitching voices effectively. The guidelines enabled all teachers to help the pupils in gaining access to the curriculum by circumventing the sensory difficulties, or by trying to limit the extent to which they impeded the learning process. Providing guidance for pupils with difficulties of this kind is likely to be more straightforward than for pupils with moderate learning difficulties. Greater agreement among teachers might be expected on the goals and the most appropriate integration for sensory impaired children than on those for children with other kinds of difficulties. Moderate learning difficulties may well call for more radical changes to the curriculum and teaching approaches, and the variety of problems among such children may indicate substantial tailoring of the provision for individual needs.

Collaboration between mainstream and learning support teachers was an important way of improving opportunities for the integration of children with special educational needs. Co-operative teaching arrangements existed in each of the mainstream schools in the case studies, although practice varied across and within schools. The most common situation was one in which the mainstream teacher taught the lesson as usual, while the learning support teacher helped a few pupils with special educational needs (with or without a statement or a record of need). The learning support teacher often provided learning materials for individual pupils. On some occasions the learning support teacher taught part of the lesson or assisted any child experiencing difficulties. The latter occurred where all pupils were working on individual programmes of work, such as in mathematics, or where the relationship between the mainstream and the learning support teacher allowed this.

Pressures on staff time restricted the opportunities to plan and discuss the curriculum together, but learning support teachers indicated that a more serious difficulty was the low priority frequently given to consultation time by the senior management of schools. Ultimately, learning support teachers sought to encourage mainstream teachers to alter their teaching approaches to take account of the needs of all pupils, including those with special educational needs. This was the most complex role of learning support teachers, requiring them to share with mainstream teachers in the planning and teaching of lessons. However, consultation occurred more often as a result of opportunism by learning support staff, than as part of a school strategy. This made it difficult to influence mainstream teachers constructively or to encourage change. In addition, learning support teachers were expected to provide support to the pupils with special educational needs, either in or out of the mainstream classroom and to prepare learning materials. They were also exhorted to provide staff development for, and act as consultants to, their mainstream colleagues.

In each of the case studies, the contribution made by the special needs auxiliaries (or non-teaching assistants) to the integration of pupils was considerable. They usually had the most frequent and regular contact with individual pupils during lessons and could respond to difficulties as they arose. This could mean ensuring that a pupil understood the task that had been set by the mainstream teacher or assisting with the recording of answers. In some ways the special needs auxiliaries could limit opportunities for integration, particularly in social terms, by being seen to be attached constantly to one child, even during break times. They said that they were aware of this possibility and tried to minimise their intervention where possible, particularly where they could see that a pupil with special educational needs was interacting with his or her peers. Overall, the contribution of the special needs auxiliaries was valued greatly by their colleagues, who expressed concern that their 'worth' was not reflected in their pay and conditions, nor in staff development opportunities.

PRIMARY/SECONDARY DIFFERENCES: THE SCOTTISH CASE STUDY

In the Scottish case study, which focused on eight pupils in a primary and its associated secondary school, there were differences in how curricular integration was approached in each school. All the eight pupils experienced moderate learning difficulties, four also had physical difficulties and all had a record of needs. There were clear differences between the staff of each school over the matter of how to integrate pupils with special educational needs. In the primary school, four of the five children were placed in the school's learning centre (a special needs base), but went into mainstream classes for part of the time. In the secondary school, where a policy of full integration operated, the three pupils with records of needs spent virtually all of their time in mainstream classes, even though the school had a learning centre. Only one of the secondary pupils was withdrawn to the centre for physiotherapy and language work; this accounted for about 10 per cent of the week.

The amount of time the pupils spent in mainstream classes varied from 30 per cent, experienced by two pupils aged 10 in the primary school, to the 100 per cent of two aged 12 in the secondary school. At one level, the differences might be explained as staff in the primary school adopting an approach aimed at the early resolution of some of the pupils' difficulties through small group tuition within the learning centre, while the secondary school teachers saw it as more appropriate for pupils to be exposed to a full range of educational experiences. Although the secondary pupils' difficulties would limit what they could achieve, a continued emphasis on the basics could be counter-productive; not only would it challenge pupils' entitlement to a broad curriculum it could also damage their motivation. It appeared, however, that there were differences that extended beyond this.

Staff in the primary school said they were concerned that unsuccessful experiences in the mainstream could damage a pupil's confidence and interfere with their progress. To minimise this risk, they built up the amount of integration of individual pupils gradually. They did this only in areas of the curriculum where success looked likely and where the level of support, from teaching or non-teaching specialist staff was adequate. They also argued that individual or small group tuition within the learning centre provided opportunities to address particular difficulties and to try to develop some of the basic skills in language and number.

In the secondary school, the widespread view among staff was that the pupils with special educational needs ought to be exposed to as many facets of the mainstream curriculum as possible, even if the actual learning that took place was minimal. They argued that the range of experiences available within a secondary school curriculum would contribute to the social and emotional development of the pupils. Benefits would also be derived from the numerous opportunities for social integration, for example in group activities. As far as pupils' individual needs were concerned, staff envisaged that there was little prospect of improvement in the basic skills by the time pupils had reached secondary school. Attention needed to be turned therefore, to helping them to find other ways to cope with their difficulties, in order to participate in various activities within a mainstream setting.

Difficulties were anticipated when pupils transferred from the primary to the secondary school. Primary staff were concerned that the pupils might not be able to cope with a full secondary mainstream timetable. Teachers in the secondary school, on the other hand, felt that the pupils' experience in primary school may not have prepared them adequately for secondary. Some criticism of the approach in each school was inferred from the teachers' comments. On the one hand, the primary was considered over-protective of its pupils with special educational needs and to display low expectations of their achievement. On the other hand, it was implied that the secondary placed excessive demands on the pupils, arising from expectations that were too high. Despite these differences in perceptions and inferred criticisms, there was no overt conflict between the staff of each school. There was, however, some compromise from the primary school staff where, for instance, the amount of time spent in mainstream by a pupil in the final year of primary school was increased before transfer to secondary. Beyond this, staff tried to ensure that the transfer of pupils was smooth and thought that any attempts to address their different understandings of integration might have a detrimental effect on this process.

The findings from the Scottish case study, with the focus on a primary and associated secondary school, had some similarities with those from the case study of a cluster arrangement in England, involving one core special school, seven mainstream cluster schools and a support service. Different perceptions of integration between primary and secondary staff also emerged in this case study: unlike the Scottish case study, however, the greatest concerns were voiced among primary staff. These emerged at the point of transfer when the differences came more sharply into focus and primary teachers were worried about children being overwhelmed by the sheer 'busyness' of secondary school life.

WAS INTEGRATION SUCCESSFUL?

It is unsatisfactory to judge the success of integration purely in terms of the amount of time the pupils spent in mainstream classes, as it provides little indication of what they have learnt. It may also discourage a consideration of the quality of the pupils' learning. It is not easy, of course, to identify the criteria on which judgements about successful integration are based, but Warnock's three levels of integration can be used in a crude way to assess the extent to which pupils were engaged in the social and academic life of the class.

The pupils in the case studies who were taught in mainstream schools could be described as locationally integrated since they were educated on the same site as the rest of their age group. Pupils in the special schools also experienced some measure of locational integration, through their formal links with mainstream schools. 'Success' was measured by the physical presence of SEN pupils within mainstream schools, either on a full- or part-time basis.

All pupils had opportunities for social integration; at the very least, this could happen at intervals or morning assemblies. However, Hegarty (1982) cautions that one must not assume that 'sheer physical proximity automatically leads to meaningful encounters' (p. 180). He suggests that teachers should manage social integration indirectly by, for instance removing obstacles that might hinder interaction, and directly through schemes such as peer tutoring which is in use throughout the United States. The only (somewhat negative) evidence from the case studies of indirect efforts by senior management and staff to encourage social integration was that they tried not to interfere with the relationships of the pupils. There appeared to be no direct attempts to manage social integration, even though evidence from the case studies suggested that this might be warranted. In the Scottish case study, for example, the children with special educational needs appeared to interact easily with their peers in the playground and in lessons. The mainstream pupils, however, seemed to relate to pupils with special educational needs in ways that differed from their usual interaction. For instance, during ball games, both in physical education and in the playground, pupils with special needs were cheered when they managed to gain possession of the ball. On other occasions, exuberance or misbehaviour on their part was tolerated in a way that it was not from other children. There is a risk that mainstream pupils could be patronising if they do not have opportunities to explore, in a focused way, their feelings about interacting with pupils with special educational needs. There could well be a place for the type of direct management of integration, described by Hegarty (1982).

As far as the staff in each of the case study schools was concerned, integration on locational and social terms was occurring successfully. Social integration was viewed as one of the most important outcomes of mainstream provision, particularly where opportunities for curricular integration were limited by the difficulties of the pupils. Both mainstream pupils and those with special educational needs were reported as benefiting from being taught together and from the opportunities to mix together socially. The parents of pupils with special educational needs also saw social integration as working well and of enormous importance to their children's emotional development and confidence.

When it came to functional or curricular integration, the question of whether success had been achieved was less clear. Hegarty (1982) argues that the main difficulty in achieving curricular integration is finding the balance between two opposing principles: on the one hand, giving the pupils the same or similar access to the curriculum as their peers and, on the other hand, providing appropriate help to meet their special educational needs. The greater or more complex the difficulties, the more onerous this task becomes and as the gap between the achievements of the pupils with special educational needs and mainstream pupils widens, claims of functional integration become more difficult to sustain.

Evidence from the case studies carried out in England and Wales suggested that the national curriculum imposed enormous pressures on teachers, particularly because of the pace of progression through the attainment targets. Attempts to involve pupils with significant special educational needs exacerbated these problems and teachers reported that the outcomes for the pupils were often unsatisfactory. The report of HM Inspectorate (DES, 1991) on the national curriculum and special needs in England and Wales, stated that the most effective lessons observed were those which had been influenced by attainment targets. Staff in the case studies, however, said that these targets militated against small steps of progression and so opportunities for reinforcement to promote success for those with special needs became difficult. They also commented that certain attainment targets were too narrow and inflexible to enable pupils with special educational needs to be accommodated readily. There was the danger that because teachers had to struggle to find novel ways of including these pupils in mainstream activities, their overall programme could become piecemeal. However, the benefits to the pupils of social integration were said by staff to outweigh any criticisms of the quality of their curricular integration.

The experiences of pupils, either in a mainstream or a special school, who were participating in the national curriculum at a stage well below their peers, were described by staff as successful, even where there were no expectations of children attaining age-related national standards. Indeed, without these pressures, teachers were able to introduce additional, smaller steps for progression and welcomed, particularly in special schools, the opportunities that the national curriculum had brought for pupils with special educational needs to attain nationally recognised standards, even if they were unlikely to progress beyond level 1. There may be a point, of course, at which the learning goals become so modified that they bear little relation to those being followed by the majority of children of a particular age group, and claims of functional or curricular integration have to be called into question.

In the Scottish case study, a number of mainstream teachers, from both the primary and secondary school, expressed their anxiety at the low achievement of particular pupils with special educational needs within their classes. They acknowledged the advantages to them of integration, particularly in social terms, but the extent of the pupils' difficulties made the achievement of mainstream goals unrealistic. Senior management and learning support staff said they had accepted that some of the pupils with special educational needs would be unlikely to achieve goals that were similar, or even close, to those attained by mainstream pupils. They regarded social integration as an acceptable substitute for curricular integration for some pupils, but did not seem to have communicated this clearly to mainstream staff.

It may be that for some pupils, social integration is seen as the most appropriate goal. Although it would be necessary for teachers to have opportunities to reach agreement on this and to plan the means of achieving the goals, the management and planning demands would be less than for functional integration. To achieve the latter for pupils with special educational needs, discussion of strategies at whole school level would be required to ensure that all teachers were equipped to make provision of this kind.

INTEGRATION: A USEFUL CONCEPT?

Calls for a much clearer debate on the nature of integration have been made by Hegarty, Pocklington and Lucas (1981), who argue that 'integration is not a self-evident goal and must be justified in a rational way' (p. 14). In a subsequent paper, Hegarty (1993) has gone further and argued that we should think in different ways and put the focus on 'participation' rather than integration. This, he suggests, would focus on what the pupil does rather than where the learning takes place. An approach of this kind would make a clear statement about the desirability of common goals and the onus would then be on teachers to justify the exclusion of any pupil from any aspect of school experience. Special education provision would then emerge as a system which ensures that children's rights are protected, rather than one which invites (rather tentatively) children with special educational needs 'to join the party' and become integrated.

Barton and Tomlinson (1984) question the uncritical acceptance of the idea that integration is automatically desirable, on the grounds that, like other forms of special education, it serves interests that are 'economic, professional and political', rather than simply arising from 'benevolent and enlightened attitudes to children' (p. 65). Recently, other serious concerns have also been expressed that integration may not be in the best interests of some pupils with special educational needs in the present economic and political climate in which local management schemes operate (Willey, 1989). Lee (1992) argues that pupils with special educational needs are left vulnerable because of the extra costs their needs impose on schools trying to compete with each other, and decisions will have to be taken as to 'whether those pupils will not be better provided for in the guaranteed special school environment of specially trained staff, low teacher to pupil numbers and enhanced funding' (p. 295). Integration is evidently being questioned, therefore, from a number of viewpoints and it is essential to develop a clearer understanding of what it involves and how it is to be judged.

As described earlier, the research reported here revealed two important factors which affected the kind of integration experienced by children with special educational needs: certain kinds of difficulties were perceived as less of a barrier to successful integration than others, and successful integration depended on effective collaboration of learning support with mainstream staff and their willingness to adapt. This required support from the senior management of the school, by ensuring that consultation time was protected for the planning of learning support. More commonly, however, learning support teachers had to seize opportunities to consult as they arose. The findings from the Scottish study also revealed how integration had been interpreted differently by staff in an associated primary and secondary school. Rather than seeking to resolve these differences through discussion, staff put their energies instead into minimising the effects upon the pupils at the stage of transfer. It was interesting that the question of whether integration is a worthy goal for children with special educational needs was not raised explicitly by the teachers in the case study. The findings, however, did raise questions about the value of integration as a construct. They drew attention to three particular problems associated with current understanding of integration, particularly the functional strand of Warnock's construct:

1 *Lack of clear definitions of integration.* Precise definitions of functional integration, which specify the matching of mainstream and special outcomes and targets, appear congruous with the language of access to the national curriculum for children with special educational needs. However, they fail to take account of those children who are likely to spend most of school careers on or below level 1 of the national curriculum or level A of the 5–14 programme in Scotland.

2 *Disagreement over what counts as functional integration.* We have to ask whether the children with special educational needs in the case study were integrated functionally when they were: (a) engaged in the same activities as mainstream pupils, but with different outcomes expected; (b) engaged in the same theme but in different activities, with different outcomes expected.

   Official documents seem to confirm these as legitimate forms of differentiation and many of the teachers in the case study clearly thought functional integration was being achieved. However, there must be a point at which the achievements of pupils with special educational needs differ so radically from mainstream pupils that functional integration cannot be realistically claimed.

3 *Hierarchy of locational, social and functional integration.* Warnock suggested that the three constructs represented overlapping, but 'progressive stages of association'. Functional integration has come to be seen officially as the most desirable form of

integration, with social and locational integration, by implication, accorded lesser value as steps along the way. Social integration may be the most realistic goal for some children, and may be viewed by professionals and parents as the most important. However, as long as the three strands of integration remain within a hierarchical framework, the achievements of such children will be undermined.

Integration is a concept with many facets. The interpretation which an individual puts on the term will depend on his or her values and especially the educational or other responsibilities which he or she carries. Some, therefore, will be preoccupied with where learning takes place, others with the processes which lead to pupils' curricular entitlement and others with day-to-day priorities to avoid stigma and facilitate an acceptable social and academic life for pupils with special educational needs. It is unsurprising, therefore, that case studies of schools in the United Kingdom throw up differences in the ways in which practitioners construe integration, even within similar contexts of legislation on special needs.

REFERENCES

Allan, J., Brown, S. and Munn, P. (1991) *Off the Record: Mainstream Provision for Pupils with Non-recorded Learning Difficulties in Primary and Secondary Schools.* Edinburgh: SCRE Project Report.
Barton, L. and Tomlinson, S. (1984) *Special Education and Social Interests.* Beckenham: Croom Helm.
Department of Education and Science (DES) (1978) Special Educational Needs (The Warnock Report). London: HMSO..
Department of Education and Science (DES) (1991) *National Curriculum and Special Needs.* London: HMSO.
Hegarty, S. (1982) 'Meeting special educational needs in ordinary schools', *Educational Research* 24: 3.
Hegarty, S. (1991) 'Toward an agenda for research in special education', *European Journal of Special Needs Education* 6: 2.
Hegarty, S. (1993) *Meeting Special Needs in Ordinary Schools.* Windsor: NFER-Nelson.
Hegarty, S., Pocklington, K. and Lucas, D. (1981) *Educating Pupils with Special Educational Needs in Ordinary Schools.* Windsor: NFER-Nelson.
Lee, T. (1992) 'Local management of schools and special education', in Booth, T. and Swann, W. (eds) *Policies for Diversity in Education.* London: Routledge.
National Curriculum Council (NCC) (1989) *Implementing the National*

Curriculum – Participation by Pupils with Special Educational Needs, Circular number 5. York: NCC.

NFER (1992) *OECD/CERI Project: Integration in the School. Reports of the Case Studies Undertaken in the UK.* Windsor: NFER.

Pijl, S. and Meijer, C. (1991) 'Does integration count for much? An analysis of the practices of integration in eight countries', *European Journal of Special Needs Education* 6: 2.

Scottish Consultative Council on the Curriculum (SCCC) (1993) *Support for Learning. Special Educational Needs within the 5–14 Curriculum.* Dundee: SCCC.

Scottish Office Education Department (SOED) (1991) *Curriculum and Assessment in Scotland. National Guidelines: English Language 5–14.* Edinburgh: HMSO.

Scottish Office Education Department (SOED) (1993) *The Education of Able Pupils P6-S2: A Report by HM Inspectors of Schools.* Edinburgh: HMSO.

Willey, M. (1989) 'LMS: a rising sense of alarm', *British Journal of Special Education* 16, 4.

Chapter 9

Special educational needs and problem behaviour

Making policy in the classroom

Derrick Armstrong and David Galloway

INTRODUCTION

Neither the Warnock Report (DES, 1978) nor the 1981 Education Act for England and Wales resulted in reduction in provision outside mainstream schools for children presenting behavioural problems (Swann 1985, 1992; Tomlinson 1985). These children illustrate the threat to a fundamental principle of the Warnock Report, namely that special needs should be defined in educational terms, rather than in terms of some deficit or handicapping condition from which the child suffers. They also illustrate tensions arising from the 1988 Education Reform Act. Local (financial) management of schools creates an obvious link between resources and pupil numbers, leading to demands for additional resources in respect of those pupils with special needs. Rational testing programmes and league tables of school results create anxiety about the impact of pupils with learning and/or behaviour problems on the school's public image, and hence on its future pupil numbers. However much they may be concerned about difficult children as individuals, headteachers have to consider the wider interests of the school. Already there are indications of an increase in the number of children excluded from school because of their behaviour (Pyke, 1992) with some groups, notably Afro-Caribbean children, being disproportionately represented (*TES*, 1992). Similarly, the number of children being removed from their mainstream schools and placed in special education on account of behavioural problems has also increased significantly over the last decade (Swann, 1992).

The Warnock Report identified the origins of special educational needs in the relationship between the child and his/her environment, which includes the school as well as home background, rather than in deficits in the child's personality. In doing so the report emphasised the responsibility teachers were expected to take for all children, including those with special educational needs. Thus, teacher professionalism was defined by Warnock in terms of skills in the management of learning for all children. More recent pressure on schools to adopt pupil selection and financial policies that maximise their competitiveness in the market place have led to tensions in the model of teacher professionalism contained in the Warnock Report. One consequence of this may be a deskilling of mainstream classroom teachers as responsibility for 'problem' children is increasingly shifted into the hands of outside 'experts', including educational psychologists and the staff of specialist schools. The deskilling of mainstream teachers in this respect can be seen as one aspect of a wider teacher deprofessionalisation as structural changes in the organisation and control of education increasingly bring challenges to the professional autonomy of teachers from those outside the profession. For example, the introduction of a national curriculum to be followed in all state schools has largely removed from teachers the control they once had over what is to be taught in schools, as well as when it is to be taught and how much. Similarly, the attempt to introduce procedures for nationally assessing the learning of all children at 'key stages' of their schooling, together with the publication of each school's results, has forced teachers to be accountable for the delivery of a curriculum over which they may perceive themselves to have little control.

In this chapter we draw on our recent research on the assessment of children identified as having emotional and behavioural difficulties to consider how recent educational reforms may affect teachers' decision-making about children identified as having special educational needs in mainstream schools. We argue that these reforms have encouraged teachers to re-define their responsibilities towards their pupils as the notion of professional competence has moved away from being defined in terms of managing and retaining disruptive pupils in mainstream classes and towards successfully negotiating their removal by formal assessment procedures. The identification of pupils whose needs cannot be met in their mainstream schools, because of their psychological disturbance rather than because of their disruptive behaviour, is prevalent and important in that it locates the problem with the child, not with the teaching. The removal of these pupils is legitimised by a growing sense that what is seen as the principal and most highly skilled work of mainstream teachers is educating more able pupils. In referring children for formal assessment, mainstream teachers may be engaged in a complex set of negotiations with other professionals in which identification of the child's pathological identity actually focuses on teachers' recognition of new work priorities and attempts to re-define their professional role as 'skilful' in the context of changes in government policy and legislation over a little more than a decade.

DISRUPTION IN SCHOOLS. AN INCREASING PHENOMENON?

Concern about the standard of children's behaviour is not new, despite the claims of those who see it as symptomatic of the declining moral standards of the late twentieth century (Humphries, 1981). Hurt (1988) has documented how, prior to the introduction of compulsory education, the Poor Law was used to transport troublesome children to the colonies. In addition the workhouse and the 'ragged' schools were used to control children whose behaviour was a 'danger to society'.

In recent years, concern over disruptive behaviour in schools has attracted renewed interest, culminating in a government-sponsored enquiry, the Elton Report (DES, 1989) into *Discipline in Schools*. Although this enquiry identified some issues as causes for concern, its overall finding was that there had been no significant increase in serious incidents of disruption in schools. Evidence from research commissioned by the Committee and undertaken in 220 primary and 250 secondary schools indicated that teachers were more disturbed by persistent minor acts of misbehaviour than by the occasional dramatic confrontation. This finding confirmed that of other recent studies (Houghton *et al.*, 1988; Wheldall and Merrett, 1988). However, it contrasted sharply with widely publicised research undertaken over the last two decades on behalf of professional bodies. Lowenstein's (1975) survey was based on a very low response rate from members of the National Association of Schoolmasters (15 per cent from secondary teachers and 5 per cent from primary) but found little evidence of teachers facing daily incidents of severely aggressive behaviour from their pupils, despite a widespread perception amongst the respondents that these incidents were commonplace in schools other than their own.

More recently, reports of research by the National Union of Teachers and the Secondary Heads Association (Pyke,1992) have suggested big increases in the number of pupils excluded from school because of their behaviour. Some caution needs to be exercised in interpreting these findings, however. First, the evidence regarding exclusions from school has not been collected systematically and there are wide variations in the type of exclusion orders made by schools and in their reporting of these to their LEAs and the DFE. Second, even where there is evidence of an increase in exclusions it is by no means clear that this reflects any increase in disruptive behaviour within schools. It may simply reflect a lower tolerance on the part of teachers of behaviour that is seen as damaging to the interests of their school. Turkington (1986), in an insightful discussion of the 'disruptive pupil', has argued that the notion of disruptiveness owes its origins more to a highly successful media campaign by the teacher unions in support of their claim for rewards to match their professional responsibilities than to any observable changes in pupil behaviour in school. He somewhat wryly observed that 'it is important to make a distinction between the apparent validity of survey findings and their publicity and political value' (Turkington, 1986: 65).

In this way it is important that there does appear to be widespread concern that the need to publish test scores will force schools to favour academically able pupils. If difficult pupils are seen as interfering with the academic progress of other children, parents of academically able children may be discouraged from enrolling them in schools which accommodate themselves to the needs of difficult children.

'DISRUPTIVE' OR 'DISTURBED' – WHAT DIFFERENCE DOES IT MAKE?

Foucault (1967), in his study of the history of insanity, argued that madness was once accepted as a part of normal society because it was believed that those who were afflicted expressed visionary insights into the experience of everyday life. It came to be seen as a disease at precisely that moment when it threatened emerging conceptions of rationality. Rationality was to provide the ideological justification for a new social order whilst opposition to that order was marginalised as an 'absurdity'. According to Foucault, the concept of insanity was primarily given meaning by the different social and political functions it served in different historical periods.

Although it is improbable that teachers ever saw 'disturbed' children as visionaries, there is, nonetheless, an analogy that can be drawn between the development of the modern concept of madness and the distinction that teachers draw between disturbed and disruptive behaviour in children. Galloway *et al.* (1982), in their study of schools and disruptive pupils, pointed out that although the concept of maladjustment was frequently invoked to remove disruptive pupils from ordinary lessons, it was unclear what behaviours this concept actually referred to. Whilst it was not a category recognised by the most widely used classification systems in child psychiatry, it did provide a label under which special education could be provided when a school was no longer able or willing to tolerate a child's behaviour. In labelling behaviour as disturbed rather than disruptive an implicit claim is made about the irrationality of that behaviour and therefore that a child suffering from an emotional disturbance needs specialist treatment that cannot be provided by a mainstream school. The supposed irrationality of the behaviour legitimises the removal of the child into special education but it also legitimises the school's failure to effect changes in the child's behaviour. This was a theme that consistently emerged in our own recent research on the identification of emotional and behavioural difficulties.

RESEARCH ON THE IDENTIFICATION OF EMOTIONAL AND BEHAVIOURAL DIFFICULTIES

In research we carried out between 1989 and 1991 in three local education authorities, we studied in detail the assessment of twenty-nine children referred to the schools' psychological service, usually by their teachers, because of emotional and behavioural difficulties. The children in the study were all of school age, ranging from 5 to 16, and were broadly representative in terms of social background and presenting problem of children attending schools specialising in the education of children with emotional and behavioural difficulties.

With the co-operation of clients and professionals, one of us (DA) observed the main parts of each child's assessment, including educational psychologists' interviews with parents, children and teachers. We also sat in on the clinical medical officers' assessments. Afterwards we talked to each of the participants separately to elicit their perceptions of the purpose of the interview and of what, and how, particular outcomes had been reached.

Our observations of meetings between teachers and psychologists, and an examination of the reports on children prepared by teachers contributing to formal assessments of special educational needs, suggest that teachers' needs, and their expectations of an assessment, are often explicitly recognised. This is illustrated by the comments of one headteacher made during a discussion with her school's educational psychologist:

> What is important is that the teachers get some support for Bryan in the classroom. We should have had the extra support before now. . . . We can't be expected to teach him without extra help . . . something will have to be done. The child has suffered and the teachers have suffered.

The expectation behind many referrals is illustrated in another school's report to the LEA

> Difficulties at high school include; threats to others, confrontation with staff, general class disruption and finally an incident with a girl that finally led to his exclusion. . . . His home circumstances are unsuitable as they do not give the right type of support necessary for him to achieve a stable emotional state. I feel a new environment in terms of school and home would be of benefit.

However, the ways in which these expectations may affect the contributions teachers make to the assessment have been relatively unexplored. The educational report that a school provides for the LEA constitutes the formal part of its contribution to the assessment, whilst an informal part is frequently found in teachers' negotiations with educational psychologists and their LEAs regarding the nature of the 'problem' and how it should be dealt with. Once a decision to request an assessment had been made by teachers two themes could be identified as consistently arising from both the formal reports and informal negotiations making up teachers' contribution to the assessment.

First, when teachers identified children as having emotional and behavioural difficulties they believed the behaviour of these children to be qualitatively different from the behaviour of 'ordinary' children. One teacher in our study was typical of many when, in requesting an assessment, she observed

> I've got a very bad class this year. A lot of difficult boys. But Damien isn't like them. With them it's because they get no discipline. With Damien that's not it. He's just strange.

Despite the conceptual weaknesses we have alluded to and the lack of empirical foundation to a distinction between 'disturbed' and 'disruptive' behaviour, teachers of sixteen of the twenty-nine children in our study explicitly identified behaviour as 'disturbed'. A common characteristic of the accounts given by teachers in these cases was a reference to causal factors for the child's behaviour over which they, as teachers, had no control: 'He's crackers, absolutely crackers. He talks to himself and answers himself. He walks around school making weird physical gestures. Psychologically the kid is disturbed. He needs help.'

The notion of the child's culpability, or lack of culpability, for behaviour is important because, where it could be shown that a child did not exercise rational control over his or her behaviour, teachers made the assumption that they could not be held responsible for that child's behaviour in the classroom. In other words, when teachers requested an assessment of a child who they claimed had emotional and behavioural difficulties, implicit in this request was a parallel claim that the child's unacceptable behaviour was not influenced by practices within the classroom or school.

Interestingly, a similar view is expressed in the Elton Report on *Discipline in Schools* (DES, 1989). Because the report was principally concerned with 'disruptive' pupils, it was necessary to distinguish these children from those with 'emotional and behavioural difficulties'. The latter were said by the Elton Committee to be in evidence when children show 'severe and persistent behavioural problems as a result of emotional, psychological and neurological disturbance [such] that their needs cannot be met in mainstream schools' (para 6:29).

In part this definition is clearly tautological. It is claimed that an emotional, psychological and neurological disturbance is evident where there is a severe and persistent behaviour problem. Likewise, a behaviour problem is judged to be severe and persistent when it is caused by an emotional, psychological and neurological disturbance. On the other hand, it is also revealing in just the same way as is the distinction teachers make between disruptive and disturbed behaviour, because it suggests that a criterion to be used in distinguishing disturbed from disruptive behaviour is that the needs of children belonging to the former category 'cannot be met in mainstream schools'. The Elton Committee recognised that

> it is sometimes difficult to distinguish between ordinary bad behaviour and disturbed behaviour, *but the distinction has to be made.* Judgements must be made by teachers, educational psychologists and other professionals in individual cases.
>
> (DES, 1989 para 6:30, emphasis added)

In our own study, children whose behaviour was disruptive but seen by teachers as manageable with the resources ordinarily available to the schools were acknowledged by their teachers as falling within their proper professional concern. Where it was felt that children's behaviour demanded the allocation of resources and facilities not normally available within mainstream schools, they were then likely to be identified as having 'emotional problems'. Thus, the second theme to emerge in our study from teachers' contributions to the assessment was that the distinction they drew between qualitatively different types of behaviour had its origins in the resources perceived to be available to their schools. This point may be illustrated by the comments of a primary class teacher who had once worked in a residential school but whose experiences there had led her to become a 'committed integrationalist'

> I was quite concerned by the difficulties presented by Tony. In attempting to teach him I would have maintained that classroom behaviour problems ultimately revolved round questions of classroom management. As teachers we are concerned with what we can affect and that is the child's learning and behaviour in the classroom. Behaviour management comes down to teacher skill. However, Tony

undermined my self-confidence as a teacher because I had not succeeded in making changes in his class behaviour. I felt emotionally drained after a session with Tony and I felt my failure to cope effectively with Tony was undermining the ethos of my classroom.

Eventually, in her report to the LEA, this teacher wrote

We have recently been allocated a classroom assistant for 9 hours a week to meet the complex needs of Tony. I strongly feel that Tony's needs will not be met in this way. Tony's disturbed behaviour patterns require full time attention. . . . I have 27 other children in my class.

These different skills were not seen as being higher-order skills. Indeed it was common for teachers, when interviewed by a researcher, to claim that if they had the opportunity to teach on a one-to-one basis they could easily cope with an emotionally disturbed child. Whilst they often added that emotionally disturbed children needed specialist counselling, this was seen as separate from their educational needs; as teachers they would be able to cope if they were not responsible for twenty-five or thirty other children.

This focus upon resources for children with learning difficulties reflects the horns of a dilemma recognised by the authors of the Warnock Report (DES, 1978):

On the one hand we are aware that any kind of special resource or service for such children runs the risk of emphasising the idea of their separateness . . . on the other hand unless an obligation is placed on local education authorities to provide for the special needs of such children there is a danger that their requirement for specialist resources will be inadequately met.

(DES, 1978: 45)

It has been argued that by defining children's needs in terms of resources those needs are individualised, inhibiting consideration of the context in which they occur, a context which includes the expectations and needs of those who request and carry out the assessment (Galloway and Goodwin, 1987). For instance headteachers in our study were particularly concerned about the negative effects on staff morale and on other children in their schools brought about by the presence of children whose behaviour was disturbed.

In consequence of there being no formal acknowledgement of the needs of other participants in the assessment process, once the procedures are invoked teachers may feel that their own needs can only be expressed in terms of the child's needs. Yet this may create a discourse which assumes a focus on the child whilst inhibiting any meaningful discussion of circumstances within the school which might affect a child's behaviour. In this way the 1981 procedures for identifying and assessing children with special educational needs may themselves contribute to a deskilling of teachers by discouraging reflexivity on practice (Armstrong et al., 1993).

EDUCATION POLICY AND TEACHER PROFESSIONALISM IN THE 1980s AND 1990s

The 1980s was a decade of major educational reform, many of the implications of which have yet to work their way through the system. Indeed, those who may have hoped for a time of peaceful consolidation have already been disappointed as the 1990s have ushered in new proposals for educational legislation along with continuing change in the arrangements for implementing the detail of existing legislation. The agenda for reform in education has shifted away from the control of the liberal and radical left and is now firmly located in the hands of the radical right. These reforms struck at the heart of the professional autonomy of teachers yet resistance to them, until the recent revolt against national curriculum testing, had been muted. It is not insignificant that the 1988 Education Reform Act followed in the wake of a widespread demoralisation within the profession that resulted from the failure of industrial action over pay and conditions.

Conservative education policy has taken the national curriculum and the devolution of resources to schools as the planks from which it has launched its bid to centralise education under the political control of government. The introduction of a national curriculum to be followed in all state-funded schools has removed the control teachers once had over what (and how much) is taught in schools. The procedures for assessing children's learning at different 'key stages' of the curriculum, together with the publication of each school's results, has made teachers accountable for the delivery of a curriculum over which they have little control. This, of course, has always been the position in virtually every other country in the world.

The devolution of resources from LEAs to schools, although giving teachers greater control over certain aspects of financial planning within their own schools, has also had the consequence of centralising power over policy-making in the hands of the DFE and the Treasury. When the ethos of teacher professionalism in LEAs was as influential as the political ideologies of elected members, teachers had direct access to policy-making mechanisms. With the downgrading of LEA control, both political and bureaucratic control over professional services in education has increasingly been exercised by central government. Without influential LEAs, teachers may find themselves in a policy-making vacuum in which individual schools lack 'clout' to do anything more than respond to government directives. The centralisation of control over education has also created external pressures on schools and teachers to adopt pupil selection and financial policies that maximise their competitiveness in the market place. It has been argued by government that by making the delivery of professional services subject to the discipline of the market place the consumer is likely to get value for money. Bluntly, if professionals don't deliver the 'goods' for which they are paid then parents, as consumers, will not want to buy. Yet research on parental choice in education suggests that it is the middle and professional classes who are most likely to be in a position to exercise genuine choice over the schooling of their children (Adler et al., 1989; Echols et al., 1990; Stillman and Maychell, 1986). Paquette (1991: 74) puts it as follows:

> The conservative doctrine of freedom of choice becomes, in education, the freedom of parents who can afford to choose among schools, but never the freedom of all parents and students to choose any learning they wish.

The concept of a 'market' in educational services may create some limited choices for those who have the power to make choices, at the expense of those who lack that power. Maintaining and improving pupil numbers will in large part be dependent upon a school's appeal to this small but influential section of the population. Schools which are unattractive to the parents of these children are in the future increasingly unlikely to benefit from the changes in school funding that are being introduced. In these circumstances, teachers may find themselves under pressure to divert resources away from children with special educational needs (unless those resources are protected by a statement) towards those whose success is likely to enhance the academic reputation of the school. Moreover, the very presence of large numbers of children with special needs, particularly where those needs arise from learning and/or behaviour difficulties, may be seen as harmful to a school's performance on national curriculum tests when compared with other schools in the locality, with the consequence that the continuation of mainstream schooling for these children is threatened.

THE NEGOTIATION OF TEACHERS' ROLES

It is important, however, to bear in mind that teachers do not necessarily form a group whose perception of professional interests is entirely homogeneous, even within the same school. Negotiations between teachers over the decision to refer a child for assessment may reflect differing professional interests as well as differing perceptions of a child's needs. This was evident in negotiations taking place between teachers in one high school visited during our research. Here, teachers with different areas of responsibility within the school revealed themselves to be conscious of different areas of concern. Simon's form tutor wanted 'some intervention-type strategy' from the psychologist: 'It was very important to get an official, an alternative view. We certainly found the psychologist useful in the past and we wanted to get her perspective.'

Bernard, head of special needs, was mindful of differences within the school's staff over what should be done about Simon. He was also conscious that if children with special needs were to be helped in the school, it was necessary for him to retain the confidence of other members of staff. Thus he could not hold out for a child where the majority of staff felt it to be a hopeless case:

> There are differences between members of staff about what should be done. On the one side there are those who want to get rid of Simon, and on the other those who feel the school is in need of expert advice on his handling. I felt the referral

might be the first step towards getting him put away, but he was referred as a last resort. This was not the option I preferred but I felt that the balance of opinion on the staff favoured this option. It's a question of whether you see it as a child-deficit model or a systems model. On balance there were more members of staff who saw it in terms of a child-deficit model.

Simon's head of year, although not expressing any strong views about Simon's needs, nonetheless was very conscious of the implications of not initiating the statementing procedures:

> To be honest I don't know what Simon's needs are but if we are going to request statementing to be commenced it is important to initiate the process before the end of a child's third year. After that nobody really wants to know. Other children become priorities for resources.

Negotiations over referral decisions may, as in this case, focus upon broader, political considerations relating to the allocation of resources within an authority, rather than solely upon how individuals perceive their own roles and skills as teachers. Therefore the decision to refer a child for assessment does not imply an absence of skill on the part of those teachers making the referral. Indeed, the decision by an LEA to initiate an assessment may reflect the success of teacher negotiations as the latter seek to define their role in terms of their skills with more able, higher-status children.

Once a decision has been taken to refer a child for assessment, this decision will be a major factor affecting future developments. Henceforward those who are involved in the formal assessment must take account of the needs of those who are disturbed by the child's behaviour. Moreover, the decision to refer a child for assessment is usually made in anticipation of a particular outcome: either the removal of a child from the school or the acquisition of additional resources. In consequence, an assessment under the 1981 Act is seen by teachers merely as a bureaucratic mechanism for effecting that outcome. Actions taken by the school prior to and during the assessment may be intended to reinforce and explicate the expected outcome. The referral of ten children for formal assessments was made at the same time as they were permanently or indefinitely excluded from school. In a further seven cases children were given periods of temporary exclusion whilst the assessment was actually in progress. In each case it was made clear that the exclusion resulted from the headteacher's perception of the inter-relationship between the child's needs, the needs of teachers with classroom responsibilities for the child, and the needs of other children in the school. After one child in the study had been excluded his headteacher argued that

> I felt we had our quota of disturbed children. . . . It was a shame he had to go home where the problems were but there was a lot of disruption in the class and other children would be affected. The class was a different place after he had gone . . . . The fact that he has been removed from school is a plus for us, the other children and the staff. We hate excluding children but our hands are tied.

In turn, this resulted in quite specific expectations about the outcome of the assessment, often that the child would not return to the school. Educational psychologists were generally very sympathetic to the position teachers were in but recognised that:

> an exclusion shuts doors in terms of possible recommen-dations, I think the headteacher was quite aware of that but at the end of the day they do it because they've tried everything else.

NEGOTIATING CONTROL: TEACHER PERSPECTIVES ON ASSESSMENT

A strong case can be made that the 1981 Education Act is not altogether consistent with the earlier Warnock Report. By tying resources to individual 'statemented' children the 1981 Act forces teachers to conceptualise children's needs in terms of deficits rather than focusing upon and supporting effective teaching interventions. The effect of this can be to deskill mainstream teachers in their work with children with special educational needs as emphasis is placed upon identification rather than inter-vention. Certainly the Act does invest teachers with considerable professional responsibilities for the identification of those child-ren. It is usually teachers who initiate 'statementing' procedures. Moreover, they are required to contribute educational advice as part of the assessment. What teachers lack, however, is the power to make decisions about the allocation of additional resources to meet needs once they have been identified. This power lies with the local authority and involves quite different issues from those involved in the professional assessment of children's needs.

In so far as teachers provide professional advice to their LEAs, their role is similar to that of educational psychologists. The two professions fulfil complementary functions in the assessment of special needs. Ostensibly, the prime responsibility of educational psychologists under the 1981 Education Act is also one of providing their LEAs with independent expert advice on children's special educational needs. Yet, as we have argued, by linking resources to individual children the 1981 Education Act has perpetuated a conceptualisation of needs in terms of available resources. The assessment of needs, therefore, can become a matter of matching needs to resources rather than resources to needs. This has important implications for professional advisers. The formal distinction between the advisory role of professionals and the administrative role of LEA officers may become blurred as professionals respond to the 'realities' of resource availability within an authority to maximise the effectiveness of their professional intervention on behalf of clients. Thus, in practice, psychologists may often fulfil an important bureaucratic function relating to the distribution of resources within an LEA. Either directly or indirectly, depending on the procedures operating within different authorities, psychologists may become the gatekeepers to resources, or at least be seen as such by teachers.

Yet the role of the psychologist is ambiguous. Other clients, including teachers, parents and children, may have interests that are very different from those of the authority, but each may have legitimate expectations of the psychologist's intervention. Consequently, the bureaucratisation of the psychologist's professional role as gatekeeper, or perceived gatekeeper, to resources may result in psychologists becoming the focus of conflict between the competing interests of different clients as each attempts to negotiate a particular outcome of the assessment (Armstrong and Galloway, 1992a). In these negotiations some clients are clearly more powerful than others. The well-documented inequality of power between professionals and parents (Armstrong and Galloway, 1992b; Swann, 1987; Tomlinson, 1981; Wood, 1988), and between professionals and children (Armstrong et al., 1993), may be contrasted with a perception of shared power frequently held by different professionals in their negotiations with one another (Armstrong *et al.*, 1991). These latter negotiations are likely to take place on the basis that each party does have a more or less equal power to influence events. Yet teacher perceptions of the psychologist's role may operate in significant ways to set the agenda for the assessment process. This can be seen, for instance, in Robin's assessment, where his teachers' perceptions of their own needs significantly affected the outcome of the psychologist's assessment even though, in the latter's 'expert' judgement, Robin did not have special educational needs.

Although senior staff at Robin's school were confident that they had the skills and resources to meet his needs, his parents were concerned about his behaviour and persuaded them to seek a psychologist's opinion. It later emerged that Robin had been referred to the school psychological service when at primary school and on this occasion his headteacher had described Robin as 'a very disturbed child'. However, when the family moved home and Robin changed schools, the psychologist decided not to initiate a formal assessment under provisions in the 1981 Education Act because at his new school the 'disturbing' forms of behaviour previously reported had not 'resurfaced'. On this latest occasion, in the absence of any great concern on the part of the school, the psychologist once again thought it unnecessary to recommend a formal assessment of Robin's needs. He did, however, arrange, for the LEA's behavioural support service to monitor Robin's progress in school. Following this recommend-ation concern was expressed by some of Robin's teachers. This focused on three anxieties. First, there was a growing concern over the suggestion made by Robin's mother that he was 'psychiatrically disturbed'. In particular they were concerned about the history of psychological involvement and began to doubt their future ability to cope with a boy who had been identified as a 'psychological case'. Second, this anxiety led to an increasing awareness of Robin's behaviour in school. Thus one teacher commented: 'there are signs that he might flip. He's become a bit more fidgety. There are signs that he's bubbling.' Other teachers expressed concern over reports that Robin had been heard talking to himself. Third, Robin's teachers also began to doubt the adequacy of the support that would be available from the behavioural support service if Robin was indeed a 'disturbed' child. These concerns led to a request for statementing procedures to be initiated after all. It was now argued by the school that this would be appropriate even if it did no more than formally specify Robin's need for extra help from the behavioural support service.

Robin's teachers put pressure on the educational psychologist and the LEA to initiate a formal assessment of his special educational needs with a view to a formal statement of those needs being issued. In response to this request the psychologist and staff from the behavioural support service entered into discussions with Robin's teachers, and eventually agreed to recommend a formal assessment under the Act. The negotiations between teachers and psychologist in this case illustrate Armstrong and Galloway's (1992a) claim that clinical criteria are not the principal criteria used by psychologists in assessments under the 1981 Education Act. The negotiations taking place between participants during the assessment may have a far more significant effect on its outcome. Although Robin's statement of special educational needs, when issued, did no more than formally endorse the existing arrangements, the school, nonetheless, saw this as a legal document which would in some unspecified way impose an obligation on the LEA to make alternative arrangements for Robin if his behaviour were to deteriorate. From the perspective of Robin's teachers, far from resulting in a transfer of their skills to the psychologist, the assessment had concluded with a successful negotiation of their own needs that gave recognition to the skills embedded in their professional role. Whilst the management of classroom behaviour was seen as comprising one of those skills, dealing with the 'disturbed' child whose behaviour, because of its irrationality, posed particular difficulties in the context of an ordinary classroom was not seen as falling within the professional responsibilities of these teachers. Robin's teachers, as was the case with others in this study, believed that in a one-to-one or small group setting they could effectively meet the educational needs of a disturbed child. However, for them this was not the issue because (a) the education of the disturbed child could not be managed effectively within the context and resources of the ordinary classroom; (b) the presence of a disturbed child in the ordinary classroom seriously impeded the learning of all children in that classroom; and (c) their skills were principally related to the 'higher-status' concerns of educating 'ordinary' children rather than to teaching children with special needs. By insisting on alternative provision for Robin if his behaviour was to deteriorate, his teachers were merely legitimising their own view of their professional role.

CONCLUSION

In this chapter we started by discussing Warnock's endeavour to abolish the distinction between children with special educational needs and others, endorsing the principle that responsibility for all children lies with the class or subject teacher. We went on to argue that government policy, far from valuing schools which are successful with children with social, emotional and behavioural difficulties, actually focuses attention on the achievements of more able children. Resulting from this policy, more pupils are being identified as having SEN and, following assessment and statementing, these children are likely to be educated in segregated settings. However, our research has identified strategies employed by teachers to legitimise increasingly high rates of exclusion; in particular, an emphasis being placed on disturbed rather than disruptive behaviour and on the professional role of teachers being concerned with educating 'normal' children.

The needs of children with emotional and behavioural difficulties may be identified in such a way that the professional competence of those with responsibility for them in mainstream schools is not brought into question. Where a child is identified as 'emotionally disturbed' teachers may view this as less threatening to perceptions of their competence as teachers than might be the case had the child merely been labelled disruptive. Whilst the latter might raise questions about the teacher's classroom management skills, the former assumes that the child's personality and emotional or family history make it difficult for him or her to respond rationally in 'normal' classroom situations. Where teachers' expectations of a formal assessment under the 1981 Act were that a child's emotional and behavioural difficulties would (or should) be formally recognised by the LEA, this outcome was seen by teachers to legitimise their decision to involve the psychologist without at the same time threatening their own professional status.

Far from undermining the professional responsibilities of

teachers, the assessment procedures may actually provide mainstream teachers with the opportunity to enter into negotiations with other educational professionals about the nature of their teaching role, resulting in a re-definition of their expertise in terms of higher-status skills associated with teaching more able children. The removal of the disturbed child is legitimised in terms of this conceptualisation of the teacher's role. In turn, this child-centred focus can constrain the type of intervention available to school psychologists who may, in these circumstances, find it difficult to develop a theoretical model for examining how the needs of all participants are constructed in, or affected by, the school context. As HMI (1990) commented, work with individual children remains central to the role of educational psychologists and this largely reflects the strong pressures placed upon them to respond to the way teachers initially define the problem.

Teachers of several pupils in our study asked for a child to be seen by a psychologist in order to establish or negotiate a particular definition of their professional skill as teachers. Some of these teachers saw their own role as crucial in the process of identifying needs and the role of psychologist primarily as gatekeeper to resources. Where this was so, they tended to adopt strategies to influence any recommendations that the psychologist might make. Thus, in seventeen cases in our study, children were excluded from school either immediately prior to or in the course of a formal assessment. In these cases, even when the psychologist considered that the child's needs could be met in that school, or in an alternative mainstream school, the chances of implementing this option were greatly reduced. Similarly, as in one child's (Robin's) case, some teachers saw statementing as necessary even though there were no specific resource implications over and above those that could be made available without a statement. The teachers' perceptions of Robin's difficulties underwent a change as they became more aware of the possible implications for themselves of decisions taken about him. Discussions between the school and the psychologist at this stage focused on the negotiation of the professional role of the teachers.

At one level this may be seen as evidence of teachers being deskilled since outside 'experts' increasingly become responsible for an area of work previously under the control of teachers (the identification of the needs of disturbing children and the planning of specialist programmes for their children). However, evidence has been presented in this chapter which suggests that teachers may counter measures that tend to deprofessionalise their role by adopting strategies aimed at re-negotiating their role with 'ordinary' children as 'skilful'. It has been argued that the referral to outside experts of children who present difficult or disturbing behaviour in the classroom may constitute just such a strategy. Responsibility for the execution of programmes for children identified as having special needs would become the task of teachers in special schools and units (or specialist teachers in the mainstream). Traditionally these specialists in behaviour problems have been regarded in mainstream schools as having lower status than those teachers working with highly motivated academically oriented pupils. Where a statement of special educational needs is provided, this is likely to be seen by teachers, not as evidence of a lack of skill on their part but as the outcome of a successful negotiation of those professional skills.

ACKNOWLEDGEMENT

This chapter is based on research carried out with Research Grant No. R 000 23 1393 from the Economic and Social Research Council and the Research Council's support is gratefully acknowledged.

REFERENCES

Adler, M., Petch, A. and Tweedie, J. (1989) *Parental Choice and Education Policy*. Edinburgh: Edinburgh University Press.

Armstrong, D. and Galloway, D. (1992a) 'Who is the child psychologist's client? Responsibilities and options for psychologists in educational settings', *Association for Child Psychology and Psychiatry Newsletter* 14, 2, 62–66.

Armstrong, D. and Galloway, D. (1992b) 'On being a client: conflicting perspectives on assessment', in Booth, T., Swann, W., Masterton, M. and Potts, P. *Policies for Diversity in Education*, pp. 193–203 London: Routledge/Open University Press.

Armstrong, D., Galloway, D. and Tomlinson, S. (1991) 'Decision-making in psychologists' professional interviews', *Educational Psychology in Practice 7*, 2, 82–87.

Armstrong, D., Galloway, D. and Tomlinson, S. (1993) 'Assessing special educational needs: the child's contribution', *British Educational Research Journal* 19, 2, 121–131.

Department of Education and Science (DES) (1978) *Special Educational Needs* (The Warnock Report). London: HMSO.

Department of Education and Science (DES) (1989) *Discipline in Schools* (The Elton Report). London: HMSO.

Echols, F.E., McPherson, A. and Williams, J.D. (1990) *Parental Choice in Scotland*, mimeograph. Edinburgh Centre for Educational Sociology, University of Edinburgh.

Foucault, M. (1967) *Madness and Civilization: A History of Insanity in the Age of Reason*. London: Tavistock.

Galloway, D., Ball, T., Blomfield, D. and Seyd, R. (1982) *Schools and Disruptive Pupils*. London: Longman.

Galloway, D. and Goodwin, C. (1987) *The Education of Disturbing Children: Pupils with Learning and Adjustment Difficulties*. London: Longman.

HMI (1990) *Educational Psychology Services in England 1988-1989*. London: DES.

Houghton, S., Wheldall, K. and Merrett, F. (1988) 'Classroom behaviour problems which secondary school teachers say they find most troublesome', *British Educational Research Journal* 14, 297–312.

Humphries, S. (1981) *Hooligans or Rebels? An Oral History of Working-class Childhood and Youth 1889–1939*. Oxford: Blackwell.

Hurt, J.S. (1988) *Outside the Mainstream: A History of Special Education*. London: Routledge.

Lowenstein, L.F. (1975) *Violent and Disruptive Behaviour in Schools*. Hemel Hempstead: National Association of Schoolmasters.

Paquette, J. (1991) *Social Purpose and Schooling: Alternatives, Agendas and Issues*. London: Falmer Press.

Pyke, N. (1992) 'Into the exclusion zone', *Times Educational Supplement*, 26 June: 14.

Stillman, A. and Maychell, K. (1986) *Choosing Schools: Parents and the 1980 Education Act*. Windsor: NFER–Nelson.

Swann, W. (1985) 'Is the integration of children with special needs happening? An analysis of recent statistics of pupils in special schools', *Oxford Review of Education* 11, 3–18.

Swann, W. (1987) 'Statements of intent: an assessment of reality', in Booth, T. and Swann, W. (eds) *Including Children with Disabilities*. Milton Keynes: Open University Press.

Swann, W. (1992) *Segregation Statistics: English LEAs 1988–91*. London: CSIE.

Times Educational Supplement (TES) (1992) 'Exclusion rates', 31 July: 2.

Tomlinson, S. (1981) *Educational Subnormality: A Study in Decision-making*. London: Routledge and Kegan Paul.

Tomlinson, S. (1985) 'The expansion of special education', *Oxford Review of Education* 11, 157–165.

Turkington, R.W. (1986) *In Search of the Disruptive Pupil: Problem Behaviour in Secondary Schools 1959–1982*, unpublished PhD thesis, Department of Sociology, University of Leeds.

Wheldall, K. and Merrett, F. (1988) 'Which classroom behaviours do primary school teachers say they find most troublesome?' *Educational Review* 40, 3–27.

Wood, S. (1988) 'Parents: whose partners?' in Barton, L. (ed.) *The Politics of Special Educational Needs*. London: Falmer Press.

Chapter 10

The role of the learning support teacher in Scottish primary and secondary classrooms

Pamela Munn

INTRODUCTION

Two documents, each published in 1978 on the education of children with special needs, had major implications for teachers' classroom practice. The Warnock Report (DES, 1978) by advocating the integration of children with special educational needs (SEN) into mainstream schools and classrooms, implied that ordinary teachers would encounter in their classes children they would not have been expected to teach in the past. Warnock's abandoning of the nine traditional categories of handicap and instead suggesting a continuum of special educational needs implied no cut-off point beyond which pupils should be segregated. Pupils simply had different kinds of needs and teachers were expected to play a major role in identifying and meeting these needs. A report by HMI in Scotland, *The Education of Pupils with Learning Difficulties in Primary and Secondary Schools in Scotland* (SED, 1978) was a radical departure from previous notions about the origins of learning difficulties. Instead of relying on pupils' ability as an explanation of their learning difficulties it drew attention to the curriculum as the main source of such difficulties. The report advocated a move away from pupil deficits towards an exploration of the school as deficient in maximising opportunities to learn. The implication was that if schools and teachers would only set about their provision for pupils with learning difficulties in the right way, then pupils' difficulties could be overcome.

It is hard to overestimate the change in teachers' thinking about learning difficulties that was being advocated by these two documents. In essence teachers were being asked to:

- cater for a wider range of pupil abilities than before;
- teach this wide range of pupils within the mainstream classroom (withdrawal was frowned upon);
- have the same curriculum aims for this wide range of pupils to avoid them experiencing failure;
- conceptualise learning difficulties differently — going beyond difficulties with reading or number *and* applying to a wider and more diverse range of pupils;
- re-examine their lesson content and teaching methods in cases where pupils were experiencing difficulty as content and methods were likely to be the source of difficulty;
- tackle 'frankly and with determination' (SED, 1978) questions of methods and differentiation.

It is no easy matter for teachers to change their classroom practice as the history of curriculum innovation shows (e.g. Fullan and Stiegelbauer, 1991; Sayer, 1987) and such changes take time (e.g. Gilbert and Hart, 1990). It certainly takes more than the publication of HMI and Select Committee reports. Furthermore, such reports are usually strong on general principles and aims and weak on how to translate these into practice. There was very little practical help and advice to assist teachers in meeting the demands that were being made on them when aspects of the Warnock and HMI reports were enshrined in the Education (Scotland) Act 1981. For example, there were very few differentiated curriculum materials and, at that time, there had been little research on whether and in what ways teachers effectively differentiated among their pupils in terms of curriculum content and teaching methods. Nevertheless, the legislation provided a stimulus to change and education authorities in Scotland moved towards the formulation of policies for the integration of pupils with special educational needs. Inevitably, they have done so at different rates and to different degrees.

This chapter reports teachers' perceptions of integration policy and practice in one Scottish region. It addresses the following questions:

- What do teachers count as a learning difficulty?
- How do mainstream and learning support teachers perceive their roles in meeting pupils' needs?
- What do mainstream and learning support teachers see as the goals of integration policy?

Before addressing these questions it is necessary to say a little about the region in which the research took place and to describe the research.

ONE SCOTTISH REGION

The regional authority in which the research, reported below, took place was unusual in that a general policy for the integration of pupils with special educational needs into mainstream provision had been in operation since 1983. When the research took place (1988–1990) all but one of the region's special schools had been closed and learning centres catering for children with moderate learning difficulties had been set up within mainstream schools.

There were approximately 118 pupils of primary school age and about 100 of secondary school age who had records of needs (broadly equivalent to a statement in England and Wales). Twelve of these pupils were being educated in the region's one remaining special school and the remainder, that is the vast majority, were in mainstream schools throughout the region. The region tried to ensure that, as far as possible, children with records of needs were educated in the local school or in the school preferred by their parents. In effect the largely rural character of much of the region meant that it was impractical for children to attend other than their local secondary school. In practice, recorded children were dispersed across the region's primary and secondary schools and no school was labelled as being predominantly for children with SEN.

Estimates of the numbers of secondary school children experiencing learning difficulties but who were not recorded varied. An average of around 18–20 per cent was cited although in some areas a figure of 30 per cent was mentioned. The estimates for primary school children were much higher with between 40 and 50 per cent being identified. Anyone making such estimates has to grapple with the question 'What counts as a learning difficulty?' This is crucial for understanding mainstream teachers' classroom practice and the role of learning support staff. It was one of the aims of the research described below.

THE RESEARCH

The research, carried out in collaboration with Julie Allan and Sally Brown, had three main aims:

- to explore what counted as a learning difficulty;
- to understand how mainstream teachers, learning support teachers and others perceived their responsibilities in meeting the needs of pupils with learning difficulties;
- to explore staff perceptions of the effectiveness of the regional policy on integration.

These aims were pursued largely by interviewing mainstream and learning support teachers in primary and secondary schools. The interviews were in two main phases for each school sector. A small number of staff in all the region's secondary schools was interviewed in phase one, in order to build up a general picture of views on policy and practice. In this phase fifty-nine staff were interviewed. Phase two involved interviews with larger numbers of staff in four schools. Thirty-two staff were interviewed. The schools selected for more intensive interviewing provided contrasts in terms of identifying or meeting the needs of pupils with learning difficulties. A similar approach was used for the primaries. Phase one involved twelve schools and interviews with the headteacher, learning support staff and a sample of mainstream staff. This was followed by more detailed study of three schools offering interesting and contrasting approaches to the identification and meeting of special needs. In all, forty primary staff were interviewed. In addition to interviewing, a small number of lessons was observed informally and some curriculum materials were analysed (see Allan *et al.*, 1991 for a fuller account).

The heavy reliance on semi-structured interviewing was not ideal. It is always difficult for teachers to talk about their classroom actions. Much of their practice is spontaneous and routine and they are rarely called upon to make it explicit. Consequently, the interviewer often obtains generalisations which provide limited insight and may reflect what the teacher thinks the researcher wants to hear. Our approach was to ask the teacher to focus on one or two pupils with learning difficulties and to tell us about how they tried to meet the needs of these pupils. We then asked how typical their strategies for meeting needs were.

This approach to interviewing elicited rich and interesting data but it has to be recognised that what teachers say they do is not always what they actually do. Classrooms are busy places and teachers select events which have the greatest salience for them. However, it is interesting that patterns among staff perceptions emerged and that a subsequent small-scale observation study of co-operative teaching seemed to confirm our findings from this research (Allan and Munn, 1991). Findings from these two studies are not, of course, generalisable to all schools in Scotland, far less to the rest of Britain. Themes did emerge, however, and they are offered as one starting point for teachers and others working in different contexts, and with different histories of integration policy and practice to reflect upon the role of learning support teachers in the classroom.

WHAT COUNTS AS A LEARNING DIFFICULTY?

It speedily became apparent that learning support staff were not expected to help all children experiencing learning difficulties. It was, therefore, important to understand teachers' categorisation of learning difficulties as an aid to making sense of their views about the role of learning support teachers. It emerged that the important distinction for both mainstream and learning support staff was whether pupils' difficulties were categorised as short term or enduring. There was a further distinction between pupils whose difficulties were enduring and who did not have a record of needs and those whose enduring difficulties were reflected in having a record. It is noteworthy that the same kinds of difficulties were seen by teachers under each of these classifications. For example, difficulties in reading, number, shape, concentration and understanding concepts were mentioned. It was not the *nature of the difficulty* that was the distinguishing feature, but rather whether the difficulty was seen as *short term and capable of remediation or long-lasting and unlikely to be remedied*. It was this categorisation that, at first glance, seemed to determine whether there was any role for learning support staff and if there was, what that role should be. How did teachers know whether pupils' difficulties were likely to be long or short term?

Interesting differences emerged between learning support staff on the one hand, and mainstream staff on the other, particularly those in secondary schools. Learning support staff tended to describe the cause of pupils' difficulties in quite specific terms. For instance, failure in comprehension might be due to the language level of texts, although within a general framework of pupils being generally slow if difficulties persisted over time. Mainstream staff, in contrast, ascribed difficulties to much more general causes. For example, pupils' short-term difficulties might be caused by the nature of the subject, changes in family circumstances or pupils' absence from school with the result that lessons had been missed. By way of contrast, the causes of long-term difficulties were seen in terms of pupils being generally slow, being physically impaired or emotionally disturbed. The mathematics teachers who featured in Weedon's study (Chapter 7, this volume) also tended to regard pupils' learning difficulties as being due to within-child factors rather than to shortcomings in the curriculum, teaching methods or the school more generally.

Four distinct categories of pupils with learning difficulties emerged from our data.

- Pupils with short-term difficulties.
- Pupils with long-term difficulties without a record of needs.
- Pupils with long-term cognitive or emotional/behavioural difficulties with a record of needs.
- Pupils with physical impairments but no cognitive or emotional difficulties and with a record of needs.

Our data suggested that teachers, particularly in secondary schools, were seeing learning difficulties as going beyond reading and number, as advocated by HMI and Warnock. Moreover, they complained that they were often unable to understand why some pupils had had a record of needs opened for them and others had not. Our categorisation implies a perception of a continuum of difficulty at least among those pupils who were categorised as having long-term difficulties. Difficulties were seen as being of different kinds. What did this mean for the role of learning support staff in mainstream classrooms? There were clear differences between primary and secondary teachers and so their views are reported separately.

THE ROLES OF LEARNING SUPPORT STAFF IN SECONDARY CLASSROOMS

As part of the process of the policy of integration, the region tried to ensure that schools had specially trained learning support staff. A specially designed diploma course was negotiated with a college of education and by the time the research was undertaken most secondary schools had well-established departments of learning support with at least the head of department (and usually some colleagues) possessing a Diploma in Special Educational Needs. In addition, the region had teachers of the hearing and visually impaired who worked on a peripatetic basis.

The training course for learning support staff emphasised a number of roles, reflecting the reality of their work. These included liaising with external agencies, ensuring that pupils with records of needs obtained any specialist help specified and a large number of other duties. The one which interests us here is the role of consultant to mainstream staff, educating them in the business of differentiation and in helping them to see pupils as having different kinds of *abilities* rather than categorising pupils more generally on a single dimension of ability. This was a role which learning support staff warmly endorsed and they were willing to be of help to mainstream teachers in any way they could as a step towards highlighting differentiation issues with them. Learning support staff believed that the most efficient and effective way of disseminating their expertise was in the joint preparation of curriculum materials with mainstream staff. However, they were willing to adopt other roles as a means to that end. It is important to stress that this educative role on differentiation issues was not seen as pertinent only to pupils with long-term learning difficulties. It was hoped that mainstream teachers would be encouraged to reflect on their teaching of all pupils drawing on their experience of helping SEN pupils to learn. We cannot say whether mainstream secondary teachers' views on differentiation or on their use of curriculum materials and teaching methods changed because of the influence of learning support staff. We, can, however, infer a good deal about these matters from the roles which learning support staff adopted in mainstream secondary classrooms. Let us first look at their role in relation to short-term difficulties.

Short-term difficulties were seen by mainstream staff as part of the everyday business of teaching. Teachers mentioned a wide range of examples, including both cognitive and emotional/ behavioural difficulties. Where pupils' difficulties were cognitive, they had difficulty in understanding a concept, for instance, or were unable to see links between old and new subject content, then it was the responsibility of the subject teacher to put matters right by using a different teaching approach, or new materials. There was no role for learning support staff since it was subject specialist staff who had the knowledge and expertise to remedy short-term cognitive difficulties. The same was true for short-term emotional/ behavioural difficulties such as caused by bereavement or family problems. Pupils exhibiting signs of these difficulties were the joint responsibility of subject specialist and pastoral care staff. It might be inferred, therefore, that mainstream staff relied on their own subject specialist knowledge and expertise or on that of pastoral care staff to remedy such difficulties. It seems that the specialist knowledge and skills of learning support were not valued in these circumstances. Nor did learning support staff themselves talk about the remediation of pupils' short term difficulties as a role they would like to perform. Our first round of data gathering produced no comments on this and, when asked specifically in the second round, very few learning support staff saw this as an important role. It may be that they saw targeting pupils with long-term difficulties as a more effective way of raising differentiation issues with mainstream staff. However, they risk their skills being seen as worthy rather than significant by adopting this approach, in a school system where school effectiveness is judged by the government largely on pupils' examination performance. Pupils with long-term difficulties are unlikely to be high achievers in terms of raw examination results and so the work of learning support staff may well be seen as relatively unimportant in terms of this key performance indicator for schools. If, in contrast, the performance indicator was expressed in terms of *pupil progress* in attainment (what is known in the jargon as the 'value-added' by the school to what a pupil would be expected to achieve) then learning support staff's skills might well be seen as both worthy and significant. In the absence of the 'value-added' approach to assessing school effectiveness, learning support teachers might reconsider their strategy of concentrating on pupils with long-term difficulties. If they were to focus on pupils with short-term difficulties their contribution to pupils' learning could be more apparent and raise their status in schools.

Having no role in remedying short-term difficulties, did learning support staff automatically provide help for pupils whose difficulties were seen as enduring? The short answer is no. Teachers reported a variety of practice ranging from there being no access to mainstream classrooms to learning support staff being viewed as valued professional colleagues who took a full part in planning lessons, in helping to develop curriculum materials and in teaching. Four different kinds of practice emerged:

- no access to mainstream classes;
- being used as an extra pair of hands in the classroom;
- being used as a technician, carrying out the instructions of mainstream staff;
- being valued as a professional colleague with distinctive skills, knowledge and expertise.

Let us look at these in a little more detail.

In cases where learning support staff had no access to mainstream classes, their lack of subject specialist knowledge was usually cited in explanation. The following extract from a subject teacher's interview gives a flavour of typical explanations for there being no access.

> I was explaining what was happening [to the class] . . . and the learning support teacher was with me . . . taking it all in. The phone rang. . . . I was on the phone listening to [the learning support teacher] explaining – with everything back-to-front and upside down . . . I said [to the class] 'Right, forget what [the learning support teacher] was saying. We'll start again'. . . . You've got to be careful. They're not specialists in the subject.

An equally disastrous experience was reported by a learning support teacher who had been trying to help in craft and design.

> I wasn't confident enough to be able to pass on confidence to the child. I was just another hazard in the class. The class teacher threw up his hands in horror, thanked me very much and didn't ask me back.

Clearly, in these instances, the specific skills and knowledge of learning support staff did not compensate for their lack of subject knowledge. Yet learning support staff can hardly be experts in every area of the secondary school curriculum. It may be that practical subjects make fewer demands on pupils' reading, writing or counting skills and that some mainstream staff see only these skills as the province of learning support staff. There may also be concerns about safety where potentially dangerous pieces of equipment, such as lathes, are in use. However, no readily discernible pattern of departments emerged where learning support staff were regularly excluded. A more detailed study of staff relationships is needed to uncover explanations for the seemingly random nature of learning support staff's exclusion from certain classrooms.

Where learning support staff were used as an extra pair of hands in the classroom, their role was defined as providing help to one or two designated pupils in the class. This freed the mainstream teacher to get through work with the rest of the class. In this role the learning support teacher played no part in lesson planning. A mainstream teacher of computing aptly sums up this role.

> The learning support teacher comes into a third year class to work with one girl who really has problems remembering what she had in previous lessons. . . . It is just a question of sitting down [with the pupil] and going through it.

In this example the subject specialist had identified the learning difficulty and relied on the learning support teacher to devise ways of helping the pupil remember previous lessons through practice and repetition. The learning support teacher had no other role.

The role of technician for learning support staff was our description of instances where they provided help to many pupils in the class but did not share lesson planning with the mainstream teacher or challenge significantly the mainstream teacher's goals. In this role, learning support staff were trusted to go around the class, helping pupils in difficulty regardless of their status as recorded or non-recorded children. In such circumstances, however, it was difficult to avoid labelling some pupils as being generally in need of help supplied only by learning support staff as these staff tended to see helping pupils with enduring difficulties as their main concern in the classroom.

This can be quickly picked up by pupils, as a mainstream teacher reported. 'The kids quite quickly split — a bright child with difficulties that the learning support teacher would not be too happy with, would automatically come to me.'

Unsurprisingly, the most effective teaching relationship in the view of learning support staff, was one in which there was joint planning and teaching of lessons with mainstream staff. This kind of relationship enabled learning support staff potentially to adopt an educative role. As mentioned earlier, they saw this as an opportunity to achieve one of their main purposes, to alert mainstream staff to fundamental questions about mixed ability teaching and differentiation. Learning support staff in secondaries saw their role primarily as consultants, helping and advising subject specialist staff on curriculum planning, teaching methods and curriculum materials. This role of pervading subject departments so that mainstream teachers automatically considered differentiation could, if successfully accomplished, lead to a decreasing need for and an eventual demise of learning support staff. Unlike other specialist staff in secondary schools, where specialists in subjects, pastoral care or managing budgets ring-fence their specialism and strictly regulate entry to it, learning support staff want to give their specialism away. An unusual position for a professional grouping!

Our data suggested that the following conditions were necessary for learning support staff to be involved in joint lesson planning and teaching with mainstream staff:

- the members of staff concerned need time to get to know each other, build up trust and see their relationship as evolving, rather than set in stone.
- non-contact time needs to be available for the learning support teacher and mainstream teacher to plan lessons together.
- learning support staff need to be reasonably confident about their knowledge of the subject matter to be taught.
- subject staff recognise the distinctive skills and knowledge of learning support staff.

It is worth remembering, however, that learning support staff believed that the most efficient way of performing their educative role was through helping mainstream staff to develop appropriately differentiated curriculum materials. They saw classroom teaching alongside mainstream staff as a means to this end, rather than an end in itself. It was a way of gaining access to departments and they were prepared to accept the role defined for them by mainstream staff on that basis.

It was also noteworthy than when both mainstream and learning support staff were asked to evaluate the effectiveness of co-operative teaching, they did so in terms of pupil motivation and quality of teaching related to the use of differentiated approaches. Criteria relating to pupil attainments were never mentioned. This suggests that the main role of learning support staff in the secondary schools researched was to educate mainstream teachers in coping strategies for the wider range of pupil abilities they were meeting. It was not to raise attainments. This is a fundamental point taken up again at the end of the chapter. For the moment, the point to notice is that if pupils are identified as having enduring difficulties, teachers' goals are directed towards coping with these, not remedying them. In this, secondary teachers provided a strong contrast to their primary colleagues.

LEARNING SUPPORT IN THE PRIMARY CLASSROOM

Primary mainstream and learning support teachers differed sharply from their secondary colleagues in three important respects. First, they emphasised their roles in overcoming pupils' learning difficulties. In many ways this is not surprising, particularly for teachers of infants where a confident distinction between short-term and enduring difficulties was hard to make. There is a general acceptance that young children develop at different rates and so there was general optimism among teaching staff that many pupils experiencing early difficulty with, say, reading or shape, would overcome these. A child of 6 or 7 with reading difficulties is a very different proposition from a child of 12 or 13. The optimism that difficulties could be largely overcome and a belief that it was important to catch pupils early meant that learning support was concentrated in the early years.

Secondly, learning support staff were not seen either by themselves or their mainstream colleagues as possessing distinctive knowledge and skills. They were seen as providing essentially the same kind of help to pupils with learning difficulties as the class teacher. The main difference was that the learning support teacher could provide intensive help to targeted pupils either in class or by withdrawal from mainstream activities.

Thirdly, and related to the above, learning support staff did not spread their efforts across the primary curriculum; they concentrated on fundamental skills of reading and numeracy. These skills were seen as keys to accessing other curriculum areas.

The educative role so strongly emphasised by secondary learning support staff was absent from their primary colleagues' discourse. Both mainstream and learning support teachers in primaries took it for granted that the dominant goal for early primary pupils was competence in reading and number work. The shared goals, skills and knowledge is evident from the following extracts from interviews. A learning support teacher commented:

> I'll often work from the top end of the group. It helps to stimulate them and lets the [mainstream] teacher work with the poorer ones.

Similarly, a mainstream teacher said:

> If [the learning support teacher] came in and I was working with the poor group, she would walk round the rest and help wherever she could. I don't think it's good for her to take [the poor group] all the time because the class teacher loses contact with them and you're not quite sure where they are or what they're doing.

This seemed to suggest a rejection of a special curriculum in the sense that pupils with learning difficulties were not viewed as requiring specialist teaching. It reinforces the notion of learning support staff as providing essentially the same skills and knowledge as the mainstream teacher. Thus, learning support staff in the primary schools played essentially the same role as the mainstream teacher except that they focused on reading and number whereas mainstream primary staff had broader curriculum responsibilities. They did not need explicitly to plan goals and methods with mainstream colleagues as these were assumed to be identical. This did not seem to match the role for which learning support staff were prepared in their specialist training. Training had highlighted the importance of an educative, consultant role as for secondary learning support staff.

Nevertheless, it seemed that the support available to class teachers was regarded as effective by both mainstream and learning support in terms of the success of resolving pupils' difficulties. Significantly, pupil attainment and progress featured in primary school teachers' interviews, another contrast with their secondary colleagues. It may be that the peripatetic nature of most learning support staff in primary schools influenced their decision to concentrate on language and number work. This is understandable given the importance of these areas for access to other parts of the primary curriculum and the optimism that, with some intensive help, pupils' difficulties could be overcome. The concern is that as pupils with long-term difficulties progress through primary, their access to the curriculum is severely restricted. As one learning support teacher commented:

> By primary 5 you get the attitude that if they [pupils] have not done it by now, you're flogging a dead horse. I find that really sad; if you've not made it by the time you've reached 10, you're on the scrap heap.

A number of primary learning support staff and headteachers shared the above view, that mainstream staff were sometimes precipitate in accepting certain learning difficulties as enduring. Nevertheless, where priorities had to be made, it was perhaps understandable that children in the early years of primary were targeted.

LEARNING SUPPORT AND INTEGRATION

The wide-ranging and radical implications for teachers' classroom practice of the Warnock Report and of the 1978 HMI report were highlighted at the beginning of this chapter. The conflicting nature of these demands needs to be highlighted too. Teachers were urged to pursue the same curriculum goals for all pupils *and* to avoid a sense of failure in comparison with others. They were urged to differentiate their teaching to take account of pupils' needs and abilities *and* to eschew a special curriculum for pupils with learning difficulties. These are difficult if not impossible demands to reconcile. Furthermore, HMI suggested that the new role of learning consultant envisaged for the learning support teacher would be professionally more fulfilling but, at the same time, HMI insisted that the major responsibility for children with special needs lies with the class teacher. They questioned whether a separate learning support department was needed in schools. Thus the demands on and expectations of mainstream and learning support staff were considerable.

In particular, the role of learning support was left unclear. While promoting the idea of a continuum of need, the role of learning support staff in helping pupils at different points in this continuum is vague. The old notion of 'remedial teachers', whose expertise lies in a capability to deal with the least able pupils and help them to achieve the limited goals of a special curriculum, has officially been dented. As we have seen, however, the new role is open to many different interpretations, between primary and secondary schools, among secondary schools, and indeed within a secondary school where the same learning support teacher can play very different roles in different subject departments.

Interestingly, Ireson *et al.*'s (1992) study of curriculum development for children with learning difficulties in mainstream primary and secondary and special schools revealed a range of roles for learning support staff. The study was based on semi-structured interviews with class or subject teachers, the teacher with responsibility for special needs and headteachers, and included an analysis of curriculum and other documents. The researchers identified three main approaches to meeting pupils' needs in mainstream schools, 'support' – (broadly speaking, integrated provision), 'withdrawal' (where special needs pupils were extracted from mainstream classes and special aims and or a special curriculum identified) and a mixture of both. In all those approaches collaboration and interaction between mainstream and learning support staff could be high but there was no clear pattern between approach and role of learning support staff. The researchers point out that the historical separation of special needs teaching may have given rise to a view of this as a 'separate curriculum area to be considered in addition to rather than as part of the traditional subject area'. This suggests that teachers' ideologies about the nature of ability is key in influencing the role of learning support staff. These ideologies could be a more important influence on practice than the different models of school organisation and curriculum development revealed by Ireson *et al.*

We are now beginning to build up understanding about teachers' classroom practice, an understanding derived from teachers' own accounts of what they value in their teaching, what they do routinely and spontaneously and why they do it. Understanding the key influences on teachers' classroom practice is essential for innovation. Only if innovations take account of these influences do they stand any chance of success. For example, we know from research on teachers' craft knowledge (e.g. Brown and McIntyre, 1993) that teachers' goals and actions are profoundly influenced by the school and classroom context in which they find themselves. The time of day, the time of year, the teacher's mood and the nature of the subject matter, for instance, are cited by teachers as influencing their plans. A recently completed study of classroom discipline (Munn *et al.*, 1992) revealed that teachers mentioned their knowledge of their pupils more than any other influence, as affecting their goals and actions. Such knowledge is not necessarily accurate or complete but it is a powerful force, shaping teachers' expectations not only about how pupils will behave, but also about what it is appropriate for them to learn. How does this help us to understand the roles of learning support staff? In secondary schools it suggests that mainstream teachers have been juggling at least three major goals as far as pupils with learning difficulties are concerned:

- goals of social integration with 'ordinary' pupils;
- goals of developing confidence in pupils with learning difficulties;
- goals of access to the mainstream curriculum.

Where teachers' knowledge of their pupils typifies them as having long-term difficulties which are unlikely to be overcome, then goals of social integration and developing pupils' confidence assume higher priority than access to the mainstream curriculum, hence the learning support teacher's role of helping the mainstream teacher develop coping strategies. The coping strategies described in this chapter have ranged from the simple provision of an extra pair of hands in the classroom to the more sophisticated differentiated planning of lessons to take account of individual differences, the development of appropriate curriculum materials and the adoption of more individualised teaching methods. However sophisticated these strategies, they are nevertheless fundamentally concerned with teachers being able to sustain a normal desirable classroom state of activity (Brown and McIntyre, 1993) not with advancing pupils' attainments. This is not to imply any criticism of either mainstream secondary teachers or learning support staff. It is to highlight the immense difficulty of holding pupils' learning and progress as a dominant goal when faced with a wide range of pupil abilities and uncertainty about the appropriate professional role for learning support staff.

In contrast, in primaries, teachers' knowledge of infant and junior pupils is uncertain and tentative. Informed by a belief that children develop at different rates, curriculum access and pupil attainment goals can be given a higher priority. Pupils' learning difficulties may be temporary and so be overcome and goals of social integration and developing pupils' confidence do not assume therefore the priority that is evident in the secondary school. These goals are not abandoned or even neglected, of course, as every primary teacher knows, but they are juggled with progress and attainment goals, hence the role of learning support staff as just like that of the mainstream teacher.

Hegarty *et al.* (1981) argued over ten years ago that the concept of integration was in need of clarification. There is a wide diversity of provision in the UK and in Europe as recent OECD studies have shown and an accompanying diversity of roles for learning support staff. This study of a small number of schools in one Scottish region highlights the diversity in an area which has had an integration policy since 1983. If, as Harold Wilson once said, a week is a long time in politics, then maybe ten years is a short time for a radical education innovation to have bedded down. Until we are clearer about what we want integration to achieve, particularly in terms of the conceptualisation of learning difficulties and pupils' attainments, and how to translate this into practical classroom strategies, then the role of learning support staff as a catalyst for changing the way teachers think about learning difficulties is likely to remain unfulfilled.

REFERENCES

Allan, J. and Munn, P. (1991) *Teaming Up: Area Teams for Learning Support*. Edinburgh: Scottish Council for Research in Education.

Allan, J., Brown, S. and Munn, P. (1991) *Off the Record: Mainstream Provision for Pupils with Non-recorded Learning Difficulties in Primary and Secondary Schools*. Edinburgh: Scottish Council for Research in Education.

Brown, S. and McIntyre, D. (1993) *Making Sense of Teaching*. Buckingham: Open University Press.

Department of Education and Science (DES) (1978) *Special Educational Needs* (The Warnock Report). London: HMSO.

Fullan, M. and Stiegelbauer, S. (1991) *The New Meaning of Educational Change*. Ontario: Ontario Institute for Studies in Education.

Gilbert, C. and Hart, M. (1990) *Towards Integration: Special Needs in an Ordinary School*. London: Kogan Page.

Hegarty, S., Pocklington, K. and Lucas, D. (1981) *Educating Pupils with Special Needs in the Ordinary School*. Windsor: NFER-Nelson.

Ireson, J., Evans, P., Redmond, P. and Wedell, K. (1992) 'Developing a curriculum for pupils experiencing difficulties in learning in ordinary schools: a systematic comparative analysis', *British Educational Research Journal* 18, 2, pp. 155–173.

Munn, P., Johnstone, M. and Chalmers, V. (1992) *Effective Discipline in Secondary Schools and Classrooms*. London: Paul Chapman.

Sayer, J. (1987) *Secondary Schools for All? Strategies for Special Needs*. London: Cassell.

Scottish Education Department (1978) *The Education of Pupils with Learning Difficulties in Primary and Secondary Schools in Scotland*. Edinburgh: HMSO.

The Education (Scotland) Act 1981.

Chapter 11

The impact of policy on practice and thinking

Sally Brown and Sheila Riddell

INTRODUCTION

In Chapter 1 we concentrated on a description of the legislation and policy literature relevant to the education of pupils with special educational needs (SEN). In this final chapter our concern is to look at the effects, as illustrated in this collection of papers, that the policies have had on practice and on thinking in this area of education. The authors of different chapters have touched on a wide variety of practical matters: the targeting of resources on some pupils while others lose out, schools' readiness to accept or exclude certain kinds of pupils, different ways of implementing integration into mainstream, collaboration among schools to improve provision and the impact of parents' involvement in decision-making. The very considerable changes in the locus of control of education over the last few years have been, of course, major influences in these matters of practice. But at the same time, thinking about special needs and about special provision has also been affected. The nature and origins of SEN, continuum or category models, the boundaries of the professionalism and competence of teachers, and the interactions between parents' and educators' constructs of learning difficulties and appropriate provision, have found themselves in the melting-pot of the debate.

The following sections look at some of the broad issues arising in this context, with the final paragraphs returning briefly to something we pointed to at the start of the book: the contrasts between policy and practice on either side of the England–Scotland border.

A CONTEXT OF UNCERTAINTY

One of the features of this collection of papers has been the documentation of the disjunctions between, on the one hand, the ways in which the influential reports of fifteen years ago (SED, 1978; Warnock, 1978) construed effective provision for children with special educational needs and, on the other hand, the ideas reflected in the policy innovations of the last five or six years. The rise in importance of a market forces approach, and the insistent encouragement of competition among schools, has had a profound effect on the way the education of pupils with special needs is viewed. The relatively high cost of such provision, schools' expectations that these young people will make limited contributions to the improvement of standards in conventional achievements, and perceptions that significant numbers of children with learning difficulties in mainstream classrooms will be seen as undesirable by the majority of parents, have changed many people's thinking. In practice, we have seen the Warnock vision of a continuum of need matched by a continuum of provision supplanted by a dichotomised system where the important distinctions are between those pupils with and those without statements or records of needs.

For the children who have learning difficulties but no statement or record, things seem to have become particularly unsettled. In the reports of the 1970s, a striking feature was the expansion of the proportion of the general population whose difficulties, it was argued, should be addressed. Warnock indicated about 20 per cent of pupils and HM Inspectorate (Scotland) about 50 per cent. Some have now gone even further; Strathclyde Region's (1992) policy document *Every Child is Special* has focused on concern for the individual needs and rights of *all* pupils. This has not been universally welcomed. Robin Jackson (1993), for example, has argued that an approach of this kind is a recipe for the

> widening (or dilution) of the definition of special educational needs to the point where it becomes virtually meaningless. . . . For if it is argued that every child is special then there must be a sense in which no child is special.
>
> (Jackson, 1993: 12)

An implication that follows is a weakening of the support

available for positive discrimination in favour of the disadvantaged who have the greatest need (which, ironically, is a second major principle of the Strathclyde policy).

As several contributors have suggested, in England there is increasing demand for statements so that extra resources are guaranteed for individual children, but this still represents a modest percentage of the population with learning difficulties. The rest of this group have, since the 1981 Act, been seen as primarily the LEA's responsibility (or problem). Since the 1988 Act (see Lunt and Evans, and Armstrong and Galloway, Chapters 2 and 9, this volume) there is evidence that schools may be trying to move even more of that responsibility towards LEAs as the schools themselves are held to account increasingly in terms of achievements typical of more able pupils. Clearly this will have an effect on the extent of integration of pupils into mainstream settings. In Scotland as well as England concern has been expressed that such integration requires a wider distribution of resources, but strict financial considerations in mainstream schools are seen as encouraging the concentration of young people with learning difficulties in special schools. Indeed, the evidence suggests that the population of special schools is not falling and may, in some areas, be increasing. The tension between that finding and the aims implied by Warnock's constructs of locational, social and functional integration is obvious. Yet these constructs have stimulated the debate about SEN over the last decade and a half. The matter of the physical location of the pupil, in special or mainstream school, is plainly something on which consideration of the child's educational and social experience (e.g. breadth and balance of the curriculum, interactions with peers and the community) is dependent and it has considerable importance in thinking about what counts as integration.

INTEGRATION

The 'principle' of integration of children with special educational needs into the community is central to the debate. While the idea of integration is generally regarded as a 'good thing', its precise meaning and translation into practice is another matter. At one extreme it can imply the demise of all special schools and inclusion of everyone in mainstream; at the other, it can mean

maintaining the status quo. Perhaps the most helpful comparisons to make, however, are between 'inclusion/desegregation'
and the more flexible 'placement in the least restrictive
environment'.

Inclusion

Jenny Corbett's account of Newham's policies (Chapter 4) has
illustrated the first of these interpretations in a context of what
she calls a 'high level of under-achievement', in an 'economically
depressed' area. Desegregation within an 'inclusive education
vision', however, was by no means a development that was
uniformly welcomed. Evident enthusiasm for inclusion as an
element of a caring, anti-sexist, anti-racist ethos, was
accompanied by concern about the pace of change at a time when
a plethora of other reforms were under way, meagre consultation
and resourcing, job security for staff in special schools, parents'
anxieties and their preferences for special rather than mainstream
provision, and the doubts of teachers and welfare staff over the
ability of mainstream schools to cope (especially with the needs
of children with severe learning difficulties). Concerns of this
kind are not trivial matters and may be as thwarting an influence
as are the market ideologies and harsh cultures of central
government which Corbett sees as endangering this 'progressive
innovation'.

While Newham provides an urban setting for its high-profile
inclusion policy, more rural areas are often contexts for
mainstreaming higher proportions of pupils with special needs.
Pamela Munn (Chapter 10) has described research in a rural
Scottish local authority where it was for the most part impractical
for pupils to attend other than their local schools, only one special
school was still open, the authority had an explicit policy for
integration and the setting up of learning centres for children
with moderate learning difficulties was seen as a part of general
provision. Within this environment there were, of course,
conflicting demands. Teachers were urged by Scottish HMI to set
the same curriculum goals for all pupils, yet shield everyone from
any sense of failure in comparison with others; to take account of
individual pupils' needs and difficulties, but to shun any notion
of a special curriculum; and to accept the consultancy role of the
learning teacher, yet have the classroom teacher take the major

responsibility for providing for pupils with special educational needs. It is clear, therefore, that even in a context which, in comparison with Newham, had few conflicts at the level of policy, the implications of integration were a major concern for practice with many tensions remaining unresolved. Indeed, Charles Weedon (Chapter 7), in discussing pupils whose difficulties are not severe enough for them to have a record of needs, has argued that existing curricular arrangements in Scotland do not provide enough flexibility even for these pupils. SOED statistics show that a higher proportion of secondary than primary pupils are educated in special schools and that placement in special schools often happens at the point of transition between the primary and secondary sectors.

In considering why this is the case, Pamela Munn reports general optimism among Scottish primary teachers that children with learning difficulties in their classes would overcome their problems, but pessimism among secondary teachers that difficulties which had persisted beyond primary school would now be remedied. That, together with the likely preference for keeping younger children in their local schools, would suggest that more primary than secondary children would be found in mainstream classrooms. In some current research at Stirling, which looks at mainstream and special provision, it appears that education authorities differ in their views of whether, on the one hand, children should have special provision at an early age before exposure to the wider world at transition or, on the other hand, be kept as long as possible in the general community and then transferred to special provision if things look bleak for their progress at the end of primary. As Corbett demonstrates in the context of Newham, the future of inclusive education is far from assured given the range of obstacles which it faces. In areas of the United Kingdom where progressive educational ideas are less easily established, opposition may be even greater. However, the move towards inclusive education is driven by commitment to an egalitarian vision and even though such visions have been battered over recent years, they have certainly not disappeared from sight. In addition, the geographic factors which have led some regions to educate almost all children in mainstream schools will continue to ensure that the problems and possibilities of this method of school organisation will be addressed.

Least restrictive environment

The alternative of the 'least restrictive environment' is a less constraining principle than 'non-segregation'. It allows for a series of providing institutions from hospital schools, through special schools (residential or day) and special units, to mainstream classrooms. The critical questions for the operationalisation of this principle are concerned with whether:

1   the child has access to his or her curriculum entitlement;
2   the support provided is adequate and appropriate to enable him or her to make the most of that entitlement;
3   the environment helps the child to identify with, and feel part of, the wider community;
4   the child's self-esteem and confidence are fostered;
5   the child's family feels secure and satisfied that the most effective arrangements are in place.

In Chapter 6 Riddell *et al.* have drawn attention to Warnock's (DES, 1978) acceptance that special schools would continue, though most children with special needs should receive their education in mainstream schools. But they also point to some of the weaknesses identified in the Scottish HMI report (SED, 1978) of pupils' repeated withdrawal from their mainstream classes for individual tuition. Such withdrawal threatens the child's curriculum entitlement. The Scottish and at least some English LEAs' strategy has been to shift the responsibility towards the classroom or subject teacher and reconceptualise the role of what was formerly the 'remedial teacher' into a consulting, supporting, co-operating 'learning support teacher'. This strategy has had by no means universal acceptance. Some parents see it as a dilution of the individual attention which they believe their children should have, and many mainstream teachers have yet to incorporate this aspect of responsibility into their conceptions of their area of professional skill.

Evaluating the effectiveness of 'least restrictive environment' strategies is, if anything more difficult than 'inclusion' approaches. The latter's 'performance indicator' focuses initially on Warnock's locational integration and success is measured by 'head-counting'. Criteria for success for social and functional integration, however, are not as obvious. While *opportunities* for social interactions can readily be observed, the evidence for effective social relationships being *established* is thin, and a basic conflict in functional integration comes from the tension between, on the one hand, giving young people with special needs the same or similar access to the curriculum as their peers and, on the other hand, providing them with the tailored help they need. This is especially obvious in the context of the national curriculum attainment targets which are for the most part insufficiently flexible to accommodate pupils with special needs. The problems that ensue from this can encourage acceptance of social integration as the realistic goal and endanger young people's entitlement to a broad curriculum.

The word 'integration' seems usually to imply that some children start 'outside' normal education. It may reflect a way of thinking that sees standard educational provision as the 'given' and looks to see whether children with particular kinds of problems can be accommodated within that provision (which is designed for pupils without SEN). What it may not do is to encourage a fundamental reformulation of standard provision which takes as its starting point the needs of the *whole* population. Whatever way curriculum entitlement is viewed, however, the characteristics of children themselves may have a substantial influence on the extent to which they become integrated into, or excluded from, mainstream settings.

The influence of pupil characteristics

Julie Allan's report of case studies in various parts of the UK (Chapter 8) made it clear that, with appropriate support (material and human), teachers accepted that many children with physical disabilities, sensory impairments and specific learning difficulties could follow the same curriculum as their peers. For children with severe and profound, and even some with moderate, learning difficulties the picture was much more pessimistic. In these cases, discrete programmes of work or major changes to the mainstream curriculum were seen as necessary, and in many cases were not regarded as feasible within mainstream classrooms. Jenny Corbett points to a suggestion that mainstreaming should *start* with those with the most severe and multiple difficulties; if successful, this would scale the teachers' worst hurdle at the start, but it also runs the risk of putting the whole inclusion process in jeopardy, if it is seen by most people as unrealistic and undesirable.

In their contribution Armstrong and Galloway (Chapter 9) have argued that recent educational reforms have encouraged the removal from mainstream classrooms of children who are disruptive. Because schools' accountability ends are best served by high academic performance, and disruptive pupils endanger that not only by the limitations of their own achievements but also by the effects they have on others, increasingly high rates of exclusion are becoming apparent without corresponding evidence of increases in disruptive behaviour. Furthermore, such children are tending more and more to be characterised as psychologically disturbed (rather than just badly behaved in class) and, as such, in need of help from 'experts' other than classroom teachers. This 'new' characterisation legitimises a move that seems counter to integration into mainstream. It also precludes the possibility of a challenge to the professional competence of classroom teachers; such competence might be expected to include the capability to deal with disruptive pupils in classrooms but not with those who are emotionally disturbed.

The way in which an individual or group views the issue of integration will depend on how the nature of special educational needs is interpreted. It is to that we now turn.

SEN AND LEARNING DIFFICULTIES: CONTINUUM OR CATEGORIES?

The chapters in this collection illustrate the variety of ways in which different groups, all of whom are intimately concerned with provision in this area, construe the terms SEN and learning difficulties. Sheila Wolfendale (Chapter 3) has drawn attention to how SEN can be seen either as an enabling term, which has removed an invidious system of categorisation, or as a term which marginalises a minority of the pupil population. She suggests it is a construct which has been politicised as it has been invoked to argue for or against certain types of provision. Since teachers are ultimately the providers, we start by addressing the ways in which they make sense of SEN.

Teachers' constructs

The combined effect of the Education Acts for England and Wales and for Scotland in the early 1980s, and the Warnock and Scottish

HMI reports of the late 1970s, might have been expected to influence teachers' thinking. These Acts and reports emphasised notions of a continuum of learning difficulties, the discarding of categories of handicap and a focus on deficits in the curriculum and environment rather than in the child. Pamela Munn's account, however, has found Scottish teachers emphasising *categories*. These categories distinguish between short-term and enduring difficulties and, within the latter, between those which do and do not merit a record of needs, and among cognitive, emotional/behavioural and physical difficulties. Apart from short-term difficulties, there was a strong tendency to see these categories as reflecting problems inherent in the child.

Considerable support for this finding comes from Charles Weedon's study where teachers saw difficulties in mathematics as predominantly pupil-based. He makes the point that too little attention has been paid to how teachers construe their classrooms and their pupils. He is not alone, of course, in pointing out that the preaching of well-meaning policy-makers or educational theorists is unlikely to bring about change in teachers' thinking unless it takes as its *starting* point the ways in which teachers already perceive and think about what they do (Brown and McIntyre, 1993: 15–16) and what they see as practical in their own classrooms. That is not to say, however, that others would accord the same privilege that Weedon gives to teachers' accounts. As McIntyre (1993: 28–30) has suggested, fluent teaching by experienced teachers requires them to develop taken-for-granted ways of conceptualising classroom situations that simplify the ways in which they think about pupils and their own actions. Unless teachers are prepared to reflect on, and continually to challenge, the simplifying concepts they use, however, there is always a danger that a comfortable and stable framework will be sustained regardless of whether it meets the learning needs and caters for the learning difficulties of pupils. Willingness to challenge one's own practice is less likely, of course, if the demands being made on one are seen as unreasonable or unrealistic. It could be argued that these Scottish teachers were reacting to a particular set of conditions and guidance (especially from HM Inspectorate) which placed too little emphasis on problems within the child and too great a responsibility on schools for the creation of the child's difficulties.

In their chapter, Derrick Armstrong and David Galloway have

argued that it is the policy of tying resources to individual statemented children that has encouraged teachers in England to think in terms of deficits within the child rather than of supportive provision. Indeed, they put considerable emphasis on the way in which teachers' constructs of pupils' difficulties, and of the extent of their own skills, have been influenced by government policies which focus on the performance of the more able and statementing of the least able. These authors do not accept teachers' definitions uncritically, but see them as shifting under the pressure of the central thrust of accountability and taking refuge in the idea that the problem resides in the child. So a move is made from describing a child's behaviour as 'disruptive' to identifying the child himself or herself as 'disturbed' and this, it is suggested, threatens the principle that SEN should be defined in educational terms rather than the child's deficit or handicapping condition.

Although the general thrust of policy in Scotland has been similar to that south of the border, more attention has been paid to the implications for classroom responsibilities and practice of adopting a continuum model. The extent to which actual classroom practice has responded to what has been proposed is, therefore, of some interest in an exploration of how SEN is being construed.

Classroom provision

A major strand of the advice offered by central government when children with special educational needs are integrated into classroom settings in Scotland has focused on collaboration between learning support staff and classroom or subject teachers. This was particularly evident in the Scottish HMI report of 1978. That report laid emphasis on the consultancy function of learning support teachers and considered the role of the whole school in supporting children with special educational needs. The practicalities of the partnership between learning support and mainstream teachers seems to have been given more prominence by central government policy-makers in Scotland than in England. This has been sustained in local authority schemes, guidelines from central bodies (e.g. Scottish Committee for Staff Development in Education, 1990) and, most recently, in staff development materials for the Scottish equivalent of the national curriculum – the 5–14 programme (Scottish Consultative Council on the Curriculum, 1993). All of these have emphasised the responsibility which the mainstream subject or class teacher has for the education of *all* pupils and the equality of the relationship with the co-operating learning support staff. The vision has been one of a planned collaborative effort which, where possible, involves two teachers working together to support all pupils in a class. In principle, such an approach could reinforce the idea of SEN as a continuum. To what extent is it apparent in classrooms?

Julie Allan has reported a mixed picture. Rather frequently, learning support teachers appeared to be dealing with those pupils who had the greatest difficulties, while the mainstream teachers taught the usual lesson to the main body of the class. Little evidence was apparent that senior management was able to give priority to consultation time for the collaboration in planning and discussing the curriculum, or to influence mainstream teachers' thinking and encourage change. Pamela Munn's findings were broadly similar. She found that responsibility for providing for pupils' short-term difficulties (often brought about by the pupil's absence) was seen by mainstream teachers as theirs, rather than the learning support teachers', since such pupils often have the potential to contribute to the raw achievement profile of the school. Enduring long-term problems, however, were regarded with pessimism and as the province of the learning support staff. Although the level of acceptance of learning support teachers as professional colleagues rather than some kind of visiting remedial staff varies, the absence of emphasis on value-added (instead of raw) achievement indicators, and the distinctive differences between many mainstream and learning support teachers' notions of what the latters' role should be, suggest that the implementation of learning support consultancy and of co-operative teaching initiatives is still in its infancy. As things stand, therefore, a substantial amount of current classroom practice seems unlikely to support the establishment of a continuum model of SEN in teachers' thinking.

But what about parents? They have a powerful interest in how their children's difficulties and needs are conceptualised.

Parents and provision

Although parents have probably welcomed the idea of locating the deficits associated with meeting their children's needs in the provision itself, they have not necessarily been attracted by the continuum model. Sheila Riddell *et al.* have shown that some at least have argued strongly for categorisation of their children's particular difficulties. They see this as a way of capturing resources in an environment where professionals may see their priority as responding to the needs of *all* pupils and so resisting the pleas of those with specific vested interests. This parental stance strikes some chords with one of the major areas of debate on disability where it has been argued that ignoring differences among different kinds of disability leads to inaction, neglect and oppression (Abberley, 1987). At the same time, however, Abberley emphasises the way in which all disabilities are experienced and interpreted in a particular social and historical context and this dimension of understanding might well be lacking among parents of children with specific learning difficulties.

The essential problem in this area, highlighted by Ingrid Lunt and Jennifer Evans (Chapter 2), is that while a continuum of pupils' needs may readily be accepted in principle, a continuum of provision is quite another matter. It is, indeed, difficult even to conceptualise, let alone implement, resources on a continuous basis. Resources tend to come in discrete bits and, in current circumstances, allocation almost certainly involves categorising the targets (i.e. particular young people with SEN) for those resources. Once that is done, there are inevitably 'losers', especially the borderline cases, and often those seem to be children with moderate learning difficulties or emotional/behavioural problems. The ways in which resources are distributed and who has control over decisions about that are crucially dependent, of course, on the general policy picture at the time. It is to that that we now turn.

POLICY INFLUENCES

The locus of control

Despite the commonalities of policy, determined by a single government at Westminster, the separate education systems have ensured distinctive differences between England and Scotland. Fifteen years ago the publication of the 1978 report on learning difficulties by HMI in Scotland, with no comparable statement from the DES, reflected the then greater centralisation of the Scottish system and the expectation that local authorities and schools would follow advice from the centre. This image of national consensus is only a crude reflection of what actually happens, but the contrast with the much more variable, almost laissez-faire approach in England and Wales in the 1970s is clear. The wide variation in local authority education policies south of the border has never been apparent in Scotland – there has been no parallel with authorities like Newham which Jenny Corbett has described as 'politically contentious', and correspondingly no comparable allegiance to what she refers to as 'visionary policies'.

In the 1990s, things look rather different south of the border with much greater control on the general framework of education being exerted by central 'government', and more of the detailed decision-making being devolved to schools. The LEAs' areas of influence and resources are correspondingly diminished. Scotland has changed less although education authorities are having to relinquish some of their control as devolved school management (DSM, the parallel to Local Management of Schools or LMS) is being introduced. The reorganisation of local government in Scotland in 1996, involving the breaking up of some large authorities such as Strathclyde, will also have an impact on the planning and delivery of educational services.

Responses to the changing policy scene have varied among the authors contributing to this collection. Sheila Wolfendale, in looking at special needs in the early years, has judged the thrust of recent legislation to be 'benign and enabling, reflecting a caring society'. From their different perspectives others are less charitable. Referring to measures like the 'absurdity' of school league tables, Jenny Corbett argues for the likelihood of a downward spiral of schools in areas of severe deprivation which cannot withstand a market culture. Jennifer Evans and her colleagues point to the growing concern, among those writing about provision for children with SEN, that the current competitive model that sees education as a delivery process is simply not able to provide for the needs of these vulnerable young people. But, as several contributors imply, or explicitly illustrate, there is no sense in which we can assume that pre-1988 was a 'golden age' for special education.

An area of considerable concern is the consequence of the moves to transfer power from LEAs to schools. Ingrid Lunt and Jennifer Evans have identified the pressure which, in their view,

LMS has produced to return to the dichotomous characterisation of all pupils as either those who have statements or records of need (and so preferential funding) or those who do not. In those circumstances, financial investment in learning support for the latter group, which includes pupils with substantial learning difficulties, is likely to diminish.

One possible way of dealing with this problem involves the establishment of clusters of schools to share resources and collaborate in planning, training and the provision of support. Jennifer Evans and her co-authors have focused their contribution on this strategy. Their finding, that effectiveness may well depend on LEAs playing a key role in encouraging schools to form such clusters and providing resources and other support, has considerable implications for the future as the authorities' influence is expected to wane and more schools may move out of the LEA bailiwick into the grant-maintained sector. This, together with increased competition between schools, the extent of breakdown of the concept of 'catchment areas' and the difficulties (even for school clusters) of dealing with multiple aspects of SEN, present a picture in which the role of clusters as a way of organising special educational provision looks somewhat pessimistic. However, recent developments suggest that, at least in theory, schools will have to continue to address the question of how they are to make such provision. The draft Code of Practice (DFE, 1993), offering guidance on the implementation of the 1993 Education Act, reiterates the expectation that children will normally be educated in mainstream schools and emphasises the responsibility of all schools to have clear policies on the integration of pupils with special educational needs. It might therefore act as a spur to the development of clusters of schools to provide staff training and specialised resources. Nonetheless, ambiguity remains concerning the curriculum entitlement of all pupils. The persistence of escape clauses is evident in Section 161 of the Act, which states that the governing body must:

> ensure that the pupil joins in the activities of the school together with pupils who do not have special educational needs, so far as that is reasonably practical and compatible with the pupil receiving the necessary special educational provision and the efficient use of resources.
>
> (DFE, 1993: 6)

In addition, parents' rights to choice of school for a child with special educational needs continue to be circumscribed. Although the Education (Special Educational Needs) Regulations 1994 state that parents may express a preference for any school in the maintained sector or 'make representations for a placement outside the maintained sector', three considerations govern the naming of a school in a statement. These are the following:

> the placement must be appropriate to the child's needs, while also compatible with the interests of other children already in the school and the efficient use of the LEA's resources.
>
> (DFE, 1993: 71)

If parents are successful in using the 1993 Act to increase the use of mainstream placements for children with special educational needs, their schools will have to think very hard about how they are to make provision and the development of cluster arrangements may become increasingly appealing.

In Scotland, education authorities have tended towards a conscious strategy of positive discrimination in favour of schools in particularly deprived areas. It remains to be seen how much this will be maintained as we move into the new scene of DSM for which each authority has now submitted its plans and funding formula to the Scottish Office. Whatever happens, it seems likely that control will move much more into the hands of schools, that co-operation with other schools with more deprived populations than one's own will not be popular (though SEN expertise in disadvantaged schools could be valued) and that the social equalising function that education authorities have been able to fulfil will not be easily overtaken by, or attractive to, individual schools.

The national curricula

Although the chapters in this collection have not included the impact of national curriculum reforms as a central theme, this aspect of the policy has a clear influence on many of educational settings described. Charles Weedon has demonstrated the very real concerns for mathematics, within Scotland's 5–14 programme, where he argues that the pressure for the entitlement to a common curriculum has militated against flexibility and choice, especially for those who have significant learning difficulties but not a record of needs. The danger that others might see in offering teachers freedom to interpret the curriculum flexibility for a wider group of pupils than those with a record is that it could result in a relapse into low expectations, notions of ceilings to pupils' capabilities and special (and limited) curricula for many young people.

In fact, possibilities for flexibility in the Scottish curriculum guidelines are probably greater than south of the border where Derrick Armstrong and David Galloway have suggested that the national curriculum has struck at teachers' autonomy and made them accountable for delivery of something over which they have little control. Harlen (1992) has drawn attention to the implications for children with SEN of the prescribed 'two-tier curriculum: the basics and the rest'. She argues that this has an inflexibility which

> disadvantages children with learning difficulties more than others, since their difficulties are generally in the areas of reading and writing. Abilities which they may have – in drawing, moving, etc. – may be undervalued because these are in the lower status tier of the curriculum.
>
> (Harlen, 1992: 2)

It has been argued that the Scottish 5–14 curriculum has some enlightened features for SEN with an approach 'in which entitlement to the Scottish version of a national curriculum is assumed for *all* children, and anything less than that has to be justified by specific arguments' (Brown, 1994).

There is still the problem, however, that although policy in Scotland has been less extreme in matters like primary school league tables, there remains strong pressure on schools to promote the achievement culture which can compound the sense of failure for pupils with learning difficulties. Scottish teachers and parents have misgivings about the emphasis in 5–14 on levels of attainment and the implications for those young people who have little expectation of meeting the requirements of the lowest level A.

Policy and parents

An important element in both government policy and much current discussion about SEN centres on the involvement and influence that parents can and should have in the education of their children. Sheila Wolfendale has described how recent policies have encouraged parental involvement and has applauded these developments. In a sector (early years education) where central planning was formerly characterised as uncertain and even non-existent, the potential for a reduction in parents' feelings of isolation and exclusion, and for the generation of new initiatives based on partnerships between professionals and parents, is clearly to be welcomed.

This encouragement of parental participation in the decision-making which affects their child has its dangers, however. Sheila Riddell and her co-authors, for example, identify a group of parents of children deemed to have specific learning difficulties (especially dyslexia) who, in powerful alliance with voluntary organisations, have had the capability and influence to press for preferential resources for their children – inevitably at the expense of others with different kinds of need. The potential for very positive benefits from the increased involvement of parents carries with it, therefore, the risk that some may act as self-interested consumers, heedless of the effects of their personal choice on others whose problems may be different but just as deserving of support. This risk is not, of course, just within the SEN part of the 'market'. Schools have to deliver what the majority or most influential groups of parents want to buy, and that may well result in the direction of resources away from pupils with learning difficulties, especially those without a statement or record of needs.

In general, however, the arguments for parents having greater access to information about their children, being accepted as having profoundly important knowledge of those children that must be communicated to (and taken account of by) education professionals, and being given real opportunities to influence the placements of their children, are extraordinarily powerful. But they bring into focus the problems to be faced when parents' views are not in agreement with those of schools or local authorities. Sometimes this may come down to problems of limited resources which preclude the provision preferred by parents; in other cases, there can be a fundamental difference in judgement about what is best for the child. Jenny Corbett makes it clear that not all parents supported the Newham policy for complete inclusion into mainstream. There are many people, especially those whose children have more severe difficulties, who regard special schools as the only places offering the safety, security and specific expertise that is necessary for their son or daughter. Whether such parents will continue to have the choice of special schools is not dependent just on the ideological commitment of the local authorities; the market economy approach, the emphasis on parental choice (majority rules) and recommendations from the Audit Commission to move resources to mainstream from special schools, could all exert pressure for the demise of the latter.

NORTH–SOUTH COMPARISONS

In Chapter 1, we identified a variety of contrasts of legislation and policy introduction between England and Wales and Scotland. Here we briefly pick up some of the points which have emerged from the collection of contributions from both sides of the border.

Looking first at the kind of research and writing which is carried out in Scotland on SEN, it seems that there is considerable emphasis on the study of classroom practice and teachers' understandings rather than on direct critical appraisal and analysis of policy. In England and Wales, the balance is somewhat different and tends starkly to confront the perspective of the policy-maker with that of the professional practitioner. To a large extent, this reflects the kinds of relationships which exist within the two education systems. The links among the Scottish Office, the education authorities and teachers have a substance which could not be said to characterise those among the Department for Education, the LEAs and the profession south of the border. Traditionally, of course, Scotland has had a more centralised system and it might be argued that people are just more used to being told what to do by the government. That seems too trite an answer, however. A more plausible explanation would take into account the ease of contact among a much smaller population, the continuing strong influence of HMIs and education authorities and, perhaps most importantly, the style with which reform is undertaken.

In general, educational reforms have had a lower public profile north of the border. There is no legislative base for the national curriculum, the Scottish Office produces guidelines rather than prescriptions (even if the distinction is not always convincing) and HMI offers support on classroom activities. Set in this lower key, adjustments can be made without anyone losing face or expending time and money on a new statute – the 5–14 curriculum, for example, can be much more flexible than the English national curriculum. The danger of this approach is that little real change may occur and the comfortable status quo is maintained.

As with the curriculum, shifts in the control of education in Scotland have been less abrupt. Power over their own budgets is only now being handed to schools, and education authorities are having a significant say in the formulae that will govern expenditure and responsibilities. Although a market economy approach is being encouraged by central government, it is being introduced in a more considered way that has avoided the sharp reactions that, as we have seen, have so often been to the detriment of pupils with special needs south of the border.

The influence of parents has probably been better co-ordinated in Scotland. They played a particularly effective role with teachers and local authorities in changing the regulations on national testing. Their choice of school placement for their children goes further in the Scottish than the English legislation. And they seem to be able to exert direct pressure on Ministers; the research study reported by Sheila Riddell *et al.* is an example of work commissioned as a result of parents' and voluntary organisations' persistent contacts with the Scottish Office.

There are prices to be paid for a slow evolutionary rather than revolutionary approach, even if the former keeps big trouble at bay. One problem is that difficult issues may not be faced up to in the short term. For example, although the Scottish Office has provided extensive guidance to mainstream schools on school self-evaluation and improvement, the performance indicators and the terms in which cost-effective arguments are pursued are not self-evidently applicable to special schools. The market forces approach discourages resourcing for those institutions which are not demonstrably cost-effective, and some heads of special schools are becoming impatient with a government that has not addressed the matter of appropriate criteria for them to fulfil and so left them exposed to the market without the tools to mount a defence or promote their cause.

IN CONCLUSION

From the preceding discussion, three central points emerge which are of crucial significance for special needs policy and provision through the 1990s and into the twenty-first century.

First, it is evident that key questions to do with the conceptualisation of special educational needs and disability remain unresolved and, indeed, until relatively recently have rarely been addressed. These hinge on the extent to which policy should be based on an acknowledgement of differences between those with special educational needs and others (and indeed among those with special needs) or whether it should assume the commonality and equality of all. Clearly, these questions are also of central importance to those involved in feminist and anti-racist initiatives, who share a concern with identifying those contexts where differences need to be recognised in order to secure additional provision, without adopting an essentialist position which denies the importance of a common humanity. Writers such as Abberley (1987) and Oliver (1990) have begun the work of developing a social theory of disability, which should contribute to the analysis of policy and the planning of future development strategies.

Second, contributors to this collection have alerted us to both the problems and possibilities of policy developments over the last decade and a half. Much has changed since the late 1970s, when the publication of the Warnock Report raised the profile of special educational needs and the prevailing climate was optimistic. In the intervening period, the growing emphasis on the market economy has aroused many fears for the education prospects of children who may be regarded as expensive and difficult to educate compared with their more academically able peers. Nonetheless, certain aspects of government policy may hold out hope for the future. The emphasis on parent power, for example, may result in individual families competing for resources for their own child, ignoring the needs of others; alternatively, as advocated by Ranson (1990) parents may come to see themselves as citizens with commitments extending beyond their own narrowly-defined self-interest. In Scotland at least, there is considerable evidence that traditional concerns with social welfare have not been jettisoned (Munn, 1992).

Additionally, even though education authorities will have to adapt to the new conditions in which they are operating, as Raab (1993) has argued, it would be premature to write them off as a spent force. Many will continue to function as equalising forces in the distribution of resources between schools and among children.

The third overarching point is that there is ample evidence of the way in which teachers continue to play a crucial role in influencing the way in which policies are finally implemented. On some fronts, they are forced to accommodate. For example, Armstrong and Galloway illustrate how teachers re-define their role in relation to children with emotional and behavioural difficulties to comply with the government's emphasis on examination results as the key measure of success. On other fronts, they continue to place the interest of children with special needs at the centre as, for example, they seek ways of including these pupils in mainstream schools. As Swann (1992) has noted, teachers' ideologies and values cannot be edited out of the educational equation and for this reason outcomes can never be read off from the original intentions of policy-makers.

As we hope this collection illustrates, policy and practice in relation to provision for children with SEN is currently an extremely interesting area for researchers. The great variety of ways in which the different facets interact has been highlighted by the different contributions to this book. Unfortunately, fertile ground for researchers and policy analysts often signals uncertainty, anxiety, inequality and problems for those 'on the ground', and there is plenty of evidence for that in reports in this collection. The challenge which faces all of us, however, is how to build on what seems to be going well and to debate constructively about how things can be improved. It has long been argued that deficit models with regard to children's difficulties are unhelpful – positive approaches which build upon what they *can* do are what result in progress. Perhaps a greater emphasis on what schools do *well*, on the *strengths* of curricular innovations for all pupils and on the *supportive* aspects of policy could avoid some of the destructive and defensive elements of the debate on SEN, and eventually ensure that standard provision means provision for *all* young people. This does not mean that we should be complacent about current policy trends. However, whilst exploring negative effects of the pervasive ethos of competitive individualism, we must continue to argue for the type of innovations which we believe will be empowering for all children, including those with special educational needs.

REFERENCES

Abberley, P. (1987) 'The concept of oppression and the development of a social theory of disability', *Disability, Handicap and Society* 2, 5–19.

Brown, S. (1994) 'The Scottish national curriculum and special educational needs', *Curriculum Journal*, 5, 1, 83–94.

Brown, S. and McIntyre, D. (1993) *Making Sense of Teaching*. Buckingham: Open University Press.

Department for Education (DFE) (1993) *Education Act 1993: Draft Code of Practice on the Identification and Assessment of Special Educational Needs. Draft Regulations on Assessments and Statements*. London: Department for Education.

Department of Education and Science (DES) (1978) *Special Educational Needs* (The Warnock Report). London: HMSO.

Harlen, W. (1992) 'Access to the curriculum for children with learning difficulties: the agenda for research', paper presented to the British Educational Research Association Annual Conference, August, University of Stirling.

Jackson, R. (1993) 'Disadvantaged by semantics', *Times Educational Supplement* 6 August, 12.

McIntyre, D. (1993) 'Special needs and standard provision', in Dyson, A. and Gains, C. *Rethinking Special Needs in Mainstream Schools*. London: David Fulton.

Munn, P. (1992) 'Devolved management of resources: a victory for the producer over the consumer?' in Paterson, L. and McCrone, D. (eds) *Scottish Government Yearbook 1992*. Edinburgh: Unit for the Study of Government in Education.

Oliver, M. (1990) *The Politics of Disablement*. London, Macmillan.

Raab, C. (1993) 'Parents and schools: what role for education authorities?' in Munn, P. (ed.) *Parents and Schools: Customers, Managers and Partners?* London: Routledge.

Ranson, S. (1990) 'From 1944 to 1988: education, citizenship and democracy', in Flude, M. and Hammer, M. (eds) *The Education Reform Act 1988: Its Origins and Implications*. London: Falmer Press.

Scottish Consultative Council on the Curriculum (SCCC) (1993) *Support for Learning: Special Educational Needs Within the 5–14 Curriculum*. Dundee: SCCC.

Scottish Education Department (SED) (1978) *The Education of Pupils with Learning Difficulties in Primary and Secondary Schools in Scotland*. Edinburgh: HMSO.

Strathclyde Region (1992) *Every Child is Special*. Glasgow: Strathclyde Region.

Swann, W. (1992) 'Hardening the hierarchies: the national curriculum as a system of classification', in Booth, T., Swann, W., Masterton, M. and Potts, P. (eds) *Learning for All 1 Curricula for Diversity in Education*. London: Routledge.

Index